BEYOND THE SELFIE

THE ART OF SELF-PORTRAITURE IN THE DIGITAL AGE

ROSIE HARDY

ilex

'And As For You...'

For my wonderful, kind, mischievous Dad.
Who never quite got the whole photography thing,
but supported me nonetheless, as I painted our front
drive yellow for a *Wizard of Oz*-inspired photoshoot.
I'm sorry it didn't wash off, but I'm glad it made the
cut as one of your favourite stories about our family.
Thank you for everything.

Philip Miles Hardy
16th July 1947–23rd August 2023

First published in Great Britain in 2024
by Ilex, an imprint of
Octopus Publishing Group Ltd
Carmelite House
50 Victoria Embankment
London EC4Y 0DZ
www.octopusbooks.co.uk
www.octopusbooksusa.com

An Hachette UK Company
www.hachette.co.uk

Distributed in the US by
Hachette Book Group
1290 Avenue of the Americas
4th and 5th Floors
New York, NY 10105

Distributed in Canada by
Canadian Manda Group,
664 Annette St, Toronto, Ontario,
Canada M6S 2C8

Publisher: Alison Starling
Commissioning Editor: Richard Collins
Managing Editor: Rachel Silverlight
Editorial Assistant: Stephanie Selçuk-Frank
Art Director: Ben Gardiner
Design: Jack Storey
Design Concept: Florian Michelet
Picture Research: Giulia Hetherington
Production Manager: Lisa Pinnell

ISBN 978-1-78157-938-1

A CIP catalogue record for this book is available
from the British Library.

Printed and bound in China

10 9 8 7 6 5 4 3 2 1

CONTENTS

INTRODUCTION

About the author 4
Why self-portraiture? 6

KIT

Getting started: Basic kit 12
Intermediate kit 20
Advanced kit 22
Extra kit: Tripods and shitty rigs 24

SHOOTING

Ambient lighting 32
Intervalometers, timers and remotes 36
Aperture, ISO and shutter speed 39
Focusing in self-portraiture 44

365 CHALLENGE

My story 50
Attempt one 51
Tim 54
Attempt two 62

PLANNING

Locations and how to find them 102
Shooting in public 112
Props and concepts 116
The role of props in photography 120
Studio lighting 122
Lighting for different moods and stories 126

PUTTING YOU IN THE PICTURE

Body image and self-reflection 130

STORYTELLING

Finding a deeper meaning 138
Viewer engagement and questions 144
Healing via storytelling 148

EDITING

Tricks of the trade 154
Before and after 162
Using AI 168
Easy, fun image-editing techniques to try 172

GETTING SEEN

Social media 180

WHAT NEXT?

From hobby to career 194
The artist emerges 206

Acknowledgements 208

INTRODUCTION

About The Author

'That's the big question, the one the world throws at you every morning. "Here you are, alive. Would you like to make a comment?"'
– Mary Oliver
Long Life: Essays and Other Writings

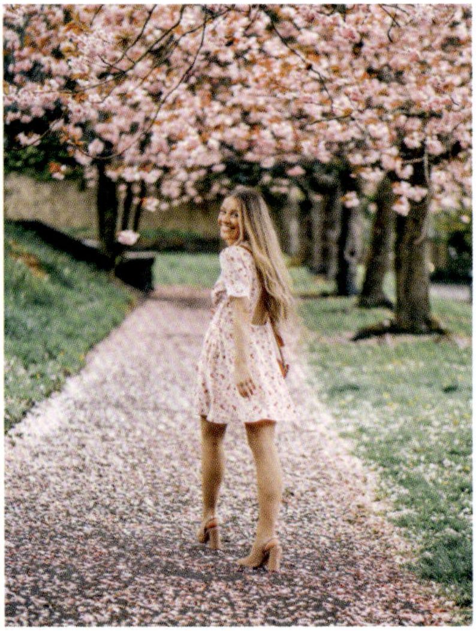

My name is Rosie Hardy. My journey with self-portraiture began at 15 years old, in my teenage bedroom, on a weird art website, drowning my sorrows somewhere, down in the deep dark internet.

It was a Bad Day.

A few months prior to my sad, late-night internet art dives, I'd woken up to the early stages of alopecia areata. My hair had been shedding in clumps, and I'd developed two large bald patches on either side of my head. This was extremely distressing, and like most teenagers, my (already fragile) identity began to crumble. My self-esteem was low, and looking in the mirror was tough. I'd struggled with disordered eating for a couple of years prior to my hair loss – the combination of the two issues led to this particular Bad Day.

As I clicked through the dark imagery in front of me, I felt a feeling of belonging. The girl on my screen seemed equally conflicted, equally disturbed, equally different. I felt connected to her self-portraits, and I too felt my inner voice start to rumble.

It seems paradoxical – the idea of taking pictures of yourself – when you already find it hard to stomach your own reflection, but my onset of alopecia was colliding with a new era, one that I found myself in, along with my peers – the world of social media, of point-and-shoot cameras and, of course, the World Wide Web.

Flicking through magazines, I would linger on pages of beautiful girls and women, and wonder why they looked the way they did. They looked so different from me. In my mirror, I saw acne, unflattering shadows, heavily applied makeup (applied to distract from my hair loss), and a round, full, teenage face. Between the paper pages, I saw perfect skin, voluminous hair, mesmerizing eyes with funny white shapes in the pupils. What were they? I became intrigued about the way these models looked, and what those little reflections meant. Why didn't the pictures I took on my point-and-shoot camera look like those? It was a curiosity that had become dislodged inside me, and I needed to figure it out.

(Spoiler: The little white blobs in their eyes were in fact the reflections from beauty dishes, softboxes, octoboxes – the very key to looking attractive in a photography studio.)

It was here that my very imperfect journey into the world of photography and self-portraiture (and self-love) began. I peered at myself through many different lenses over the years that followed – my internal reflection changing along with the physical. My hair was to fall out three more times after the first incident, and later I would go on to lose an incredible man and partner to cancer. Throughout my life so far, my camera has been an unintended companion and compass along the way. They say that 'the opposite of depression is expression', and I have found that to be very much true for me.

Taking self-portraits has led me to many amazing experiences – breathtaking scenery, some cool career highs, not to mention being in the position to write this book. But these self-portraits have also documented and comforted me at my deepest lows, and kept me company during the losses and the grief that all of us will eventually experience.

With this book, I hope to equip my fellow life-passengers with the knowledge and abilities that I've come to gather – to pass on what has been passed to me, for you to use in any way that brightens and nourishes your life or art. I believe that self-portraiture is a wonderfully unique tool to have under your belt, and that to study your own soul is quite the privilege.

I hope you enjoy this book.
– Rosie

WHY SELF-PORTRAITURE?

'I always take a close look at those who lose themselves in self-portraits. They are solitary souls, prone to introspection, who have really grappled with their existence.'
– Young-ha Kim
I Have The Right To Destroy Myself

Self-portraiture has been a significant and well-recognized method of artistic expression throughout history, both in traditional art forms and, of course, in my favourite medium – the medium of photography. It offers us artists and photographers a unique opportunity to delve into self-reflection, self-exploration and self-representation. And – hold the narcissism – self-portraiture doesn't equal self-obsession. Exploring our minds, hearts, thoughts, feelings and behaviours is the foundation of self-awareness, one of the most important Pokemon cards in the game of 'Being A Better Person'.

Here's an in-depth explanation of just why artists have turned to self-portraiture as a method of art and photography, along with some examples of famous artists who have chosen to embrace it.

SELF-EXPRESSION AND IDENTITY

Self-portraits allow artists to depict themselves and communicate their personal experiences, emotions and perspectives. By capturing their own image, we can convey our inner thoughts, struggles and joys, giving our viewers a glimpse into our identity and self-perception. Self-portraits can also reflect cultural, social and personal aspects of the artist's life, touching on the topics that affected them in that era. It's also fascinating to see the changing landscapes, politics, fashions and social norms reflected in Rembrandt's work, which can make us think about how different life must have been then.

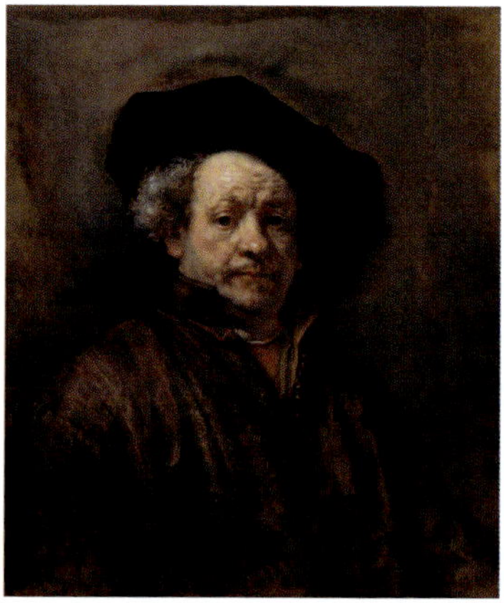

Self-Portrait, Rembrandt van Rijn, 1660

Notably, Rembrandt van Rijn, a renowned Dutch painter from the 17th century, created many self-portraits throughout his career. His self-portraits evolved over time, showcasing his immense skills when it came to the depiction of light, shadow and facial expressions in particular. These works provide insight into not only Rembrandt's artistic development, but also his self-reflection – his changing perception of himself.

The cultural documentation in my own early work is, unfortunately, much less historically significant. You can, however, see the trends of the times – the bad hair extensions, the layers of fake tan that you can almost smell through the image and the heavy eye makeup. That being said, I like to think my emotional evolution has been captured quite thoroughly.

INTROSPECTION AND PSYCHOLOGICAL EXPLORATION

Self-portraits offer artists a means to explore our own psyche, inner conflicts and personal growth. Through the process of creating self-portraits, we can confront our own image, explore our vulnerabilities and engage in a form of deep self-introspection. Throughout my personal journey, this self-observation has played a huge role in helping me overcome my own struggles. Self-portraits can easily become a way to express and process your emotions and self-doubts and lead to self-discovery.

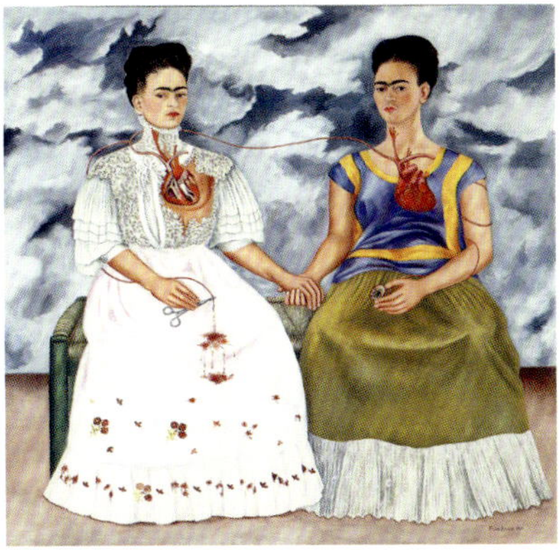

The Two Fridas, Frida Kahlo, 1939

Frida Kahlo, a Mexican artist, extensively painted self-portraits that incorporated many symbolic elements, and explored themes of her own identity, pain and the female experience. Her self-portraits were deeply introspective and reflected her physical and emotional battles, as well as her cultural heritage. She explored many topics that affected women in her time, including miscarriage, abortion, birth and breastfeeding. Kahlo's self-portraits serve as a visual diary, capturing her innermost thoughts and experiences during her lifetime.

AUTOBIOGRAPHICAL DOCUMENTATION

Self-portraits can eventually become a visual record of an artist's appearance throughout their life. They provide historical documentation of what that person looked like and preserve the artist's likeness for future generations. Self-portraits can convey an artist's ageing process, the changing styles and fashions at the time, and the evolving cultural context in which they lived.

You may have heard of Vincent van Gogh, the iconic Dutch post-impressionist painter. He created numerous self-portraits during his career, and these self-portraits didn't just showcase his unique style and use of colour, but they also documented his physical and mental state, providing insight into his artistic journey and his struggles with mental health.

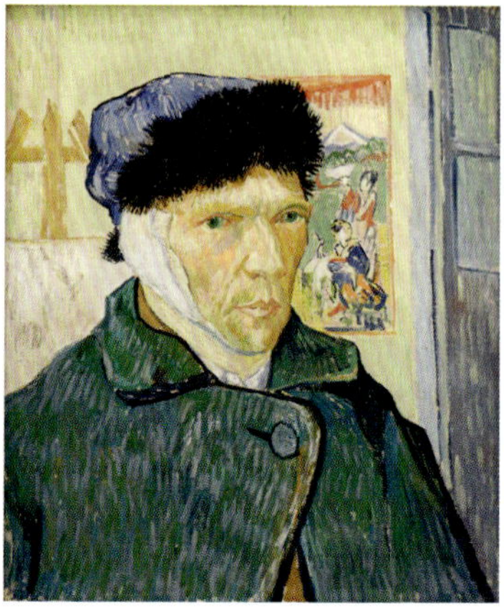

Self-Portrait with Bandaged Ear,
Vincent van Gogh, 1889

EXPERIMENTATION, PERFORMANCE AND ALTER EGOS

Self-portraits allow artists to experiment with different techniques, compositional elements and lighting conditions. For example, Juno Calypso. Calypso is renowned for her conceptual, stylized self-portraits. My favourite series of Calypso's is the series *Joyce*, where she dresses as a fictional alter ego of the same name. Calypso quotes Joyce as being a 'bored, frustrated, lonely housewife of her imagination,' and photographs herself in various hotel rooms. I was immediately drawn to the colouring and composition within her work – the flat pops of pink throughout the series gesture towards traditionally feminine themes. But as you examine the series more closely, you find that Calypso is exploring the oppressive side of femininity, its 'restrictive beauty regimes and modern rituals of seduction'. She has said, 'I'm trying to make a perfect photograph of a woman trying to create a perfect vision of herself'.

THE BENEFITS OF EXPRESSION IN SELF-PORTRAITS

Shooting self-portraits encourages someone to explore their own identity, their emotions and their own personal experiences. As Edith Eger says, 'I understood that feelings, no matter how powerful, aren't fatal. They are only

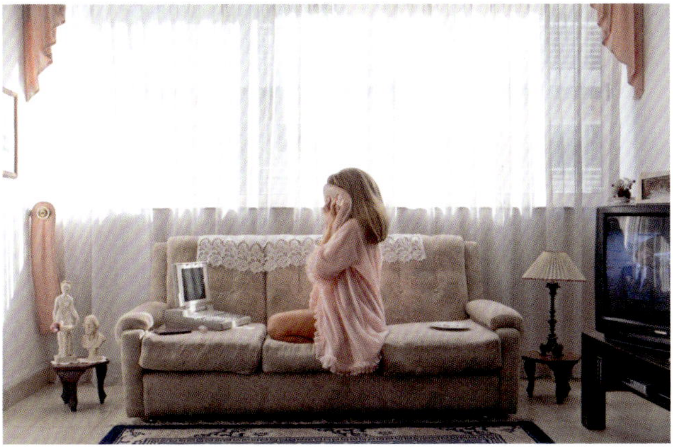

Disenchanted Simulation, Juno Calypso, 2013

temporary. Suppressing the feelings only makes it harder to let them go. Expression is the opposite of depression.'

The catharsis and emotional release that comes with creating a self-portrait is one of the reasons I perservered with them, once I'd mastered the skills I wanted to with my photography. The act of self-expression through self-portraits provides a safe therapeutic outlet for people to process and communicate their emotions, and has been a form of diary-style therapy for me.

Personally, taking self-portraits has been an empowering experience, and has led me on a journey of self-acceptance. They can be a tool for us as individuals to express ourselves authentically, and to embrace and discover our own unique quirks and personalities. Self-portraits have also created a space for genuine connection to others. The images that revealed vulnerability were, more often than not, those most engaged with. Shared human experiences can resonate with our viewers, which fosters connection and empathy, and a sense of community.

If those aren't good enough reasons to indulge in a self-portrait, then I'm not sure what else is. To partake in something that has been a powerful artistic practice across history – something that allows you to express your own identity, to introspect, to document your own life – all the while experimenting with different artistic techniques! Through self-portraits, many artists have left behind a visual legacy exploring the human condition, and you could join them. Sounds pretty good, hey?

01.

KIT

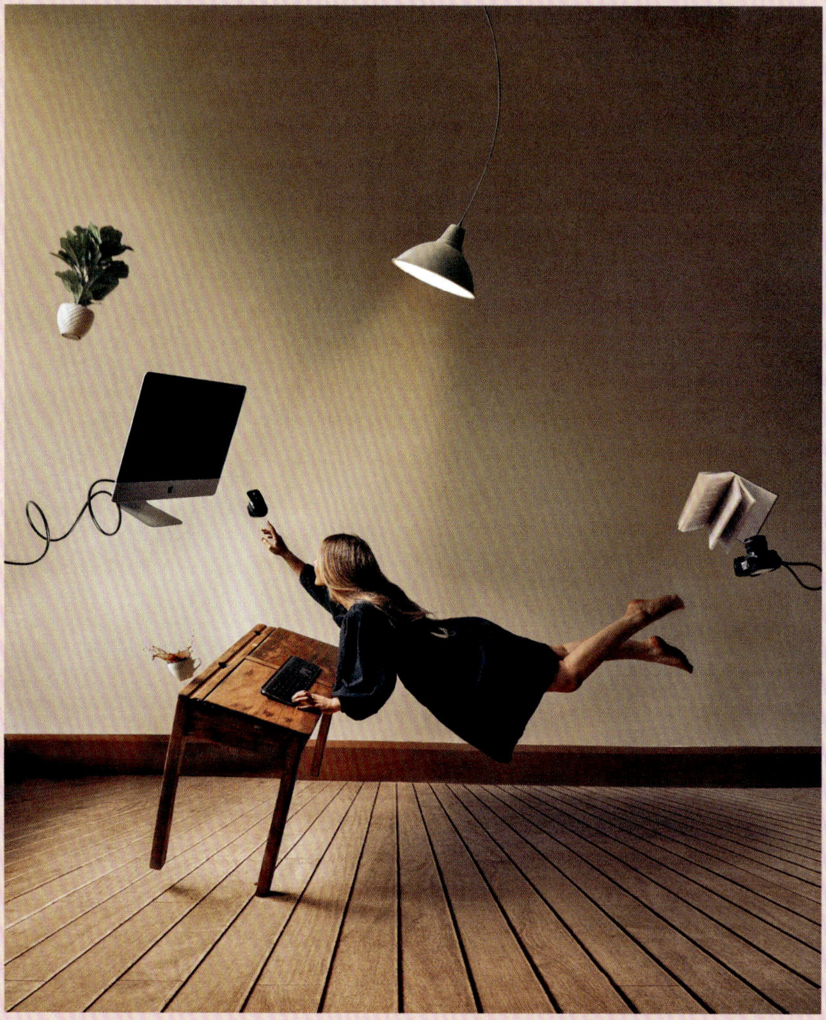

'There are many ways to be free. One of them is to transcend reality by imagination, as I try to do.' – Anaïs Nin
From my 'Workspace' series, commissioned by Logitech.

GETTING STARTED: BASIC KIT

So, you've decided to venture into the world of self-portraits. Welcome to the chaos.

First of all, you should expect to be overwhelmed by the amount of options that lie in front of you, especially for your number one tool of choice.

THE CAMERA

The good news is, you can relax. At 15 years old, I chose my first camera based on three very eyebrow-raising qualities – it was silver, it was small and it was one of four I could afford at the time. Since buying my first camera (a Canon point-and-shoot), I've gone on to become an ambassador for Canon, representing the brand across Europe and speaking on its platforms at photography events. Therefore, my first tip for my fellow camera-curious friends would be this:

Don't get overwhelmed. You can make any camera work. Years ago, a photographer called Lara Jade took part in a series where photographers were challenged to create their style of work in a camera chosen by the public. Imagine her surprise when she was handed a toy camera made for ages three and upwards. If she can take stunning fashion photographs on that, the rest of us can definitely work with a cheap point-and-shoot.

QUESTION: WHAT DO I NEED TO THINK ABOUT WHEN I CHOOSE MY FIRST CAMERA?

There are three main issues to take into consideration when choosing your initial camera. They are:

THE CAPABILITIES: What do you want to shoot with this camera? A self-portrait camera requires the ability to fix it to a tripod, some kind of timer or intervalometer or remote function and, of course, a quality picture result. This can be achieved by everything from a smartphone to a professional DSLR.

YOUR BUDGET: What are you prepared to spend? When people ask me what a good beginner camera is, I tell them about my first DSLR, the Canon EOS 500D. This currently retails at around £200 or so. However, cheaper options are absolutely available. Especially for those looking to dip a toe into the film-development water, it's worth considering an option that won't paralyze you with pressure cost-wise, nor will it limit your abilities to create what you have your mind set to.

PRACTICALITY: Are you looking to hike mountains with your camera? Hoping to take it on far-away trips stowed in hand luggage? If so, it's worth considering a camera that is light, compact and durable.

When looking at different cameras, you'll also be up against a lot of gobbledy-gook tech terms. I'm going to explain many of them below, so you can decide what is most important for you.

1. WHAT IS AN APS-C CAMERA?

An APS-C camera is another name for a camera with a smaller sensor. The sensor is what 'captures' your photographs, and a camera with a big old sensor is, generally speaking, going to create a better-quality image. This explains why full-frame cameras are more expensive and why APS-C cameras fill much of the budget market.

2. WHAT NUMBER OF MEGAPIXELS SHOULD I CHOOSE?

Megapixels refer to the number of individual pixels, or picture elements, that make up an image captured by a camera sensor.

Each pixel is a tiny dot of colour and brightness information, and the more pixels there are, the higher the resolution (size) of the image. The resolution directly affects the level of detail, sharpness and the ability to enlarge or crop the photograph without losing quality.

While more pixels can be useful, it's important to consider other factors such as the camera's sensor size, the lens quality and image-processing capabilities, as they all contribute to overall image quality. Additionally, a greater number of pixels can often result in large file sizes, meaning you'll need more storage space, and a computer/editing software with higher processing speeds, all of which costs money.

3. LENS COMPATIBILITY

Check the camera's lens mount system to make sure it supports a wide range of lenses, as this expands your creative options in the future. We cover more about lenses later in this chapter.

4. WHAT MAKES A USER-FRIENDLY CAMERA?

Simply put, what makes a camera user-friendly is how YOU feel about it. When camera shopping, look for a camera that you find easy to navigate. The menu and interface should feel natural and accessible to you when you explore it. There's nothing worse than spending precious shooting time trying to find out how to set the self-timer.

5. MIRRORLESS VS NON-MIRRORLESS (THIS ONE'S A BIGGIE!)

The key difference between a mirrorless camera and a non-mirrorless camera – commonly known as a DSLR (digital single-lens reflex) camera – lies in their optical design and the way in which they handle light.

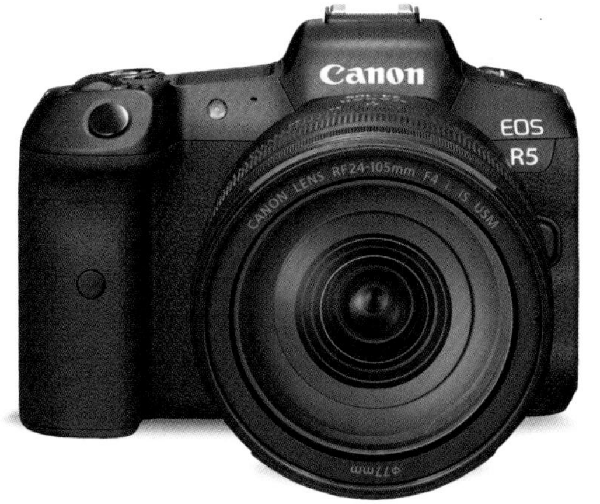

MIRRORLESS CAMERA:

- **OPTICAL DESIGN:** Mirrorless cameras, as the name suggests, lack the mirror mechanism found in DSLR cameras. Instead, they use an electronic viewfinder (EVF) or the rear LCD screen for composing and previewing images.
- **LIGHT PATH:** In a mirrorless camera, light directly reaches the image sensor when the shutter is open. There is no optical path redirection through a mirror to the viewfinder, which allows for a more compact camera body design.
- **AUTOFOCUS:** Mirrorless cameras typically use 'contrast detection' or a combination of contrast and phase-detection autofocus systems. Some advanced models offer rapid and accurate autofocus performance, especially with continuous tracking.
- **SILENT SHOOTING:** Due to the absence of a mirror and the use of an electronic shutter, mirrorless cameras often have silent shooting modes, making them suitable for discreet shooting situations. Personally, for self-portraits, I actually prefer to hear my shutter clicking – it lets me know when to pose and when to move.
- **LENS COMPATIBILITY:** Mirrorless cameras usually have their own lens mount systems, and they require adapters to accommodate lenses from other brands or lens systems.

DSLR CAMERA:

- **OPTICAL DESIGN:** DSLR cameras consist of a mirror and a pentaprism or pentamirror that reflects light through an optical viewfinder. The mirror flips up when the shutter is released, allowing light to reach the image sensor.

- **LIGHT PATH:** In a DSLR camera, light first enters the lens and passes through the mirror, which redirects the light to the viewfinder. When the shutter is released, the mirror quickly moves out of the way, enabling the light to reach the image sensor.
- **AUTOFOCUS:** DSLR cameras traditionally employ phase-detection autofocus (PDAF) systems, which use a dedicated autofocus module located at the bottom of the camera body. This system excels at tracking moving subjects and is known for its speed and accuracy.
- **OPTICAL VIEWFINDER:** DSLRs feature an optical viewfinder that offers a real-time, through-the-lens (TTL) view of the scene. The optical viewfinder provides a direct optical representation of the subject, without any digital processing or lag.
- **LENS COMPATIBILITY:** DSLR cameras have specific lens mounts designed for their respective brands, and lenses are generally not interchangeable between different systems without the use of adapters.

Both mirrorless cameras and DSLRs have their own advantages and can cater to different shooting preferences. Mirrorless cameras tend to be more compact, offer advanced features like in-body image stabilization and are well-suited for video recording. DSLRs, on the other hand, often excel in autofocus performance, offer a wide range of compatible lenses and provide a traditional optical viewfinder experience. The choice between the two depends on the photographer's specific needs, shooting style and personal preferences.

6. IMAGE STABILIZATION

Choosing a camera that offers in-body or lens-based stabilization helps reduce blur caused by camera shake, especially when shooting handheld or in low-light conditions. If you're shooting self-portraits on a tripod, this shouldn't be a huge issue, but it is still handy to know.

7. WHAT IS A GOOD ISO RANGE?

The acronym ISO stands for 'International Organization for Standardization', which is the organization that creates various technology and product standards. In photography, ISO was originally created to provide a single numerical measurement of a film's sensitivity to light, replacing previous disparate standards such as ASA and DIN. Today, it is also used to indicate a digital camera sensor's sensitivity to light, with higher ISO settings indicating greater sensitivity. It is important to consider a camera's ISO range, as a wide range offers greater flexibility, especially when it comes to low-light photography. We'll explore ISO in chapter 2.

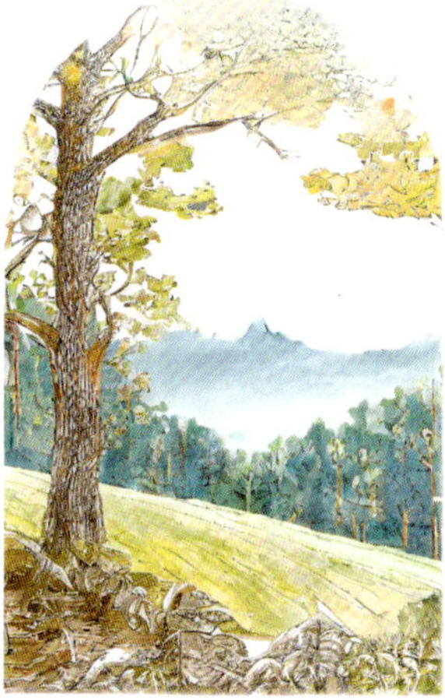

ISO 100

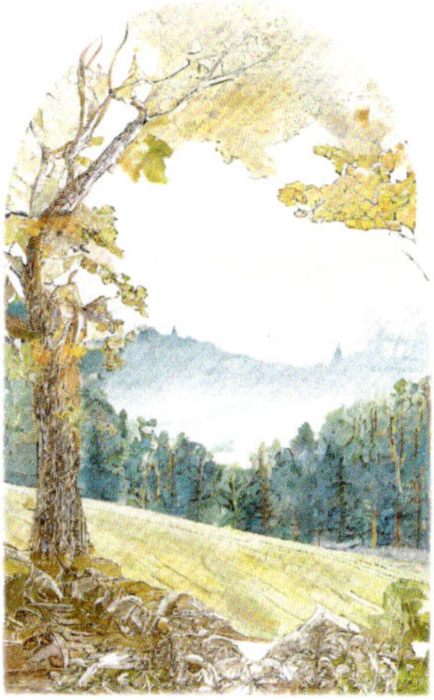

ISO 800

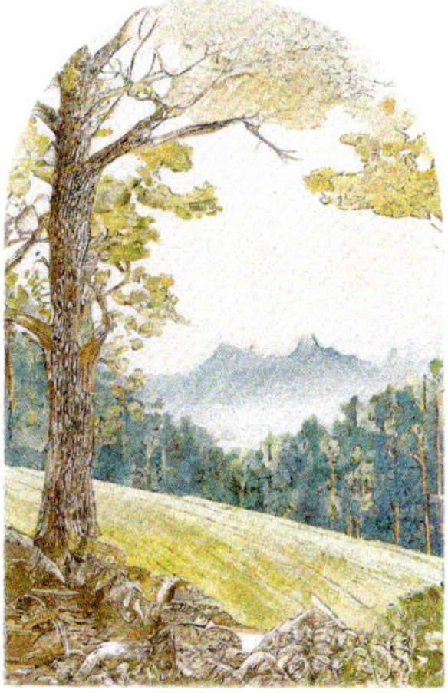

ISO 25,600

8. CONNECTIVITY OPTIONS

A camera that has the necessary ports (USB, HDMI) and wireless features (Wi-Fi, Bluetooth) for transferring images, remote control or sharing content with other devices helps hugely when shooting self-portraiture. Being able to link your camera to your phone means you'll have the option of seeing how you look on the other side of the lens before you shoot using certain apps. (Read more on intervalometers, timers and remotes in chapter 2.)

9. BATTERY LIFE

It's worth noting the camera's battery life, and the availability of spare batteries, especially if you plan to shoot for extended periods without immediate access to charging. Although batteries can be expensive, I would suggest that it's always best to buy spare batteries from the camera brand itself, rather than cheaper lithium-ion alternatives from unknown sources.

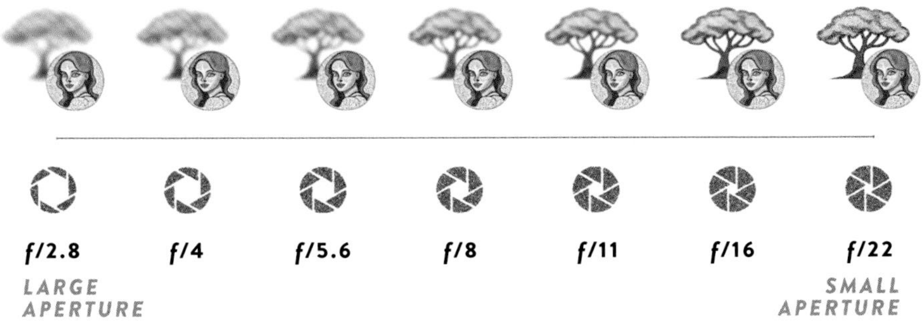

LENSES

Once you've selected a camera, you might like to explore the world with different lenses. Simply put, a lens is a way to change the overall look and feel of a photograph. Many photographers argue that it is better to have an amazing lens than an amazing camera body (I'm one of them!), and it's important to point out that you cannot always mix and match lenses. For example, some Canon cameras will only mount specific Canon lenses, and this includes APS-C cameras vs full-frame. Mixing brands of lenses is also a grey area – you can often use third-party lenses such as those from Sigma and Tamron, providing they have the correct mount for your camera, but you generally can't use lenses from other camera manufacturers. If you're unsure of whether your lens will mount your chosen camera body, simply check the spec online of that specific lens. It will tell you what it is compatible with.

APERTURES

Every lens has a maximum aperture sertting, which is expressed as an *f*-number or *f*-stop. When explaining what aperture is, I always tell people to imagine the pupil of an eye.

When it is dark, the pupil gets bigger and wider (a lower aperture – say, *f*/1.2 or *f*/1.8). This lets more light enter the pupil (or in this case, camera sensor), and allows the overall image to be brighter. A side effect of a wide aperture is that you'll lose 'depth of field' – a term that refers to the amount of a photograph that appears sharply focused. For my own personal style, I tend to only shoot on lenses with a maximum aperture of *f*/1.2, *f*/1.4, *f*/1.8 or (at most) *f*/2.8. A general rule of thumb is that the better a lens is, the wider its maximum aperture will be (and the more expensive it is).

LENSES – THE FOCAL LENGTHS AND WHAT THEY'RE GOOD FOR

As a beginner, the focal lengths you are most likely to encounter (and what they perform best at) are as follows:

Most APS-C cameras are available with a kit lens that offers a focal length range of around 18-55mm and a maximum aperture of *f*/4 at the widest focal length, and *f*/5.6 at the longest setting. When I first bought a DSLR, this was the lens I used for the first year of my photography life. It's not great, but it is functional. This lens is a zoom lens and will allow you to capture more or less of your chosen scene without the need to move the camera (or tripod).

The 18mm end (wider angle) will provide a very basic landscape shot. You won't need to be too far from the camera to be fully in the frame, plus there will be enough scenery around you to create a 'scene'. The 55mm end (at full zoom) will create a portrait shot, and the landscape around will not overpower the person in the photograph. However, take note of the maximum *f*-stop (aperture). At *f*/4–5.6, this is what holds the lens back: your portraits will have most of the scene in focus, which can lead to a chaotic, busy feel in the overall image.

My personal dream combo for beginners is a full-frame Canon EOS 5D with a 50mm *f*/1.8 lens.

Remember, as a beginner you don't need to start with a DSLR. Smartphones have come so far with their camera technology, and you can create great portraits using portable mini-tripods and Bluetooth remotes.

If you're going to stick to taking selfies on your phone, head over to the Ambient Lighting section in chapter 2 (see page 33) for tips and tricks to make the most of the lighting you have available.

INTERMEDIATE KIT

If you're quite familiar with how cameras work, or have owned a DSLR or mirrorless camera for a while, you might be looking to upgrade to a new camera body or lens. My recommendations for intermediate photographers/hobbyists that are looking to turn pro are:

1) Canon EOS 6D Mark II
2) Nikon D780
3) Sony Alpha 7 III

An intermediate photographer looking to shoot self-portraits should also consider adding more lenses to their bag. This will allow for a variety of styles. Here are my favourite lenses, and when I would use them for my self-portrait photography:

CANON 35MM F/1.4 LENS: This is my go-to lens. It gives me the ability to capture a full scene, but doesn't distort or stretch out my body/face by being too wide angle. It has a wide aperture (*f*/1.4), is fantastic quality and produces reliably sharp images.

50MM F/1.4 OR F/1.8 LENS: If you aren't able or ready to invest the extra money into a *f*/1.2 lens, then one of these is a great alternative. It's an intermediate price tag with great results. The 50mm *f*/1.4 is a wonderful portrait lens and allows for both full-body portraits and close-ups.

SIGMA 24MM F/2.8 LENS: This lens is the widest I will go for portrait-style self-portraits. This lens is great if you're looking to capture more of a location and less of a person. The *f*/2.8 aperture means it's not the best in low light, but the price tag means you'll be staying in a lower budget.

USED VS NEW

Along with a good selection of lenses, intermediate photographers should also consider investing in a full-frame camera. If you're looking for good quality without blowing your budget, buying used is a great option. My preferred sites for sourcing used kit are mpb.com and eBay. I've used both throughout my photography career, and luckily never bought dodgy goods. When buying cameras, it's worth looking for good–excellent condition, and hunting for a lower shutter count. When buying lenses, check for any detail about issues with the lens, or look for scratches/cracks that could interfere with the images produced.

Personally, I've favoured buying used equipment for a long time. Buying used kit supports my photography style, and I can find cameras and lenses that support my budget, while still being reliable and good quality.

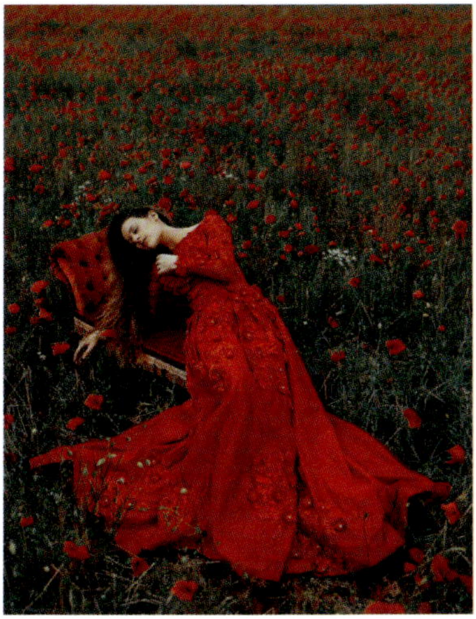

'Self-portrait in Poppies' – Shot using a Canon 35mm f/1.4 lens.

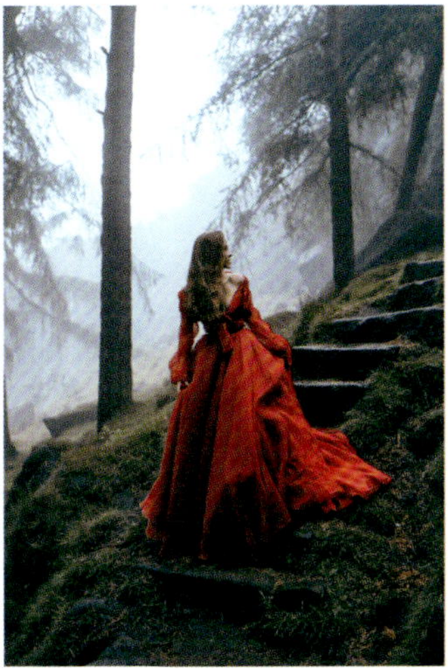

'The Escape' – Shot using a Canon 50mm f/1.4 lens.

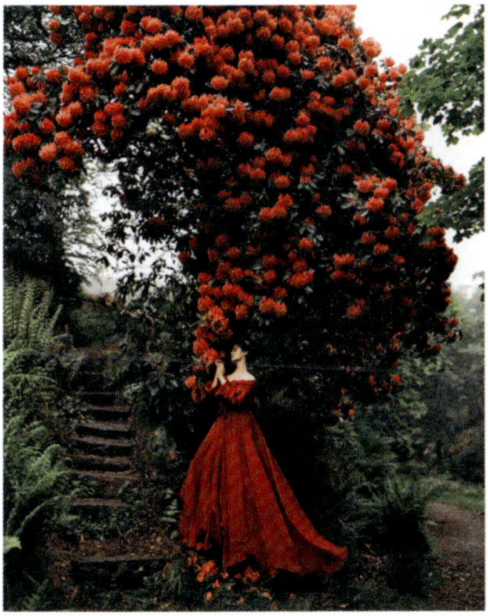

'The Way My Heart Grows' – Shot using a Sigma 24mm f/2.8 lens.

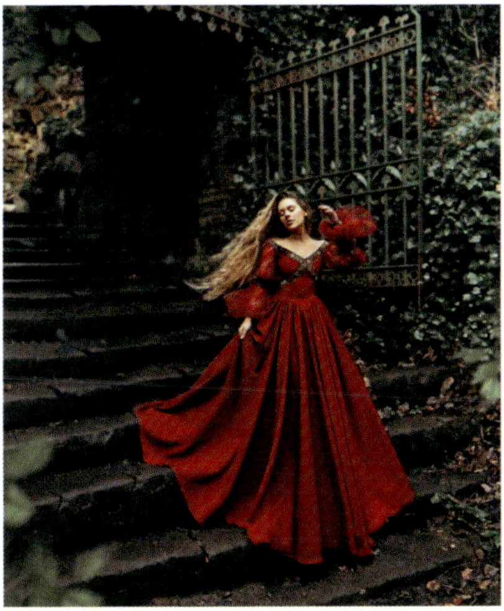

'The Runaway' – Shot using a Sigma 35mm f/1.4 lens

ADVANCED KIT

Expert professional photographers often require top-of-the-line equipment to meet more demanding standards in their photography. Here are some examples of expert professional photography kits, including the wonderful (and expensive) world of medium-format cameras, and some of the best full-frame DSLRs, along with the notable features that make them the top choice for professionals:

MEDIUM-FORMAT CAMERAS:

- **HASSELBLAD X2D 100C:** This medium-format mirrorless camera boasts a 100-megapixel sensor that provides exceptional detail and image quality, with a wide dynamic range, superb colour accuracy and impressive low-light performance. The system is backed up by an array of high-quality lenses, making it suitable for various genres, including landscape, commercial and studio photography.
- **PHASE ONE XF IQ4:** The Phase One XF IQ4 is renowned for its extraordinary image quality, thanks to its 150-megapixel medium-format sensor. It delivers exceptional resolution, dynamic range and colour depth. The camera's modular design and extensive lens lineup make it highly adaptable for commercial, fine art and high-end fashion photography.

FULL-FRAME DSLR CAMERAS:

- **NIKON D850:** The Nikon D850 is a highly versatile full-frame DSLR camera favoured by professionals. It features a 45.7-megapixel sensor, excellent dynamic range and superb low-light performance. Its advanced autofocus system, high-speed continuous shooting and 4K video capabilities make it well-suited for a wide range of genres, including landscape, portrait and sports photography.
- **CANON EOS 5D MARK IV:** The Canon EOS 5D Mark IV is a popular choice among professionals due to its 30.4-megapixel full-frame sensor and exceptional image quality. It offers excellent dynamic range, low noise performance and impressive autofocus capabilities. Its robust build, weather sealing and advanced video features make it suitable for various applications, including wedding, documentary and commercial photography.

MIRRORLESS CAMERAS (FULL-FRAME):

- **SONY ALPHA 7R V:** The Sony A7R V is a mirrorless camera that combines a 61-megapixel full-frame sensor with advanced autofocus and image stabilization, as well as an AI processing unit that offers advanced subject and face-recognition capabilities. It offers superb image quality, impressive dynamic range and excellent low-light performance. The camera's compact size, silent shooting mode and high-resolution electronic viewfinder make it well-suited for landscape, portrait and travel photography.
- **PANASONIC LUMIX S1R:** The Panasonic Lumix S1R is a full-frame mirrorless camera known for its high-resolution 47.3-megapixel sensor and exceptional image quality. It offers advanced image stabilization, a robust build and weather sealing. The camera's 187-megapixel high-resolution mode, wide dynamic range and excellent video capabilities make it suitable for professional still photography and videography.
- These examples are just a few of the many professional-grade cameras available on the market. It's worth noting that the choice of equipment ultimately depends on an individual photographer's specific needs, shooting style and preferences – there isn't a need to splash the cash on these cameras unless your shoot really does require it. If you decide to move into the professional sphere, prioritizing factors such as image quality, resolution, dynamic range, autofocus performance, durability and versatility is the key when selecting your photography kit.

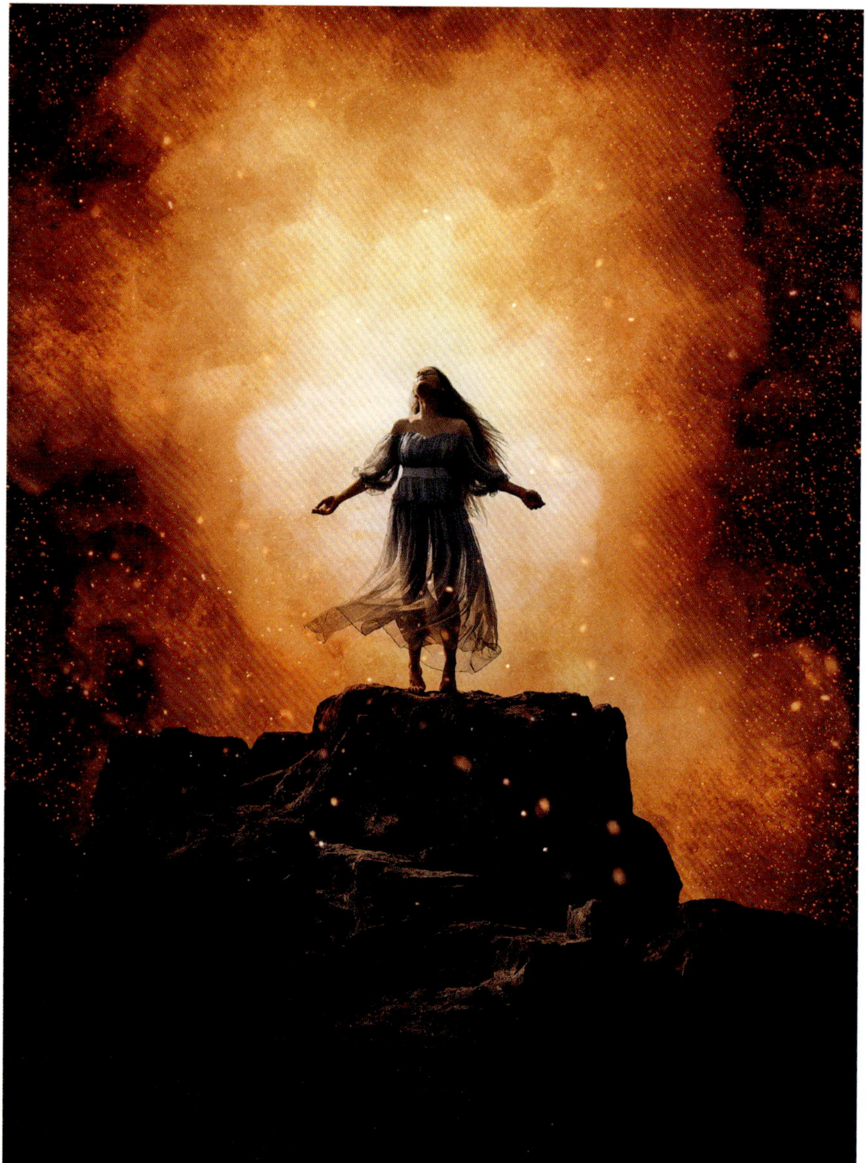

Make sure your tripod can withstand all terrain.
And, of course, the raging flames of hell!

EXTRA KIT: TRIPODS AND SHITTY RIGS

TRIPODS

As you can imagine, it's pretty hard to take a self-portrait without using a tripod. Their role in photography is to provide stability and support to the camera, allowing you to shoot hands free. Having a stable camera has the added benefit of ensuring sharper images in a variety of shooting situations, whether that be on a cliff edge, in a rushing river or in the safety of your own living room. Tripods offer even more benefits, like reducing camera shake, enabling long exposures, allowing you to create the composition you want and, most importantly, letting you feature in your own shot. So, let's dive in.

STABILITY AND CAMERA SUPPORT: Tripods provide a stable platform for the camera, minimizing unwanted movement and ensuring sharp images, especially in low-light conditions or when using telephoto lenses. They help eliminate camera shake caused by hand-holding the camera, resulting in sharper details and better image quality. The downside of this, of course, is that you are limited to 'setting up' for every shot you take – there's a lot more freedom for candid imagery when hand-holding your camera. However, in the world of self-portraiture, the set-up is part of the fun.

LONG EXPOSURES AND LOW LIGHT: In situations where longer exposures are required (for example, if you want to capture night scenes or create silky smooth water effects), tripods are brilliant, if not essential. They keep the camera steady during the extended exposure time, preventing blur, and allow precise control over the amount of light entering the camera.

COMPOSITION AND FRAMING: Tripods allow us to compose and frame our shots exactly as we wish. By keeping the camera in a fixed position, we can carefully adjust our framing, align horizons and create any composition we desire. The only limitations are the more 'quirky' angles, a bird's-eye view being one of them. We'll cover some more exciting and imaginative tripod-free solutions in the next part of this chapter: Shitty Rigs.

TRIPODS IN SELF-PORTRAITURE: Tripods allow self-portrait artists to capture themselves without the need for assistance. They can be equipped with all kinds of fun features, like adjustable legs and extendable centre columns, providing some flexibility in achieving a variety of heights and angles. With self-portraits, it's important to choose a tripod with good durability – as there will be no one to man it, you don't really want something that will easily blow over, taking your camera with it.

TRIPOD OPTIONS ACROSS BUDGETS

BEGINNER:

- **JOBY GORILLAPOD:** A tripod that is flexible and compact with bendable legs that can be wrapped around various objects. Ideal for lightweight cameras and beginners on a tight budget.

INTERMEDIATE:

- **MANFROTTO 190XPRO4:** A sturdy aluminium tripod with adjustable leg angles and a centre column that can be tilted horizontally, allowing for versatile shooting positions and angles.

EXPERT:

- **GITZO GT3543LS SYSTEMATIC:** A professional-grade carbon fibre tripod known for its exceptional stability, durability and precision. It offers advanced features like a reversible centre column, detachable leg sections and a high weight capacity.

Other factors to think about when choosing your tripod are things such as its weight, maximum load capacity (I've made this mistake before), height range (very important), stability and the material (aluminium or carbon fibre tend to do better than plastic). Additional features like quick-release plates, leg locks and ball heads also come into the equation, but it's important to find a tripod that suits your specific needs and shooting style.

Investing in a tripod that matches your skill level and shooting requirements is important. As your skills and demands grow, you may find it beneficial to upgrade to a more robust and feature-rich tripod. However, always remember to consider your camera's weight and lens set-up when choosing a tripod, to ensure it can support your equipment effectively.

SHITTY RIGS

'Shitty Rigs' was the name of a funny blog many years ago, dedicated to all the terrible and creative alternatives that photographers found when their tripod or boom arms didn't cut it. Here are some of my favourite personal shitty rigs:

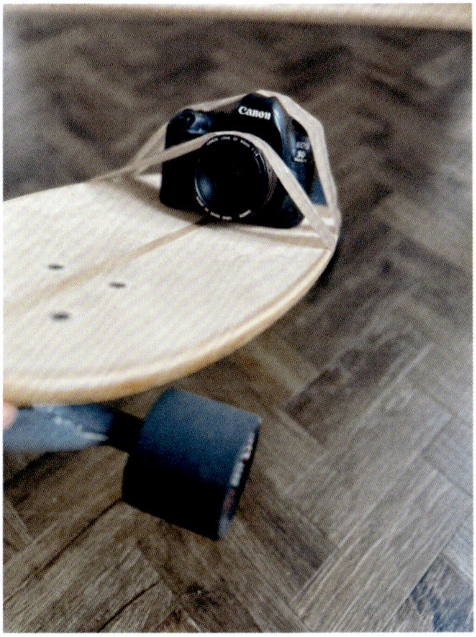

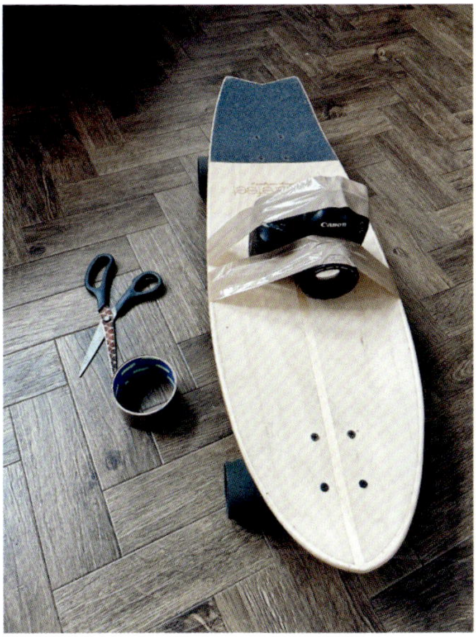

Skateboard shitty rig for when you can't afford a camera dolly. Bikes, trolley carts and cars are also useful alternatives.

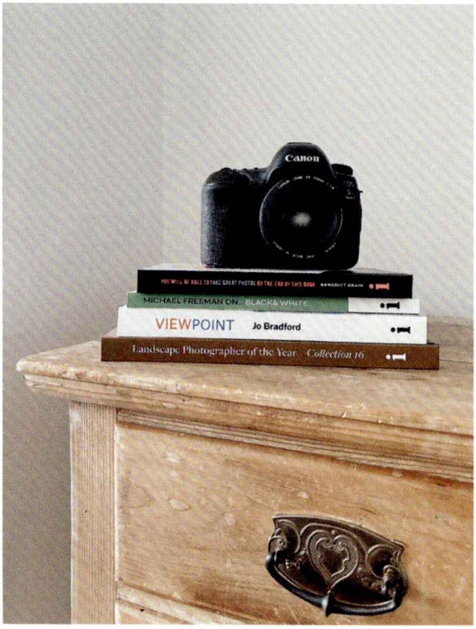

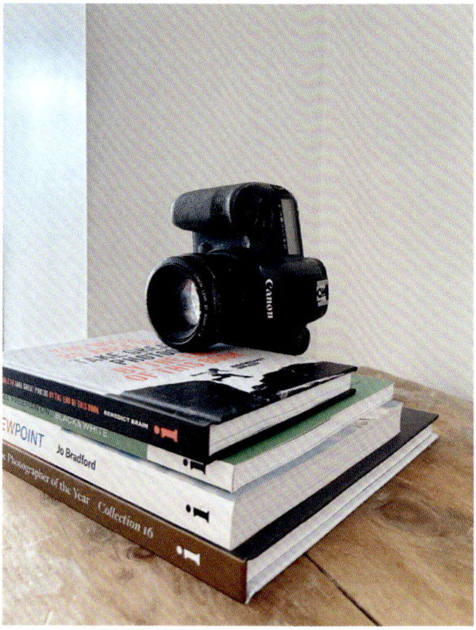

Book-stack shitty rig – configured for both portrait and landscape shooting styles. A book or a wallet can be used for lens support. This is a classic shitty rig for beginners without a tripod.

If you find yourself without your tripod quick-release plate, or in a beautiful location without the tripod itself (at least you have your camera), here are some great tips for making the most of your self-portrait opportunity.

In nature, try and find a flat surface that you can balance your camera on. Walls, tree stumps, big rocks – use whatever you have with you to flatten the surface out as much as possible.

Using a smartphone under the lens will prevent the image from shooting too much of the floor – any kind of similar depth rock or branch will also work. Consider shooting landscape and then cropping the image afterwards for a portrait-style result. It's hard to shoot portrait style without your tripod!

If you can, use things like duct tape to your advantage. It's easy to feel restricted when using a tripod, so getting creative without your essentials is a fun way to connect with the 'play' aspect of shooting. If the shot doesn't work, worse case you'll have a fun story, best case a new method of shooting!

And finally, remember the three important laws of shitty rigs: Adapt, Overcome, Camera Insurance. The greater the photographer, the shittier their rig.

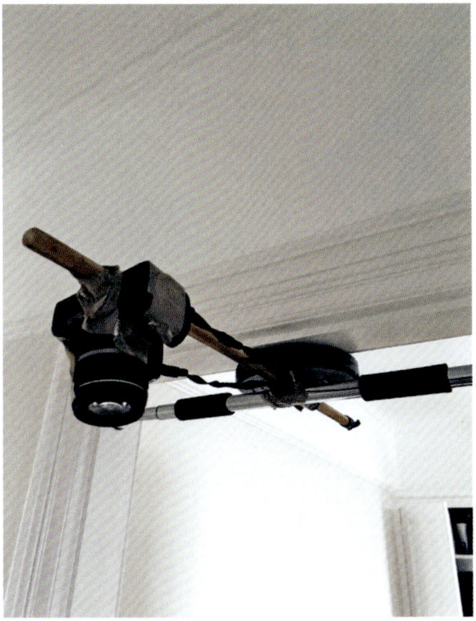

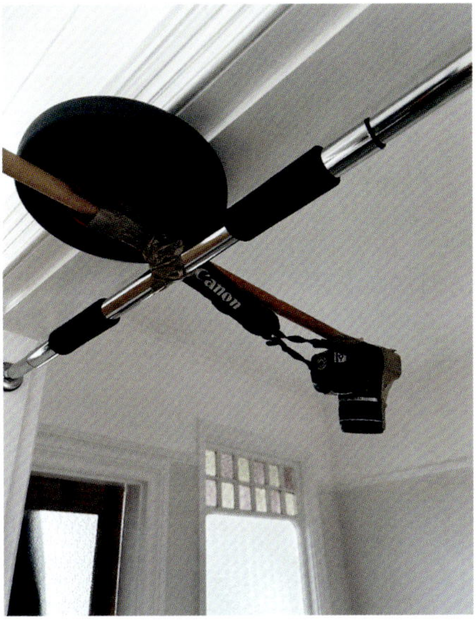

Pull-up bar shitty rig for when you are boom-armless and need a bird's-eye view. The camera is duct-taped onto a pole (broom handle, mop, anything will do) and a weight is used to counterbalance the weight of the camera.

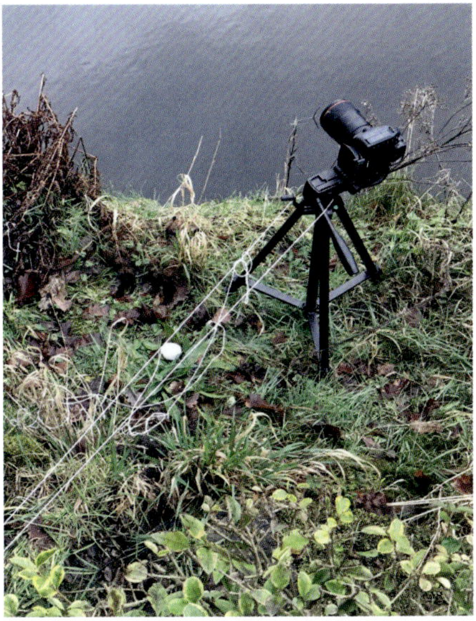

String shitty rig. No water risk is complete without a scrap of string stopping your camera from going for a swim!

02.

SHOOTING

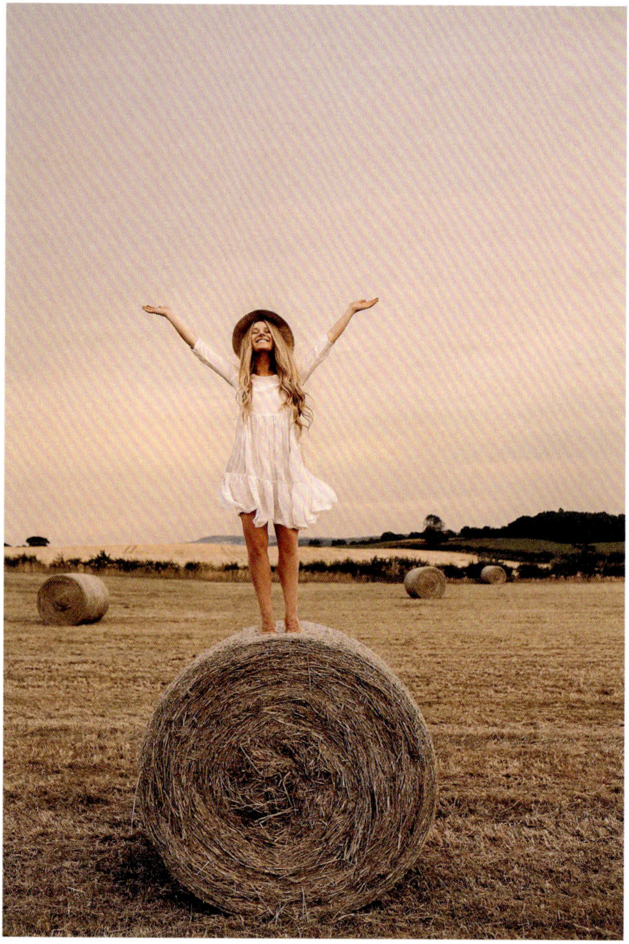

This self-portrait was shot in overcast lighting – the golden glow to the clouds behind me was added in post-production, to create the illusion of sunset lighting.

AMBIENT LIGHTING
Beginner & Intermediate

Once you have your kit sorted out, the next big influence on your images will be the light you choose to shoot in. 'Photography' translates to 'painting with light', after all! Different ambient lighting conditions can impact the mood, exposure and overall aesthetic of a photograph. Understanding and utilizing various lighting situations allows photographers to adapt and create images with different atmospheres and visual effects.

In this chapter, I will walk you through many of the common ambient lighting situations you might encounter, and how you can maximize them in your work. Let's begin by categorizing them by 'outdoor' and 'indoor'.

OUTDOOR

SHADE: On a sunny day, shooting in shade is a life-saver. You'll find it created by buildings and trees, and often this can be some of the most flattering lighting for portraits of any kind. Shooting in the shade produces soft, diffused lighting with reduced contrast. It minimizes harsh shadows and creates even illumination, resulting in a balanced and natural-looking image.

DIRECT SUNLIGHT: Direct sunlight is one of the harder ambient lighting situations to master. It creates strong contrasts and deep shadows, and can sometimes lead to overexposure or harsh highlights. If you're shooting in white clothing, be prepared to lose all the detail in the highlights. If you're shooting with a busy background (like woodland), hard light can often leave the image looking chaotic. While direct sunlight can produce vibrant colours and a sense of warmth, it may also cause squinting and harsh facial shadows, and it generally has a less flattering overall result. Careful exposure and positioning can help mitigate this, but it's definitely one for the brave.

BACKLIGHTING: Backlighting occurs when the main light source is behind the subject, creating a silhouette effect or a halo of light around the subject. I personally love backlighting, and it is my preference on a sunny day, all day long. Think fairytale, angelic vibes and an ethereal look. Some people find backlighting challenging, as while it can produce a rim of light around the subject's outline, emphasizing their shape, the front of the subject may appear darker. Proper exposure adjustment, shooting in Raw or using reflectors can help balance the lighting and reveal details in the subject.

AN OVERCAST DAY: As I am based in the UK, I usually shoot self-portraits on cloudy, overcast days. Many photographers prefer the depth and opportunity that comes with harder light, but personally I love the consistency and soft lighting that comes with a big dose of cloud. An overcast day also means that more locations are up for grabs – it's less likely you'll hike a mountain only to find the direction you want to shoot in looks busy or chaotic in the bright sunshine. It's easier to stitch different elements together in post-production when shot on cloudy days, and generally makes my life easier. Long live cloudy days!

INDOOR

Shooting indoors is generally more challenging than outdoors – you have less ambient light to begin with, so you'll need to raise your ISO or lower your shutter speed, or drop your *f*-stop to increase the amount of light entering your camera sensor. Here are some light situations that I've commonly encountered, and how to use them to your advantage.

CEILING SPOTLIGHTS: Spotlights are focused light sources that direct a beam of light onto a specific area or subject. They're becoming more common in modern homes, and create strong contrasts between light and shadow, emphasizing certain details or creating dramatic effects. When photographing a person under spotlights, it's important to manage the exposure carefully to avoid blown-out highlights or underexposed shadows. The direction and intensity of the spotlight can also influence the mood and overall look of the image. If there isn't a good ambient light source (like a window) nearby, I would always turn off any spotlights in a room to avoid false-looking lighting and unwanted shadows/highlights.

WARM-COLOURED LAMPSHADES AND LIGHTS: Lamps and lights with an orange or warm-toned light source can cast a warm and cosy glow. This type of lighting can create a nostalgic or intimate atmosphere – it tends to enhance warmer colours, such as reds and yellows, which sounds lovely in theory, but when you extend this to a person's skin tone, you can accidentally leave people looking more orange than they really are. Again, my preference (with a good light source from, say, a window) is to turn any external warm lights off. However, if it's nighttime and any other light sources are low, the warm glow of a candle or lamp can produce soft and romantic-looking results. Uncovered bulbs will generate more light, but at the cost of harder, less flattering lighting.

WINDOW LIGHT: Window light creates soft, diffused lighting with gentle shadows. As a photographer, this is my absolute favourite kind of indoor lighting. When you photograph a person or take a self-portrait near a window, the light will fall evenly on your face, which produces soft highlights and shadows that accentuate facial features. It is some of the most flattering lighting you can find.

AND FINALLY, THE ULTIMATE NATURAL LIGHTING SET-UP: THE GARAGE

In my opinion, the most flattering lighting known to wo/man is the lighting that is created by a garage, porch or bus stop set-up. When you block off the light source from all areas except front on (and shoot in shade or overcast light), you create your own personal photography studio. Adding a backdrop into this situation takes your result to another level, and will leave you or your clients very happy indeed.

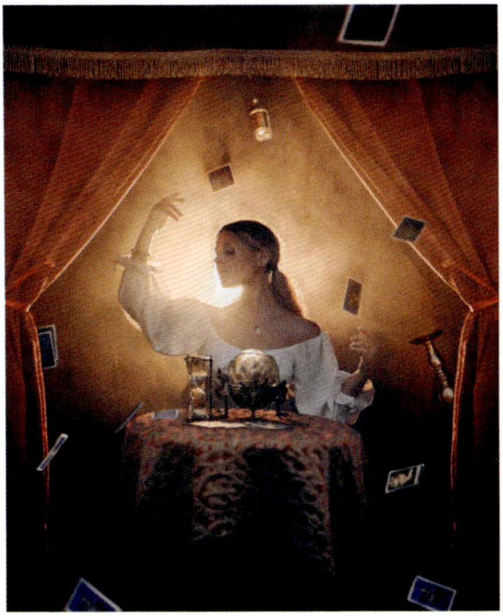

I was asked to create this fortune teller-themed shot for a perfume brand. The tent mimicked my garage lighting set-up, creating an enclosure for me to stand in. I placed my portable Interfit Badger Beam LED light on a light stand behind me to backlight my hair. A smoke bomb behind me mixed with the lighting set-up to create this magical haze.

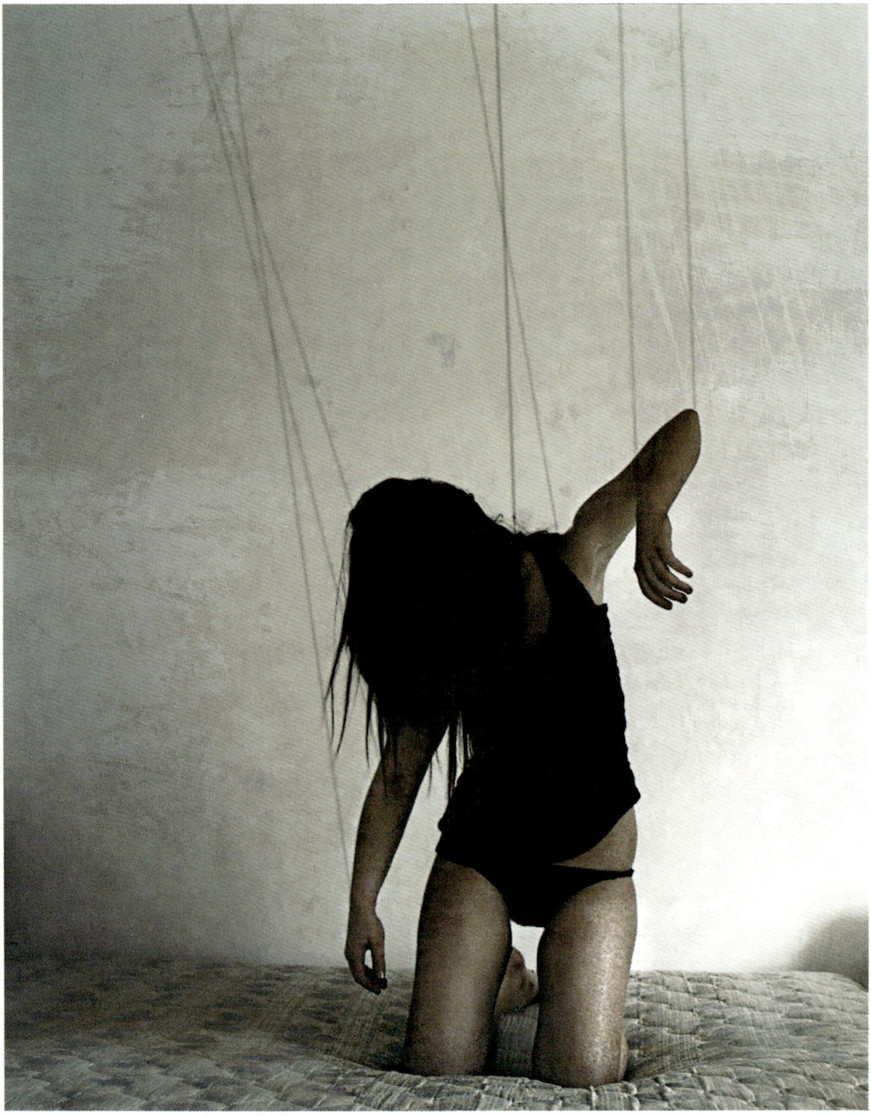

'Not Your Puppet' – One of my first self-portraits, taken in 2008. Shot using a Canon EOS 400D with an 18–55mm kit lens.

INTERVALOMETERS, TIMERS AND REMOTES

Intervalometers, timers and wireless-remote systems are built-in features found in many modern cameras, offering photographers enhanced control over their shooting process. Luckily, the technology in this area of photography has much improved in recent years. When I first started shooting my self-portraits, it was me vs the ten-second self-timer.

In this image (circa 2008), I had ten seconds to press the shutter, get myself over to the bed and throw myself into this pose. I did about 50 takes, and was exhausted by the end of the session.

So, here's an explanation of these very useful features and their handy pros for self-portrait photography.

INTERVALOMETERS

Intervalometers are camera functions or accessories that allow photographers to schedule and automate the capture of images at predefined intervals, for example, every one second, two seconds, five seconds (the choices really are endless). If not shooting for a self-portrait, they are also useful for creating time-lapse sequences, capturing long-exposure shots or documenting gradual changes over time. My preference, of course, is using them for selfies. The intervalometer allows me to go as far away from the camera as I like (as I'm not dependent on Wi-Fi, Bluetooth remote distance or a ten-second dive limit), and taking images every second or so means I'll capture a range of poses and motion. You can set your intervalometer to stop whenever you'd prefer or keep going until you switch the camera off.

SELF-TIMERS

Timers are features that allow photographers to set a specific delay before the camera captures an image. They can be used to create self-portraits or group photos by giving the photographer time to join the scene after triggering the shutter. For example, cameras such as the Canon EOS 5D Mark IV or the Fujifilm X-T4 offer customizable self-timer settings. You can set a delay (such as five seconds or ten seconds) after pressing the shutter button, allowing you to get into position for a self-portrait before

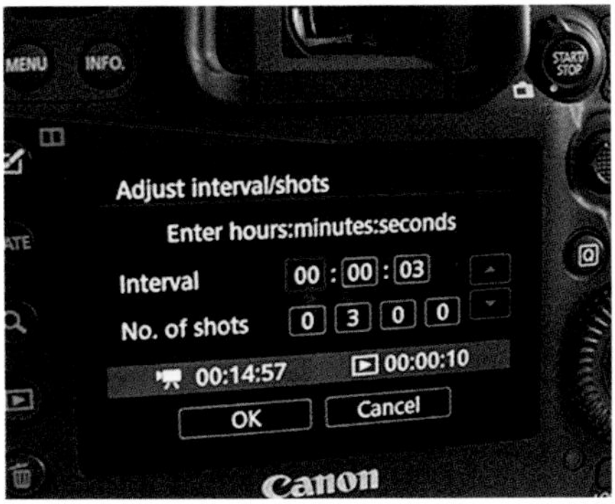

The settings of the intervalometer function on a Canon camera.

the image is captured. This feature is particularly useful for beginners who may not have access to a wireless remote or when shooting in a location where using a remote is just impractical. Self-timers were my go-to for at least three years of my photography career.

WIRELESS REMOTE SYSTEMS

Many cameras are compatible with wireless remote systems, which allow photographers to remotely control their camera's shutter release. Wireless remote systems can include dedicated remote controls or smartphone apps that connect to the camera via Wi-Fi or Bluetooth.

The Sony PlayMemories Mobile app and the Canon Camera Connect app are popular examples of smartphone apps that enable wireless remote control. These apps provide features like Live View, touch focus and the ability to trigger the shutter remotely, allowing photographers to view themselves on their phone's screen before capturing a self-portrait. This functionality helps provide aid in your composition, making sure that your desired pose and framing are on point. You can always edit your phone out of the picture afterwards or camouflage it in the scene. This feature is also incredibly useful for checking focus, and saves plenty of time and frustration.

Utilizing these features and settings in self-portrait photography offers several advantages:

INCREASED CONTROL AND CONVENIENCE: Intervalometers, timers and wireless remote systems provide photographers with greater control over the timing and execution of their shots, enabling more flexibility and creative possibilities.

ENHANCED COMPOSITION AND EXPERIMENTATION: With wireless remote apps, we can preview our poses or compositions on our smartphones, which allows for subtle adjustments and some experimentation before taking the final shot.

CAPTURING MOVEMENT AND PROGRESSION: Intervalometers set to shorter intervals (like one second) can capture a series of images that showcase movement, gradual changes or time-lapse sequences, which adds a cool dynamic element to your self-portraits.

By leveraging all these wondrous built-in features and technologies, we photographers can achieve far more precise and creative self-portraits, all while expanding our artistic vision.

APERTURE, ISO AND SHUTTER SPEED

Understanding the basic pyramid of aperture, ISO and shutter speed is crucial for photographers. These three elements are the pillars of exposure control, meaning without them, you risk not having a picture at all!

By mastering these concepts, photographers can achieve proper exposure, control the depth of field in their images, manage image noise and capture motion effectively. Let's delve into each topic and explore their meanings, control methods and, of course, their pros and cons:

APERTURE

Aperture refers to the opening of the lens diaphragm through which light enters the camera. It is measured in *f*-stops, represented by numbers like *f*/2.8, *f*/4, *f*/5.6 and so on. A wide aperture (small *f*-number) means a larger opening, while a narrow aperture (large *f*-number) represents a smaller opening.

CONTROL: Aperture is controlled by adjusting the lens's aperture value or *f*-stop. A wider aperture (e.g., *f*/1.8) allows more light to enter the camera and results in a shallower depth of field (blurry background). A narrower aperture (e.g., *f*/16) restricts light, leading to a deeper depth of field (more in-focus background).

PROS AND CONS:

- **WIDE APERTURE (LOW F-NUMBER):** Pros include shallow depth of field, pleasing background blur (bokeh) and the ability to shoot in low-light conditions. Cons include narrower focus range, potential for focusing errors and limited depth of field control in certain situations.
- **NARROW APERTURE (HIGH F-NUMBER):** Pros include a larger depth of field, sharper focus throughout the image and increased chances of capturing details in the background. Cons include reduced light reaching the sensor, longer exposure times and potential diffraction softening at very high *f*-numbers.

When shooting self-portraits, I tend to keep my aperture set at *f*/1.4 or *f*/1.8, depending on the lens I'm shooting with. I will only increase the depth of field and shoot at *f*/4 if I need to include details of the background in the shot. On the following page are some examples of my self-portrait work, shot with a wide aperture (*f*/1.4) and a narrower one (*f*/4).

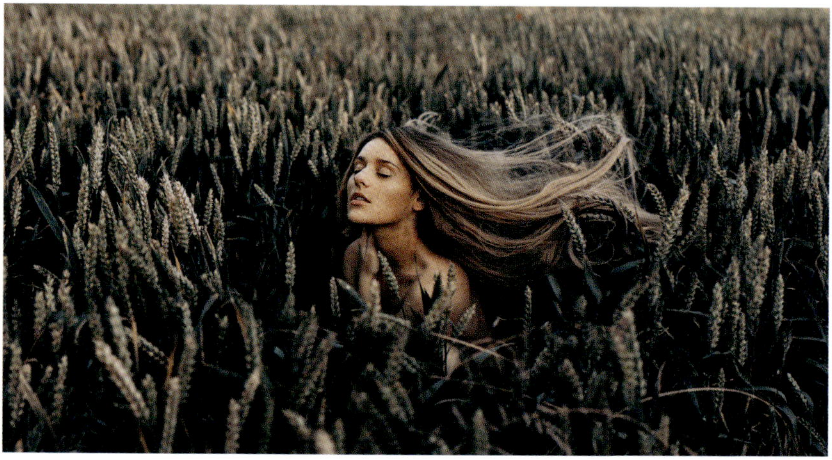

Shot using a Canon EOS 5D Mark II with 85mm f/1.2 lens, 1/800 sec. shutter speed, f/1.2 aperture, ISO 400.

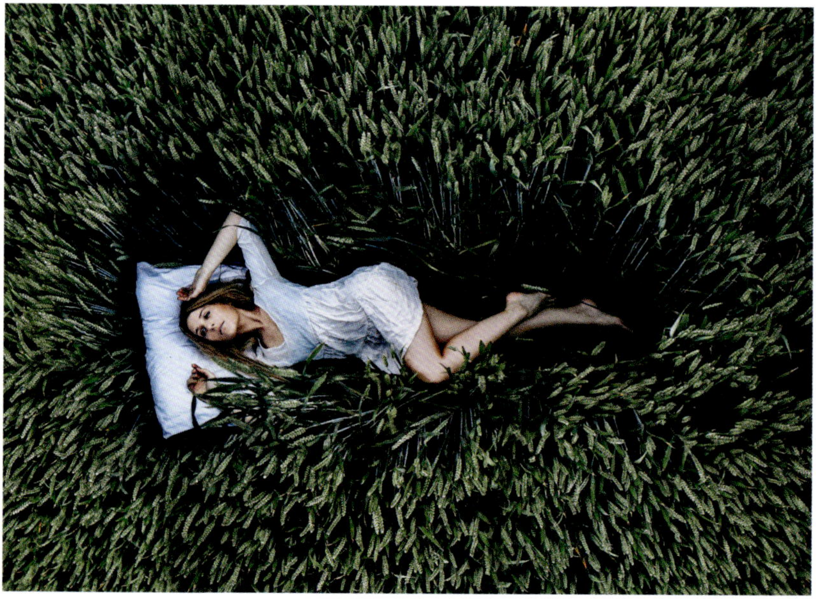

Shot using a Canon EOS 5D Mark II with 35mm f/1.4 lens, 1/200 sec. shutter speed, f/4 aperture, ISO 640.

ISO

ISO represents the sensitivity of the camera's image sensor to light. It determines how well the camera captures details in low-light conditions, but also affects the amount of noise in the image. Common ISO values include 100, 200, 400, 800 and so on.

CONTROL: ISO is adjusted through camera settings, with higher ISO values increasing sensitivity to light and lower ISO values decreasing it. However, raising the ISO also increases the visibility of noise in the image, making it look lower quality and compromising the detail in the shot.

PROS AND CONS:

- **LOW ISO:** Pros include less noise, improved image quality and sharper details. Cons involve the need for more light, limitations in low-light shooting without a tripod and longer shutter speeds to compensate for lower sensitivity.
- **HIGH ISO:** Pros include better low-light performance, faster shutter speeds and increased flexibility in challenging lighting conditions. Cons would be increased noise, reduced dynamic range and potential loss of image detail.

When shooting outdoors on a typically overcast day, you'll be able to keep your ISO low – think 100, 200 or 400. The darker it is when you're shooting, the more likely it is that you'll need to increase your ISO. But remember that pesky noise can damage the overall image. Consider adjusting your aperture (lowering the *f*-stop) or reducing your shutter speed if possible.

Did you know that the Nikon D6 has a maximum native ISO of 102,400? It also has an extended ISO range that goes up to 3,280,000. Crazy!

SHUTTER SPEED

Shutter speed refers to the length of time the camera's shutter remains open, exposing the image sensor to light. It is measured in seconds or fractions of a second.

CONTROL: Shutter speed is controlled by adjusting the camera's settings, with longer durations (e.g., 1/4 sec., 1 sec.) allowing more light to reach the sensor and shorter durations (e.g., 1/1000 sec., 1/4000 sec.) reducing the amount of light reaching the sensor. Shutter speed also controls the appearance of motion blur, with fast shutter speeds freezing motion and slow speeds enabling you to create intentional motion blur.

PROS AND CONS:

- **FAST SHUTTER SPEED:** Pros include freezing fast-moving subjects, capturing action with minimal motion blur and increased sharpness. Cons include reduced light reaching the sensor, potential underexposure in low-light

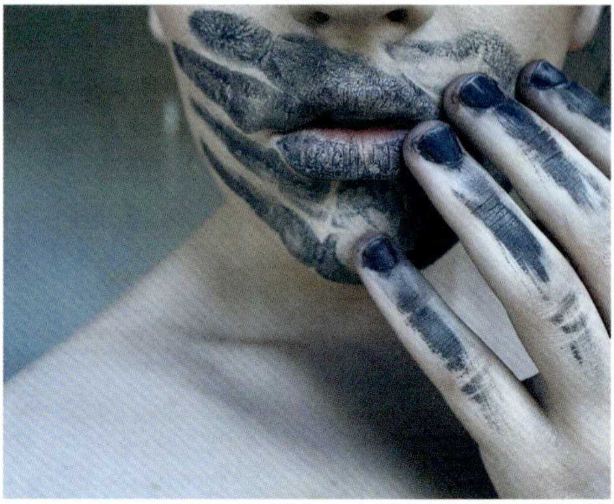

Shot on a Canon EOS 400D with 18–55mm kit lens, 1/60 sec. shutter speed, f/5 aperture. These were the Auto settings generated by my beginner kit, and I used editing to blur the background and create the shallow depth of field. I now use my wide-aperture lenses to achieve this.

conditions and limited depth of field control in bright situations.

- **SLOW SHUTTER SPEED:** Pros include creating intentional motion blur, creating light trails, long-exposure imagery (think rolling clouds or gushing water turned into silky smooth waves) and conveying a sense of motion. Cons involve the risk of camera shake without stabilization, potential overexposure in bright light and slow shutter speeds not being ideal for fast-moving subjects.

SHOOTING STYLES:

Once you've understood how each function works, you then have the opportunity to control them. As a beginner, I shot for the first year in Auto mode. I have and continue to have no shame in this – I wasn't shooting for a love of technicalities, and just wanted to create. Learning the ins and outs came naturally to me later, as I became more curious about my favourite tool. Don't feel bad if this is something you want to learn later too – it's better to remain excited on Auto than become overwhelmed with the controls.

That being said, if you do decide to explore, here are your given modes:

- **MANUAL MODE:** This mode provides full control over aperture, ISO and shutter speed, allowing photographers to adjust all settings manually for precise exposure control. I shoot exclusively in Manual mode now, something Beginner Rosie would be terrified of. It's not so scary after a couple of weeks!

- **APERTURE PRIORITY:** In this mode, you decide on the aperture setting you want to use, and the camera automatically sets the shutter speed needed to achieve the correct exposure. This isn't foolproof, though. If you use Auto ISO, the camera might choose a high (noisy) setting or it simply might not be able to set a slow enough or fast enough shutter speed based on the light levels and your ISO/aperture combination.
- **SHUTTER PRIORITY:** Here, photographers select their desired shutter speed, and the camera automatically adjusts the aperture to achieve proper exposure. Again, sounds great in theory, but as a photographer with a preference for wide apertures, I'd be gutted to shoot in a beautiful location and find that the images are over-detailed with no depth, when I actually wanted a beautifully shallow depth of field.
- **PROGRAM MODE:** This mode sets both aperture and shutter speed automatically, but allows photographers to adjust other settings such as ISO, exposure compensation and white balance.

Here's a quiz to get to learn the functions of aperture, ISO and shutter speed.

Q) IT'S A DARK NIGHT, AND I WANT TO PHOTOGRAPH MYSELF JUMPING IN THE AIR, WITHOUT BLUR. WHAT SHOULD I CHOOSE?

A) FAST SHUTTER SPEED, LOW ISO (100), WIDE APERTURE (F/1.4)

B) SLOW SHUTTER SPEED, HIGH ISO (2,000), WIDE APERTURE (F/1.4)

C) FAST SHUTTER SPEED, HIGH ISO (1,000), WIDE APERTURE (F/1.4)

ANSWER: C gives the best combination for an image in low light, without motion blur and without too much image grain. A would produce an underexposed image, and B would produce a potentially exposed image, but with undesired motion blur.

Remember, trial and error are by far the best tools in understanding how aperture, shutter speed and ISO connect. You don't need to be able to memorize or know exactly what settings to shoot at – you can feel your way and use whatever feels best based on your environment and available lighting.

FOCUSING IN SELF-PORTRAITURE

One of the first questions people ask me about my self-portraits is 'How on earth do you get yourself in focus?'.

Luckily, I have many secrets and answers to that and I'm going to spill them now for you. But first, a little more about the focusing system hiding inside your camera.

The focusing system is responsible for achieving super-sharp focus on the subject (or area of interest) in an image. It determines how the camera measures and adjusts focus to ensure the desired elements of your shot are in sharp focus. When shooting a self-portrait, you have the option to use either autofocus or manual focus – and each has its own advantages and considerations.

AUTOFOCUS (AF)

Autofocus relies on the camera's internal mechanisms to automatically adjust the lens position and achieve that pin-sharp focus. It uses various focusing methods and modes to detect and track subjects, some of which you can choose in your camera menu. Some common autofocus modes include:

- **SINGLE AF (ONE-SHOT AF):** This mode is suitable for stationary subjects. The camera locks focus when the shutter button is pressed halfway, and the focus is maintained until the picture is taken.
- **CONTINUOUS AF (AI SERVO AF):** This mode is useful for capturing moving subjects or when the camera and subject are both in motion. The camera continuously adjusts focus as long as the shutter button is half pressed, allowing for continuous tracking of the subject.

WHEN SHOOTING A SELF-PORTRAIT USING AUTOFOCUS:

- Use a focus point or area selection mode to ensure the camera focuses on the desired area of your face or body.
- Utilize face-detection or eye-detection autofocus (if available on your camera, of course) to ensure super-sharp focus on your face or eyes.
- Use a tripod or a focus-and-recompose technique to ensure that the camera focuses accurately on your desired position. Keeping the camera still helps massively, and controls at least one variable.

AUTOFOCUS POSITIVES:

- Autofocus is best known for being quick and convenient, especially when capturing spontaneous moments.
- Advanced autofocus systems can accurately track moving subjects, which is a big winner for self-portraiture. You can walk into the

shot and out again, knowing no matter where you stand and move, you'll be tracked and in focus.

- Features such as face-detection and eye-detection autofocus aid in achieving sharp focus on specific facial features. As a rule of thumb, I always tend to aim for focus on the eyes above anything else.

AUTOFOCUS CONS:

- The camera may focus on the wrong subject if it's not properly selected or if there are distractions in the shot (for example, other people in the background).
- In low-light situations or low-contrast scenes, autofocus may struggle to lock on to subjects.

MANUAL FOCUS (MF)

Manual focus (as the name suggests) allows for manual adjustment of the lens focus ring to achieve sharpness. This means the camera/lens is set to focus at one specific distance, and this won't shift during your shoot. Pro tip: always remember to switch your manual focus back off if you've got another photoshoot the next day. Learn from my mistakes!

Shooting self-portraits with this method provides full control over focus and is especially useful in situations where autofocus may struggle, such as low-light or low-contrast environments.

MY TIPS FOR USING MANUAL FOCUS:

- Use Live View mode and zoom in on the screen to accurately adjust focus on specific facial features. Live View has been a life-saver for me over the last five years.
- Consider using a remote shutter release or utilizing the camera's inbuilt intervalometer function to prevent camera shake when manually focusing.

MANUAL FOCUS POSITIVES:

- Allows precise control over focus, especially in challenging lighting conditions or situations with limited contrast.
- Useful when shooting with a tripod or for achieving a specific creative effect.

MANUAL FOCUS CONS:

- Requires careful attention and practice to achieve accurate focus.
- Can be time-consuming, especially when shooting fast-paced action or capturing multiple images.

In self-portrait photography, the choice between autofocus and manual focus depends on things like your shooting conditions, your desired level of control and, of course, your personal preference. I recommend experimenting with both methods, and understanding how they interact with your camera's specific focusing system to achieve your vision. Personally, I prefer to shoot mainly manual focus when it comes to my self-portraits, but would switch to the autofocus tracking system on, say, a Canon EOS R5 if I wanted shots of me running/moving in a ballgown.

Shot using manual focus on a Canon EOS 5D Mark II with a 35mm f/1.4 lens.1/500 sec. shutter speed, f/2.8 aperture, ISO 320.

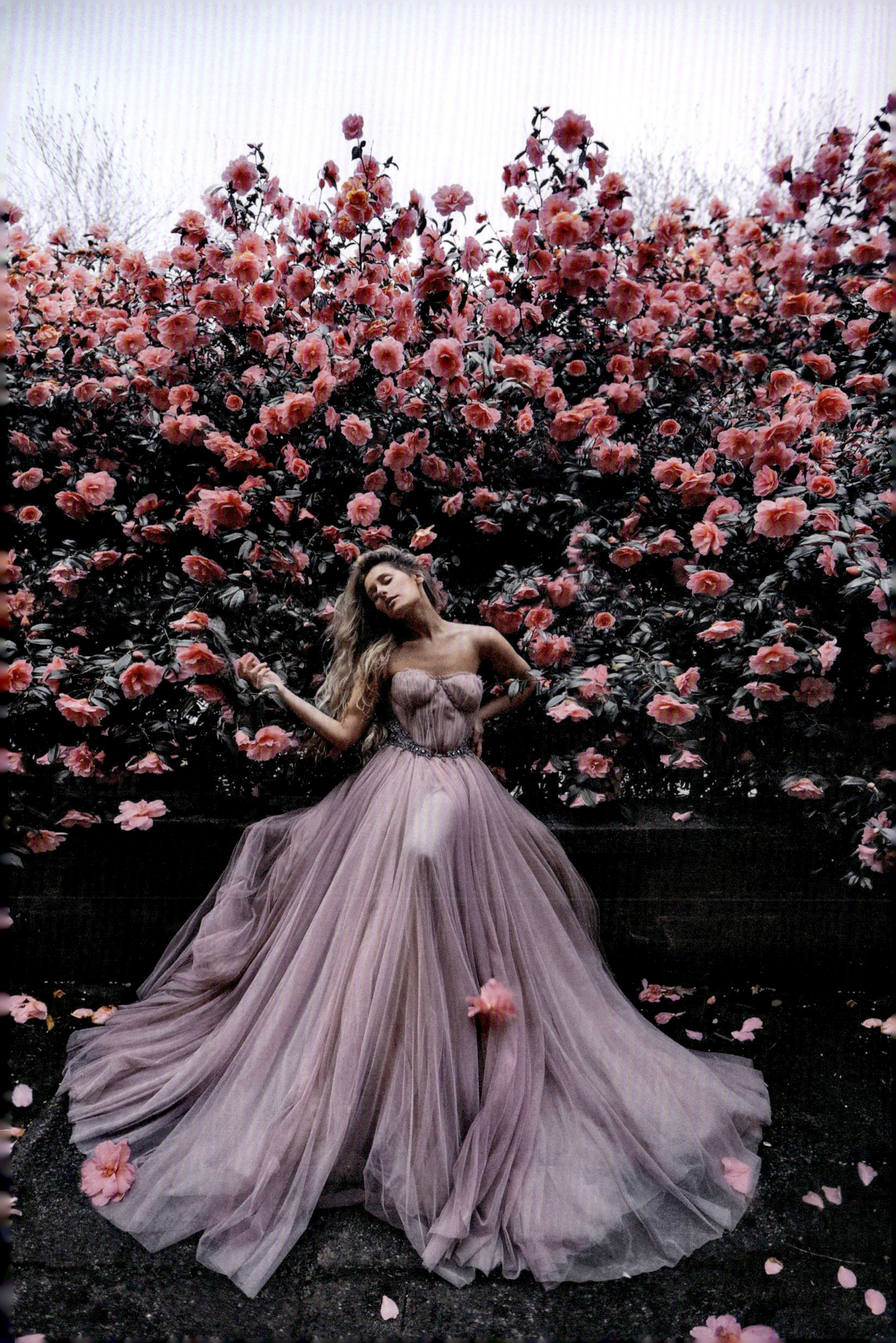

03.

365 CHALLENGE

MY STORY

'As long as I kept moving, my grief streamed out behind me like a swimmer's long hair in water. I knew the weight was there but it didn't touch me. Only when I stopped did the slick, dark stuff of it come floating around my face, catching my arms and throat till I began to drown. So I just didn't stop.'
– Barbara Kingsolver
The Poisonwood Bible

The 365 Challenge originated in the depths of the internet, and I stumbled across it in around 2006. Also known as a 'Photo-a-Day' or 'Project 365', this challenge is a personal project where photographers aim to capture and share one photograph every day for a year. It gained popularity and became more widely recognized with the rise of social media platforms like Flickr and Instagram, which provided forums for photographers to share their daily images. As time went on, self-portraiture became a branch of the 365 challenge, and it was a branch I was happy to climb.

Many photographers have embraced the 365 Challenge as a means to develop their skills, explore new techniques, document their lives or simply enjoy the creative process. The project allows photographers to experiment with different styles and showcase their progress throughout the year. As a teenager, I was drawn to the idea of shooting self-portraits each day for many reasons, the first of which being the outlet to express myself, with the undercurrent of an expectation not to be any good at it. After all, this challenge is about growth – to see how much your style, technique and message evolves in a year.

In my journey, I also liked the idea of creating a new identity for myself online. At school, I felt like a misfit – I didn't feel I fitted into any particular set or group, and found myself drawn to escapism from the struggles I was facing. Luckily, my escapism was centred around creativity and somewhat delusional thinking (in a nice way). The dawn of sharing your personal life on the internet came naturally into my life, and the online 365 photography community provided a place of inclusion, connection and support.

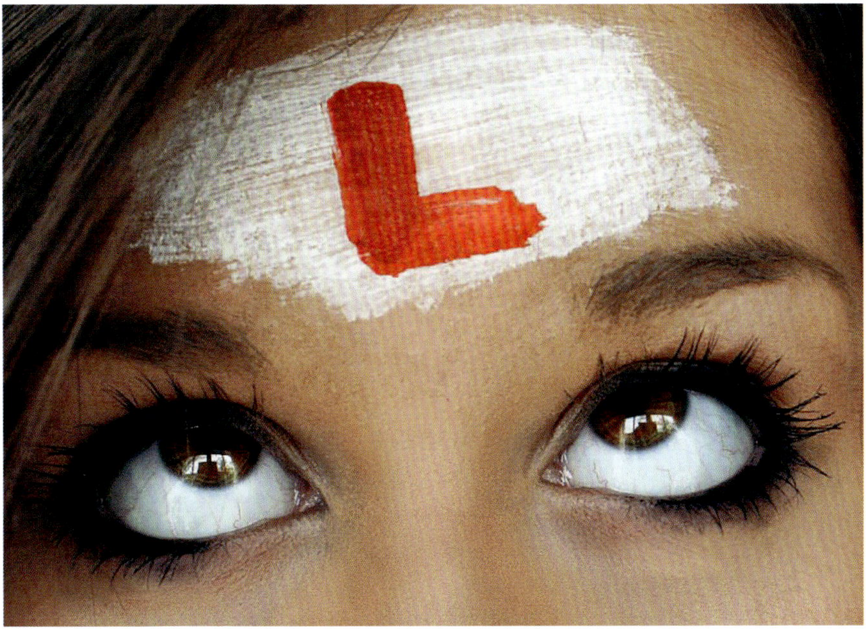

ATTEMPT ONE

8/365

Before my alopecia took hold, I'd struggled with (and would continue to struggle with) heavily disordered eating. I kept online food diaries, became obsessed with imagery of super-slim models and ricocheted in cycles of starving followed by big food binges. I told no one, but my strange behaviour around food was noticed at home and at school. I'm still not entirely sure what I was trying to control, but the feeling of being an outsider never left me until I found my home on Flickr. My art teacher, Mr Oates, encouraged me to pursue photography and self-portraiture in my work. When I produced a photo series on eating disorders for my GCSE coursework, he encouraged me even more to create. I don't know whether he intended to support me in the monumental way he did, but praising my photography and expression (as 'beginner' as it was) helped add a healthy lifeline into my big bag of unhealthy coping mechanisms. Over the years, I moved through my eating disorders and alopecia, and invested more and more time and energy into my self-portraits. Expressing my struggles through them has served me as much as professional therapy.

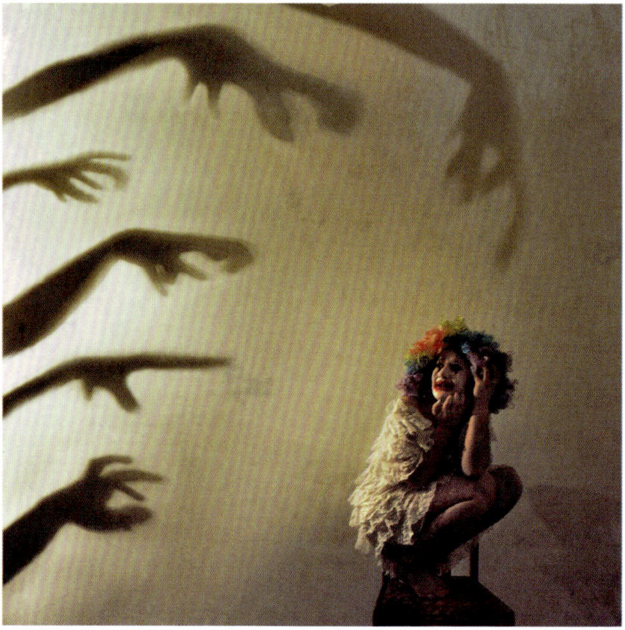

135/365

In my first 365 attempt, I made it to around 186 days before giving up. I want to stress that this wasn't a failure – the process was enough for me to realize that I loved photography, and wasn't going to live a life without it. I became overwhelmed by the attention (positive and negative) that my daily photo diaries were getting online. The internet is a Wild West of its own, and I was sharing myself very openly on there. I'd met another photographer, who lived in North Carolina, USA, thousands of miles from me. He was also doing the 365, and we bonded over imaginative self-portraiture. We began sharing our relationship with our online audience and the attention swelled again. As I began to learn more technicalities from him, my editing abilities also grew. We would Photoshop ourselves into images together, still having never met. Though we were far from the first people to have an internet romance, it felt like we were the first to have their relationship develop entirely in front of an audience, and have these people follow our every thought and move every single day. Eventually, we met, and continued our 365s together, documenting the first time we saw each other in the flesh, the first trips abroad and eventually me moving to North Carolina from the UK.

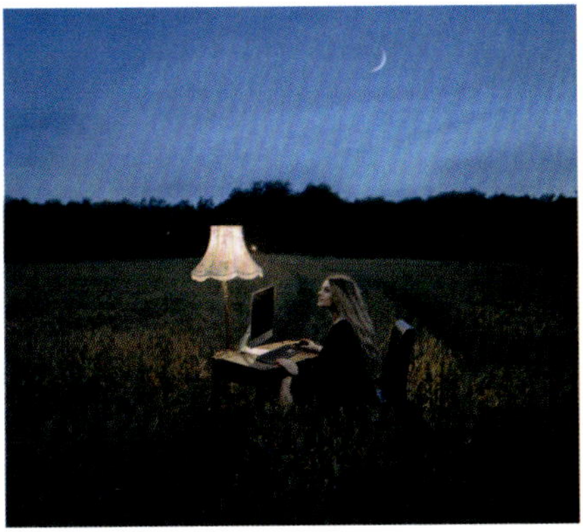

171/365

The support and encouragement was overwhelmingly loud, but it became harder and harder to not focus on the occasional mean comment. Eventually, the online negativity began to take its toll on me. The comments grew and grew, and the unrestricted internet did its thing. On top of this, I found it difficult to come up with a new concept and idea for a photo every single day, and often felt like I was rushing my work, or having to lift concepts from other people, without properly creating a more original concept. Understandably, doing this did not go down well online. I struggled to feel inspired, but felt addicted to the rush of posting and sharing, and receiving validation for the 'me' I was on the internet. I decided to stop my 365 after an online hate campaign was started – it wasn't worth the energy, the depression or the nastiness. What started as a healthy escape from exactly those things began happening all over again. I remember sitting in my biology class, and thinking to myself, 'I can make all of this go away if I just never pick up a camera again'.

If I had to pinpoint it, I'd say that moment is where I knew that being a photographer was the direction I wanted to take my life in. I loved the validation I found online so much – I loved feeling liked, accepted, included. And in equal measure, I despised the opposite – being bullied, disliked, rejected. It felt like hell on earth reading through the hate mail that was landing in my inbox and in my comment section on Flickr, but I just couldn't give up creating. There was no price too high to throw the towel in on the one thing that had given me purpose, an identity, some healing. So, I stopped the 365 but continued to create. I took the time to learn from my mistakes, to apologize and to begin again.

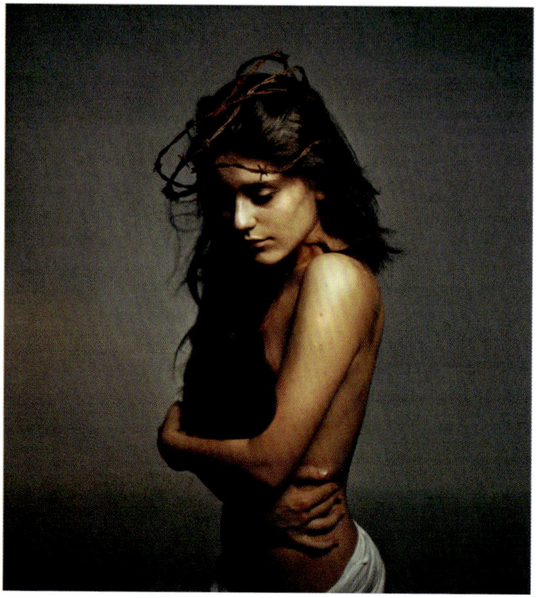

TIM

My second 365 Challenge took place almost ten years after my first, for very different reasons. Most of the photography world had shifted from Flickr to Facebook and Instagram, and so had I.

It was 2015, I was 24, and I was costume hunting for fantasy-themed ball gowns and costumes in my local theatre costume hire shop, The Royal Exchange Costume Hire, in Manchester. I was in my element – rows and rows of beautiful fabrics, magical costumes, headpieces. Heaven to me! A man came in to buy his own costume, and we acknowledged each other happily. I carried on skipping round the rails of costumes. Eventually, he asked for my help choosing a ringmaster's jacket – I told him the ragged, tattered black one, of course. He was older than me, but had that charisma and energy that seemed a little bit magic.

I have a principle in life, based on a wonderful quote:

'If you want to get warm you must stand near the fire: if you want to be wet you must get into the water. If you want joy, power, peace, eternal life, you must get close to, or even into, the thing that has them.'
– C.S. Lewis
Mere Christianity

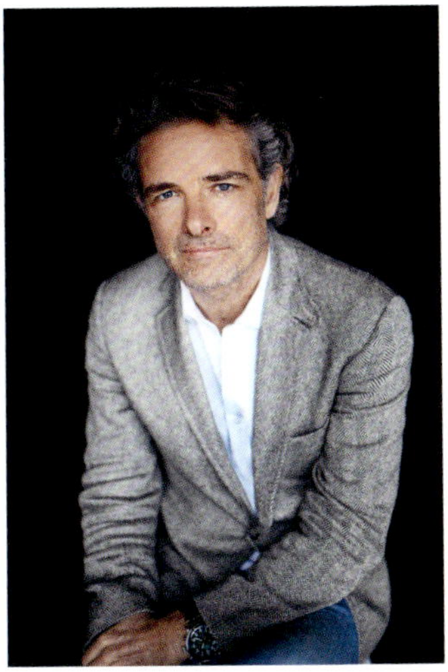

My motto is quite simple: follow the magic, and your life will become magical by default. Tim, as I later learned was his name, embodied that mischievous and playful spark that I loved so much in life. I decided that I would ask what his costume was for (assuming it was a play or theatre production) and go and see it, convinced something wonderful would happen to me there, wherever it was.

He told me that his costume was in fact not for a theatre production but for a work event – a circus-themed costume ball, and he was the ringmaster. And, with a smile at my disappointment, he remarked that he'd 'have to hire me to get me in'. Ever the one to leap at a random opportunity, hiring me was absolutely the right thing for him to do – the costume ball seemed a good alternative to a play, and a bonus to be paid to be there! He left the costume shop with my phone number, and I carried on burying myself in layer upon layer of tulle dresses. I didn't really expect to hear from him, thinking it was probably a lovely but polite conversation, but a few days later my phone beeped.

It was an invitation – me plus a friend, if I wanted to bring one, to 'The Circus'. We'd have our own room at the hotel in Liverpool, along with all the other staff attending. I liked following the stepping stones that were unexpectedly unfolding in front of me. I didn't think much more of the job, or of Tim, until the night of The Circus.

Checked into my hotel room, I dressed in my own circus costume, ready to shoot. Tim sent me a message, asking if I needed to get any shots of him getting ready. I popped into his room and told him that brushing his teeth was the only suitable shot we needed – and snap, I unknowingly took one of my favourite photos I've taken this lifetime (see page 56).

I spent the rest of the night surrounded by brilliant, imaginative costumes, stilt walkers, smoke and candyfloss, acrobats and friendly faces enjoying their night. I knew Tim was the boss, but didn't know how well loved he was by all those who worked for him. I watched and photographed as he spoke to every single person there, shook their hands and listened to them intently. He threw me the occasional glance, which I brushed off, and carried on hopping into dark corners to shoot my pictures. He came up to me as I chatted with another person, and asked what we were talking about. Tinder, of course, was the topic at hand. 'I wouldn't know,' he said. 'I'm recently divorced. Do I need to sign up?'

It was a subtle conversational drop, and I laughed and made my excuses to dart away into another corner. For as charming and lovely as he seemed, he was older than me and not someone I'd considered romantically. I enjoyed the rest of the night, a big smile on my face, snapping away merrily at all the spectacular sights. I went back up to my room, closed the door, and put on my pjs for bed.

An hour later, there was a knock on my door. It was Tim, also in his pjs, and a bottle of champagne, along with a bucket. 'Smooth,' I thought, 'but absolutely not.' I didn't mind the idea of sitting up and talking with him, as he seemed to have lived a fascinating life, but that was where I drew the line.

What followed was probably one of the most honest and vulnerable conversations I've ever had in my life. Tim explained, to my sadness, that he had cancer, and was supposed to be dead right now. He'd been given six months to live six months before, and yet here he was. I asked him questions: how had staring directly into his mortality affected him? He was so positive, so nonchalant, so simply glad to be alive. By 3 a.m. we were listening to music. He sang along, we sang together, it was so pure and innocent and lovely. I showed him my favourite poems, he enjoyed them and asked for more. He asked why I wasn't in a relationship, I shared some dark experiences from my past that I usually wouldn't tell anyone, not even the internet, not even my family, things that would usually take me months to open up about with a partner. But Tim might not be here tomorrow, or next week, so why not tell him? He responded with such lightness to something I carried that felt so, so dark. It was as though he held up a map to another way of thinking – a way of forgiving others, forgiving myself. All of a sudden, it didn't seem so bad. 'I have terminal cancer. I win,' he said, with a wink.

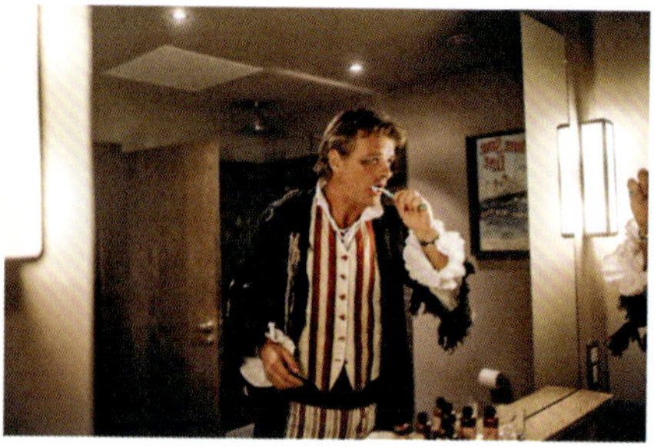

The early hours of the morning came and went in a haze of connection and endless talk, and ended with an unexpected kiss. It was a sweet moment, and as we lay there talking, fingers intertwined, he said, 'This is one of those Rebecca moments.'

'Huh?' I was confused.

'On your Instagram post. You wrote a quote from Daphne Du Maurier's *Rebecca*. This is one of those moments.'

Ah, yes it was. More than I could ever have imagined.

'I wanted to go on sitting there, not talking, not listening to the others, keeping the moment precious for all time, because we were peaceful, all of us, we were content and drowsy even as the bee who droned above our heads. In a little while it would be different, there would come tomorrow, and the next day, and another year. And we would be changed perhaps, never sitting quite like this again. Some of us would go away, or suffer, or die; the future stretched away in front of us, unknown, unseen, not perhaps what we wanted, not what we planned. This moment was safe though, this could not be touched.'

– Daphne Du Maurier, *Rebecca*

The Circus was gone by the morning. Tim and I went our separate ways, and I thought to myself, I will always remember my magical night at the show, and the deep, human connection I felt with a stranger. How funny and wonderful, how we can connect together so deeply just by showing a little more of our hearts than we usually dare. I smiled for the rest of the day, and carried on with my stepping stones.

A week later, I delivered the pictures, and got another message from

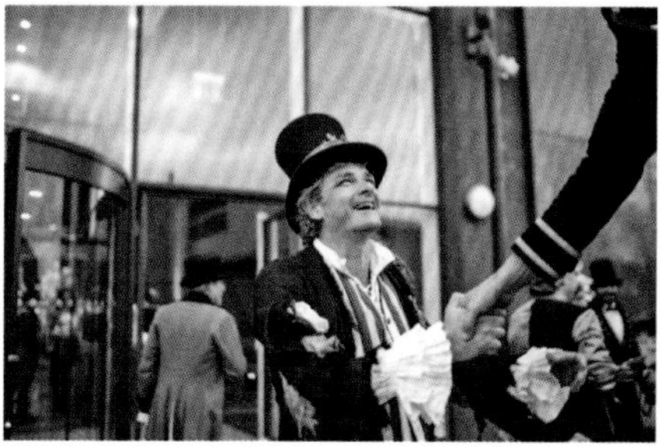

Tim. He was thrilled. 'They came out beautifully! And you made me look quite good.' He asked if he could take me to an art gallery followed by lunch at one of his restaurants as a thank you. I was quite happy at the idea of seeing my new friend, but mentally made a note that there wouldn't be any more stolen kisses – just friends felt good.

We spent the day wandering around at the art gallery, giving our terribly inexperienced opinions on all the different art. Tim had moved into a new place, and explained the walls were horribly bare and that I should choose a new art piece for his snug. Hungry for the challenge, I settled on a piece that felt the most 'me' – a weird-looking girl wearing a Victorian ruff, a dead look in her eyes and, most bizarrely, holding a bag of popcorn. The popped kernels were clutched in her hands, falling from her fingers as her empty gaze met that of the viewer. It was weird, it made us both feel uneasy. I loved it.

We went to lunch, he told me he was on a strictly vegan diet for the cancer. 'No fun at all.' He told me that the cancer was all he ever was asked about these days – not only had it taken over his body, but even worse, it was dominating all his conversations, too! So, we made a rule – no cancer talk, unless absolutely necessary. And there was so much we had to talk about. Hours had passed, and we'd barely scratched the surface. I went to walk back to my car, gave him a hug goodbye and, this time in public, he leaned in and I politely gave him the cheek, just as planned.

What didn't go to plan was that over the following months, I began to fall completely in love with Tim. Every day, we would text each other, asking questions about the other, telling stories, sending poems and quotes on the harder days, sending music recommendations to blast on the good.

A month after our first meeting, Tim was told he needed to spend the week in hospital; he wasn't doing well. He was on a new kind of immunotherapy, and the steroids had caused his lips to go black, making him look like he'd been stranded up on Everest for a few days. He said that the nurses loved him (I didn't doubt it), and would I like to swing by for a visit? So, I did. I vividly remember exiting the lift at the hospital, getting to his floor. Walking along, wondering what room number he'd be in… and when I listened, I could hear music. Rock music, to be exact. As I got further down the corridor, the music got louder – it was The Doors, one of

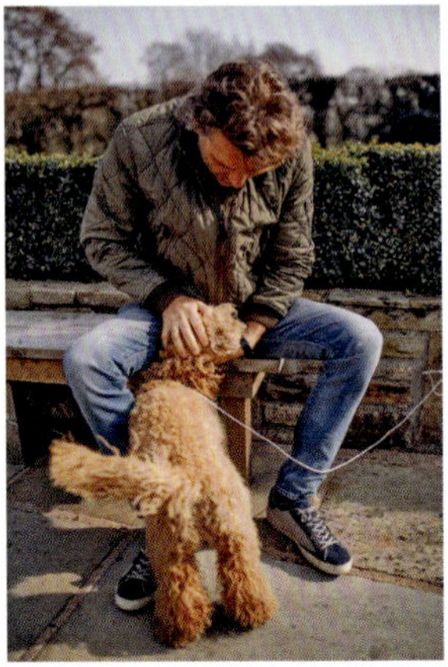

Tim's favourite bands. Blasting it in his hospital room in total style – I couldn't help but smile.

A week passed after my hospital visit, and Tim got quieter. His texts became less and I got a little sad. I loved talking with him, and didn't really want our friendship to be so fleeting. Eventually, he apologized, said that he didn't want to drag me into this and that he was very poorly and would be back in touch to see me when he was better. I told him I understood, that we could keep in touch via text, and tried to carry on with my stepping stones, a little sad that Tim's would probably come to an end long before mine would.

To cut a long, happy, heartbreaking story short, Tim and I continued to keep in touch. I ended up going over to his place to see the unveiling of his new art piece, *The Weird Girl With Popcorn*, hanging on his wall and to talk some more. No cancer talk, though. It was late November, we lay on the grass outside his house and looked at the stars. We talked about the Fermi Paradox, watched Neil deGrasse Tyson on YouTube, and talked some more. We threw the vegan diet out of the window and ate chocolate ice cream together. He told me stories of his life, the crazy things he'd seen and been part of. The way he'd approached the obstacles that had reared their heads was nothing short of remarkable. It was clear that he was an incredible, very special person. And he thought I was, too.

Our friendship eventually turned into a relationship, and despite both of our hesitations about what people would think (me worried I'd be seen as a gold digger, Tim worried that he'd be seen as a creep or a fool), we decided we actually didn't care that much at all. It seemed to make much more sense to seize love while we both still could, and I couldn't imagine a better person to live out an unexpected love story with. He was gentle and kind, and treated me as a complete equal. As the months flew by, and the reality of his illness became increasingly apparent, I began to experience what I now know to be 'anticipated grief'.

I remember taking the train alone to London to spend the day with him, and sobbing quietly in my seat the whole way down. I didn't want him to vanish from my life. I didn't ever plan on falling in love with him, but to know him was to fall in love with him. I began to start frantically scanning every moment we spent together, trying to log every memory into my brain so that I'd never forget. I wrote poem after poem, was inhaling art like a drug addict, and had never felt more alive and connected to my soul than in those months.

Eventually, we had to talk about the cancer. Tim told me that he hated the idea of gradually getting weaker, becoming unable to talk, walk and look after himself. He told me his Grand Plan: to go into a hospice and not see anyone again until he died, except his best mate, Dave. I was so upset at this idea. The concept of saying goodbye to him, knowing he was still alive, and not having access to talk to him and care for him, as though his only benefit to anyone was him in fully functioning order, was unbearable. More tears.

He told me that he didn't plan to die any time soon, that I didn't need to worry, and so, I didn't. We made plans. The last night we spent together, I didn't know it was the last night. The rain was heavy, thunderstorm-worthy rain. It poured down his windows very much in the way my tears had poured down my face days before. He had a cough. A pneumonia diagnosis, from his doctor. The rain continued, and I suggested that we go lay outside in it together. 'It'll kill me if I do that,' he said with a smile, 'but you go.'

I didn't look behind me, but I have a feeling that he watched. I walked out into the garden, took off all my clothes, and sat crossed-legged on the wet grass.

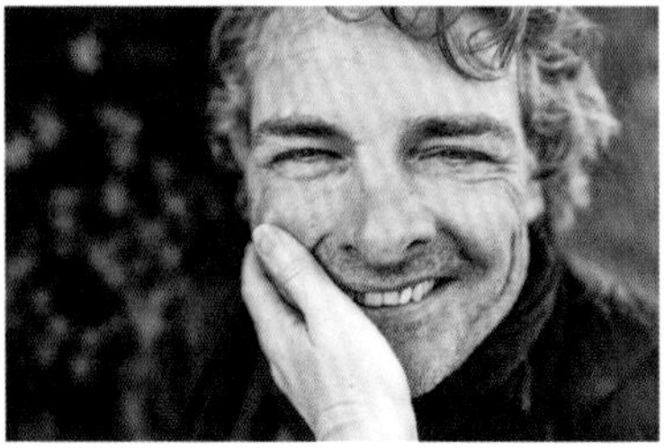

I felt the raindrops pooling on my arms and legs, I felt the coldness and the goosebumps. I felt so alive, and wished so much that he would sit with me and feel it, too. My inner brain-voice said to me, 'Rosie, you have to do this on your own'. So, I did. I sat there, eyes leaking, trying to soak in every moment where Tim was only in the other room, when all I had to do was turn around, go inside and fall into his arms. It's very corny, but a huge rainbow came out as the rain stopped. I saw it as a little sign that I had done my grieving, that I had got 'it' out of me, and the moment was safe, the moment could not be touched. I went inside and we ate a can of peas in bed.

The next night, I sent him the poem 'What Can I Say?' by Mary Oliver.

'Nice poem,' he replied. 'Goodnight Darling xx'

The next morning, I got a phone call. Tim had passed away at some point during the night. My body forgot it had knees.

The minutes, hours, days, nights, weeks and months that followed were some of the hardest to bear you could ever imagine. I had known all along that Tim would pass away, but I had not anticipated just how much I would miss him, and just how huge a hole his absence would leave in my life. I sobbed through most of the day, and struggled to sleep most of the night. I was constantly looking for signs he was still here, seeing him in my dreams, searching for some kind of meaning in the absolute despair and grief. I've never felt the weight of time more cruelly than in those first weeks. Every second that passed felt like a second further away from him, and I wanted nothing more than to crawl back in time, back into his arms. I became wracked with anxiety at the idea of losing any kind of memory of him, terrified that I would forget some important detail, an interaction or joke that we shared, a memory of his face in a certain lighting. I felt like I was entirely responsible for keeping him alive inside of me.

The days passed by and took me with them. I felt directionless, staring down at my future with nothing but sadness. Even though I knew Tim wouldn't have ever been in my life for longer than a few years, the reality of living each day without him was harder than I could ever have imagined. I had known him, I had known life with him. I couldn't picture a world that I could ever be as happy in without him. I later found out that this world does exist, and Tim is always with me, albeit in a different form. At the time, I thought loss meant letting someone go, and forgetting them a little more each day. Now, I remember him with fondness and love, and carry him with me in the pocket of my heart, as I live the fullest life I can with the time I've been granted.

Around seven weeks after his death, I was struggling with both the lack of purpose in my life, and another aspect of grief that I hadn't thought to consider at all. That was the shame and judgement other people had of my own grief. It shocked me – I couldn't contemplate a world when, after losing your boyfriend, anyone would think to leave hurtful comments about sharing pictures together, or a poem.

'YOU SHOULD KEEP THESE THINGS PRIVATE.'

'JUST MOVE ON AND LET IT GO.'

'THIS ISN'T APPROPRIATE.'

It was another difficult reality to swallow. I had to accept, for as much as it felt cathartic, helpful and healing for me to express my grief openly, it wasn't that way for everyone else. And I had to be okay with that. But (and this was much harder to do), for as much as I wanted to be as emotionally safe from any more pain as possible, I had to continue to grieve in my own way.

There's a great saying in times of struggle, which is, 'There is more than one way up the mountain'. I found

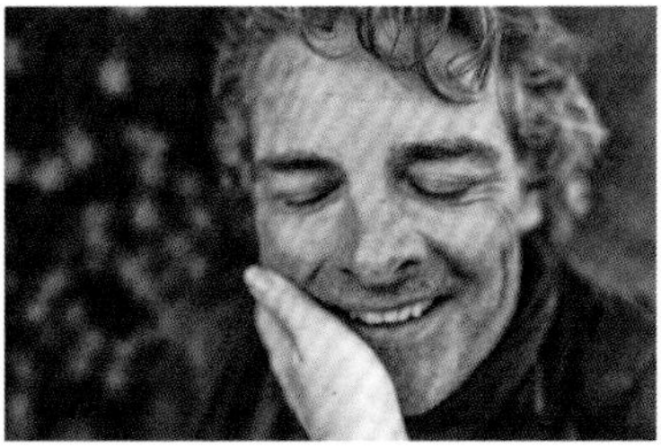

myself coming back to it over and over again, knowing in my heart that I am a person of external processing and external expression. I believe many people are equally authentic internal processors and internal expressors. I believe some people do not internally process, nor feel comfortable expressing even within themselves. And I believe there are more ways than just mine up the mountain.

One of the most humbling parts of grief was trying to withhold my own judgement of those who judged me. They were not me and they didn't have my experiences, but I didn't have theirs either. Learning to let go of their opinions, cruel words and lack of support was incredibly hard. But it did drive me forwards and made me even more sure of what I needed to do, which was to take up the same project that I had started all those years ago.

ATTEMPT TWO
365 Days Of Grief

I started Day One with no more than a burning desire to get the feelings *out*. I didn't want to become numb, I didn't want to take pride in feeling nothing. For me, I wanted to feel every inch of the pain, go to the very depths of the abyss, and know I could survive it. Here are some of my 365 creations, and their accompanying journal entries.

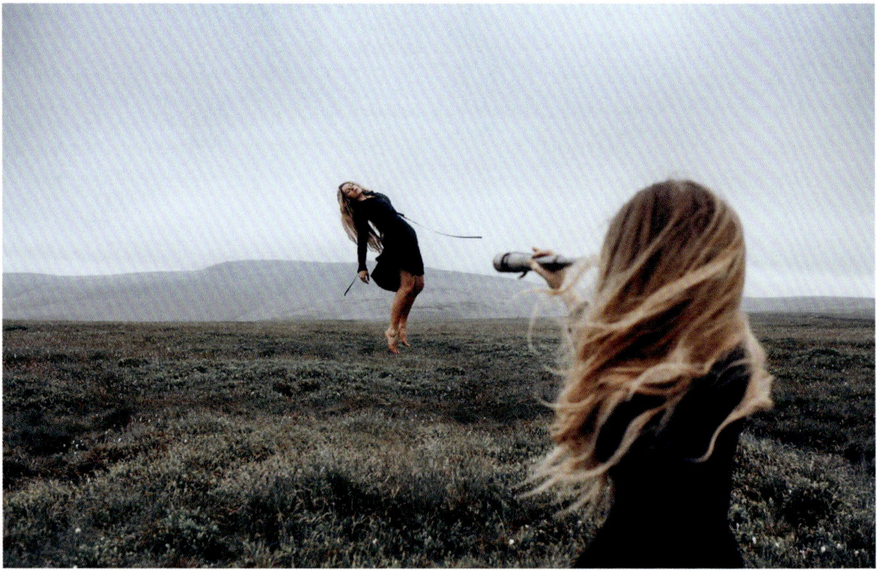

1/365

Eight years ago, I picked up a camera and joined Flickr. I was a normal teenager, who mused on my everyday life, and on this site I found a little outlet for the buzzing that went on inside my head. I found friends, a community, support, creativity and inspiration. Flickr became my home. My self-portraits and subsequent 365 project not only developed a skill that has since become my career, but allowed me to create my own little worlds to hide in – small pockets to live in and call my own. Whenever I was sad, I would think of an image to fit the feeling. Whenever I needed somewhere to bury my lonely mind, I created a scene, and you lovely people looked at it and looked at me in there, like a snowglobe.

Seven weeks ago, my life changed. I got the call to say my beautiful, kind, magnificent human being of a boyfriend had died.

I am looking at those words on the screen and they break my heart.

That day I fell in the most unimaginable hole, I kept waiting for my toes to hit the floor, and it never came. I'm realizing that grief, and missing someone, never really has a floor to hit. You're kind of always in freefall.

I haven't been able to write about it on my social media channels, but I feel like Flickr is a safe place. It's out of the way and it's safe with you guys who know me, who support me; it's a safe way for me to express all this sadness and to write about this, and us (though I'm not sure when I will be ready to do the latter).

My instinct, when I get hit with darkness, is to feel it and write about it and photograph it, and look at it as words on a page or a picture on a screen. This is my way of living, it's as essential to me as breathing. Without my wonderful boyfriend, I feel like I am missing a part of my heart, but without expression in whatever form, I feel like a ghost. I don't recognize myself.

So, here we are. Eight years later, starting again.

My goal is to have something to focus on every day, whether it's an edit or a self-portrait or just *something*. I'm seeing what has happened as a rebirth, as an entirely new life. And I intend to do wonderful things with the one life I have – I don't intend to stagnate, to exist through the days, to let the wonderful parts of me close off in fear of pain. I can withstand it, and pain is just as important as joy. I must first rip and tear before I can heal, let it all drain out of me before I can allow in the light. If I block the sadness then the happiness is blocked, too. To be human is to feel, and I am not ashamed of that; I am not ashamed of feeling my darkest moments. I *will* make something good come from them.

As ever, thank you anyone who is reading this for your eyes, for your words, for your witness to my life. Anyone who wants to share in this journey is welcome along the way. xx

*

And so, 'Attempt Two' began. And, spoiler alert, it was one of the hardest, saddest, happiest, most heartbreaking and heart-healing years of my life.

Here are some notable images, from notable days.

4/365

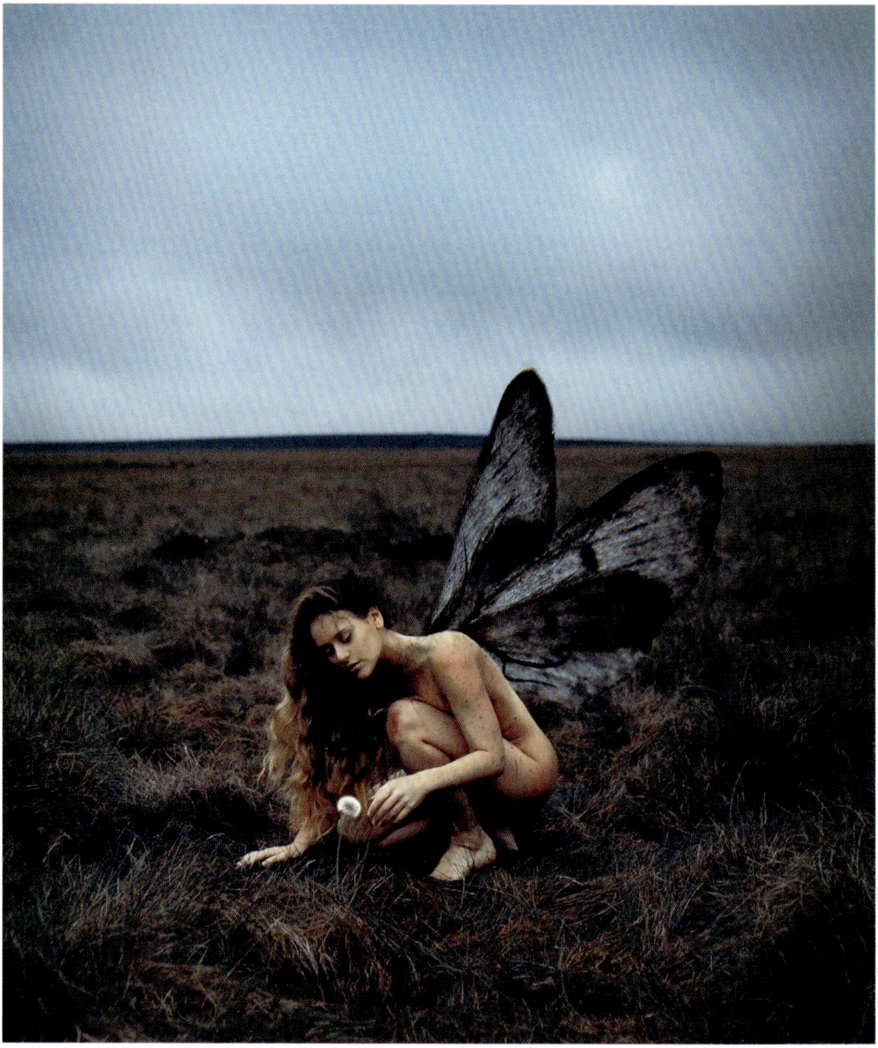

A SINGLE GLORIOUS THING

'In my own worst seasons I've come back from the colourless world of despair by forcing myself to look hard, for a long time, at a single glorious thing: a flame of red geranium outside my bedroom window. And then another: my daughter in a yellow dress. And another: the perfect outline of a full, dark sphere behind the crescent moon. Until I learned to be in love with my life again. Like a stroke victim retraining new parts of the brain to grasp lost skills, I have taught myself joy, over and over again.'
– Barbara Kingsolver
High Tide in Tucson

This is partly inspired by the flower fairies illustrations. I grew up with these as a kid and always identified with the Blackthorn Fairy most, because she looked totally badass! Climbing on thorns, tattered clothes, my kinda fairy.

Today has been lovely. I woke up pretty shattered from yesterday's wedding and went to do some couple portraits about an hour's drive away – I'm able to sing in the car again (loudly) and I feel like this last week I've felt really grateful to be alive again.

That was one of the hardest things to get my head around after he died – I had no idea how I was going to ever *want* to be in this part of my life again. I read somewhere that life is only ever comparisons – the state of oneself with an old self, circumstances with other circumstances, and so on. I loved life *so* much before him, with him, that I couldn't see how it would ever compare. Letting go of the idea of comparison has been huge. Moments are only ever moments, so if I want to sing loudly in the car then I will damn well sing until the moment comes to an end. And as my collection of wonderful moments grows, hopefully so will my overall perspective on the 'enjoyableness' of my current present. Boom.

And yes, I was totally naked in a boggy moor on the roadside here. RIP, my dignity.

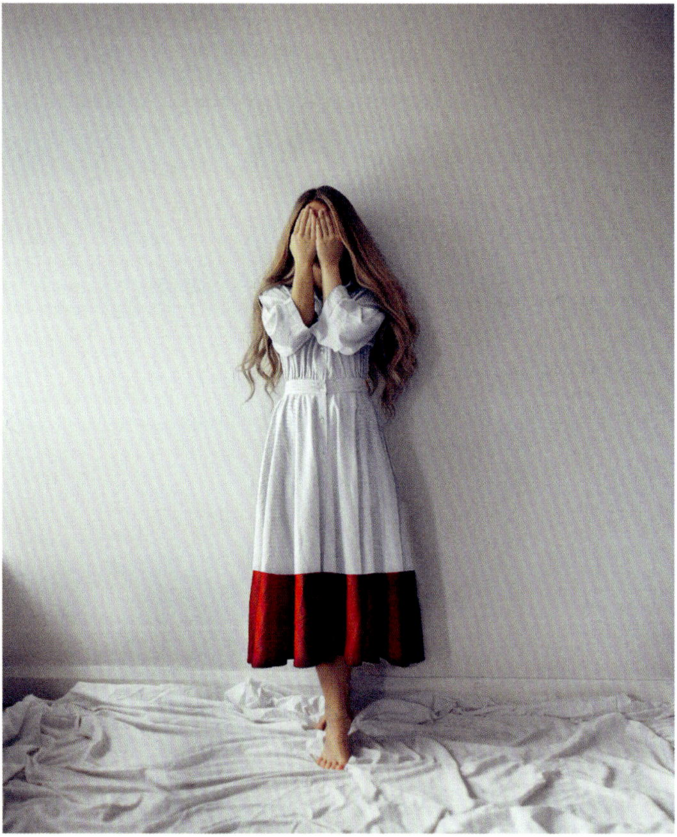

LOW BATTERY

Last night, after I went to bed, I just plummeted. What charges you? For me, it's being outside, when the air smells like campfires. Lying alone in a meadow of grass and letting the insects march all over me, like a tiny orchestra of little legs. It's watching the sunlight dance on my walls, doing a little soul work every day. When my battery is low, sometimes I don't recognize myself. Time to recharge.

(Sorry Mum, I haven't cleaned my room, all the clothes are just chucked on the bed.)

9/365

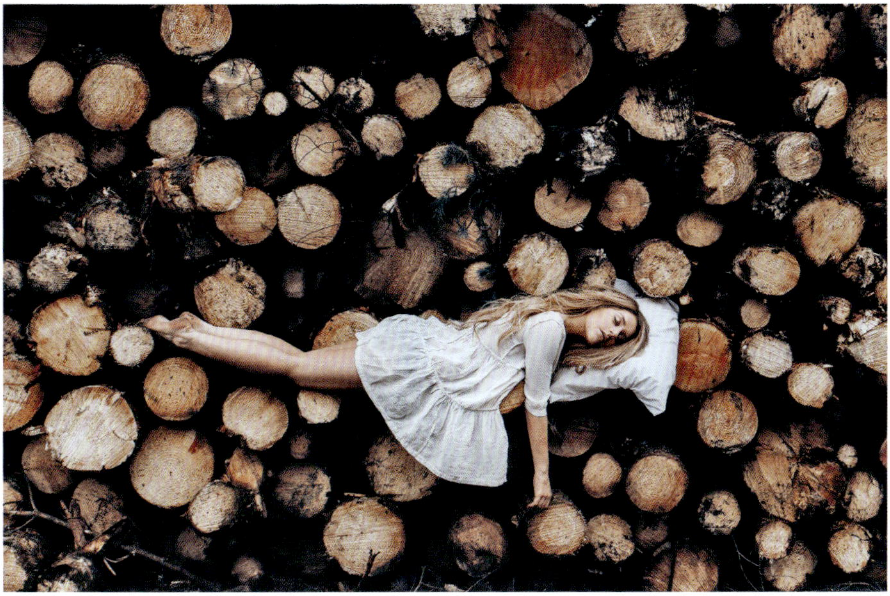

The last week, my sleeping pattern has gone right out of the window. My mind is clattering, thumping down stairs, banging pots, and you can't shout a lullaby.

In a way, it's a good thing – my mind is on this project, my mind is focused on any state it finds itself in. I shall study it and turn it into a photograph. However, it means that come the morning (or early afternoon, don't judge me), I'm rendered exhausted and useless.

This whole process has been exhausting. It's been exhausting to constantly feel, to constantly try and verbalize it all, to stay on top of my grief so it doesn't fuck me up when my mind is resting and turned.

Anyway. Today, I feel exhausted, so I decided to nap through today's 365.

The very bare minimum of editing has gone into this! I held this pose like a friggin' core-strength maniac. 2/10 for comfort, do not recommend.

28/365

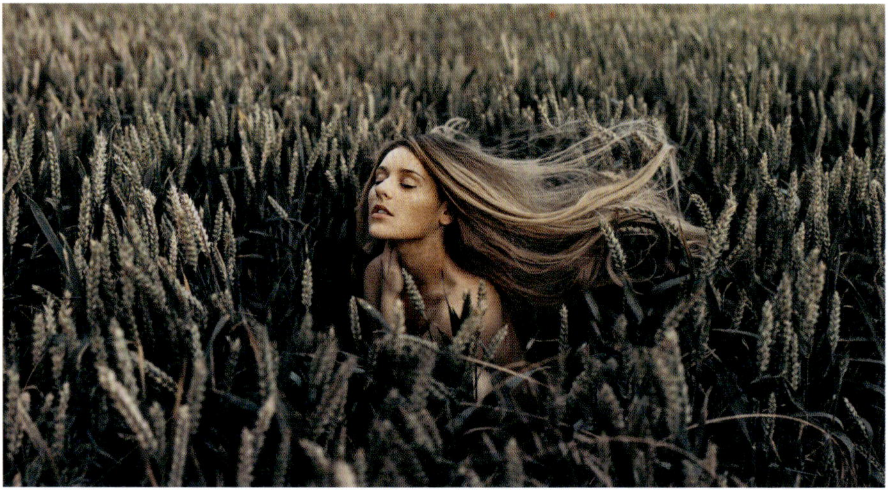

'To live in this world
you must be able / to do three things:
to love what is mortal;
to hold it
against your bones knowing / your own life depends on it;
and, when the time comes to let it go,
to let it go.'
– Mary Oliver, 'In Blackwater Woods'

On the drive home last night, I drove past a rabbit that had been knocked down and lay in the middle of the road. I pulled over and used an old shirt to pick it up and move it to the side of the road.

I got back in my car and for about four hours straight, I cried and cried and cried. Something about seeing that rabbit without any life, feeling the weight of its body in my arms, it triggered all this grief in me.

For some minutes, it was pathetic, sad, feeling-really-sorry-for-myself-right-now crying, all the missing him from the last couple of weeks just welled up inside of me and I had to let it out. This crying eventually broke into 'he would cuddle me and smile at the fact I care so much and am so emotional and tease me about this' crying, and then I was laughing through my tears at all the times he teased me and all the times we let our personalities play with each other, and then I cried some more because I missed him again and because I miss my best friend. I heard his voice in my head reassuring me that he was in everything tonight, and to look how handsome he looked lighting up the sky with all those colours. And then I cried some more because for me, crying is healing, grieving is healing. And then I felt soothed, and I carried on driving myself home.

49/365

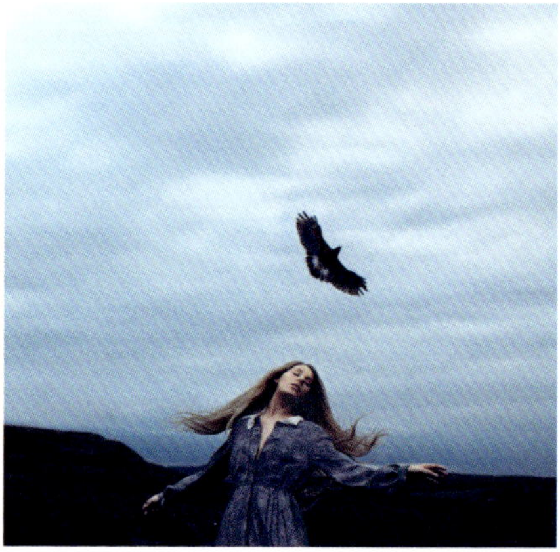

'I hope that you do not let the world condemn you for being too loud, too expressive, too soft; that you do not let it convince you to be perfect instead of real. I truly hope that you celebrate the fact that you are not for everyone, that you are not impressing the kinds of people built on the foundations of a sad world. If there is anything you do, please, let yourself rejoice in the fact that you do not fit in, that you think differently, because there is a chaos inside of you and it is going to change lives. It is going to make even the cynics believe again. It is going to grow love from thorn and glass.'
– Bianca Sparacino, *You Are Not For Everyone*

Nearly 50 days in, and finally my mind is wrestling itself free of the claws of rumination!

I had such a wonderful dream of him last night. We went on a date to a pub and I asked him what was good to eat. He told me to try the 'buttered hog'. I have no idea where that came from whatsoever, but I found it hilarious when I woke up, and it made me realize that we haven't ended at all – I'll still have new funny things to have with him, even if in my imagination or dreams. I skipped off to my shoot today full of beans, as though I'd really been on a date with him last night. I drove home and felt back to myself again! It was just wonderful.

So, happy Rosie today! I'm off out to make the most of the misty weather and maybe hop in a lake!

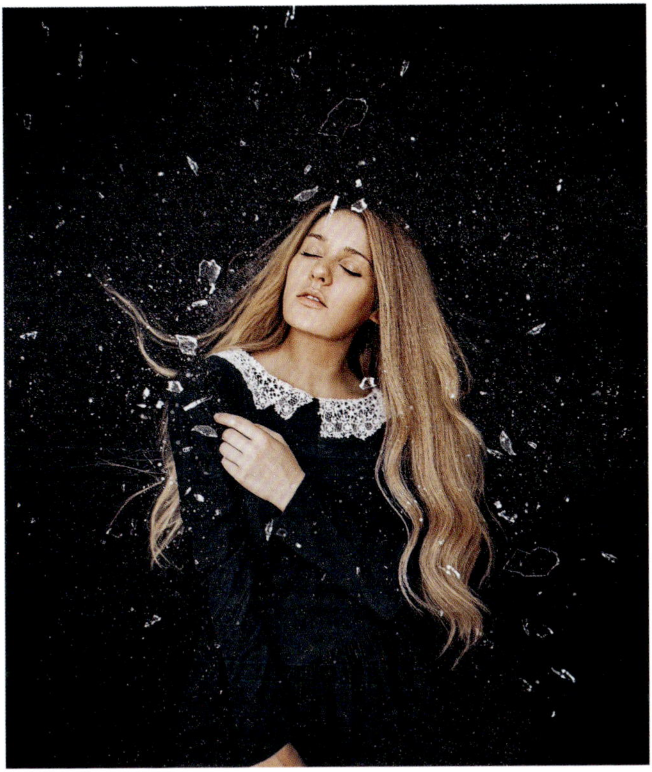

SHATTERED

shatter
ʃætə/verb

1. To break or cause to break suddenly and violently into pieces, to explode, damage or destroy.
2. To feel greatly upset.
3. Extreme tiredness.

Today, I scored a bullseye on all of the above. I'm going to bed.

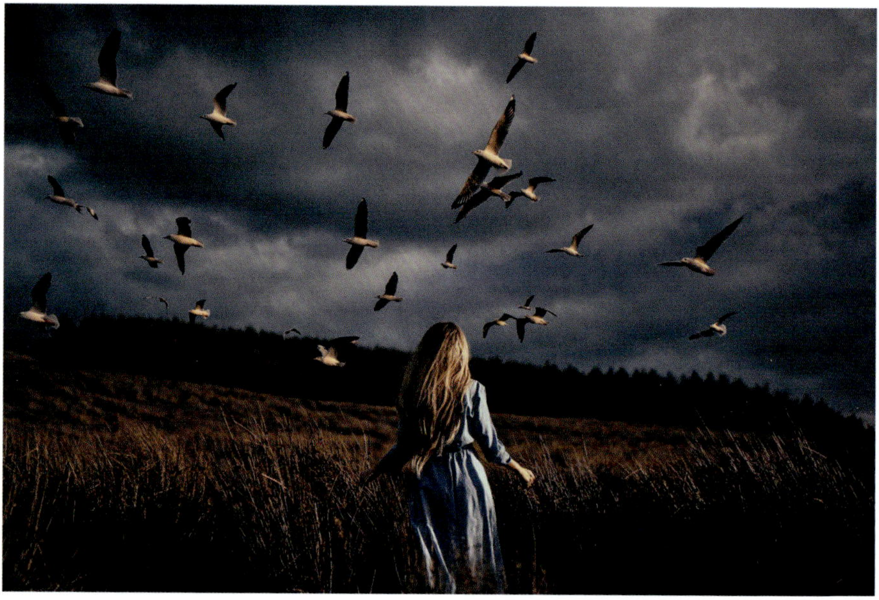

Something spectacular happened exactly a year ago today. I woke up with a spring in my step, a sparkling mind, the skies were blue and there was a faint quiver of wonder in the air – autumn was just about to begin, and I felt extremely happy.

A set of entirely unforseen circumstances had seen me cancel my appointment at the Royal Exchange costume hire place the week before, and reschedule for 10 September. I went to hunt for costumes, and was excitedly rummaging through the racks, when at about 2 p.m. I laid eyes on the most wonderful person I'd ever encountered. Someone spectacular.

Of course, I didn't know it at the time, he was just a man with a twinkle in his eye, blue jeans, a white shirt, and a confidence I recognized and gelled with immediately. I didn't intend to fall in love with him. In fact, I didn't intend for anything to happen at all, but when he told me about his costume ball, I couldn't resist being playful with him and accepting his invitation. He looked too interesting to pass by. He told me his name, Tim, and we shook hands and glowing smiles, exchanged numbers and went our separate ways.

Of course, I had no idea what was to come. No one ever does. It's better that way, because it makes the future ever so exciting, and had I known all the brilliance I'd encounter, I'd have been far too overexcited and probably spoilt the whole thing :-) Instead, I held him at arms length, questioned him, challenged him, opened him up and poured myself in, and let him do the same. Falling in love with him was like being a child again, and 'climbing a tree without any idea of how I would get down', as Lang Leav would say.

As the autumn rolled into winter, sometimes I cast my eyes back to that day, and wonder just what the bloody chances were that someone who fit me so beautifully would intersect my life so spectacularly like that – exactly the right time, exactly the right day. At a point in our lives when we were both free to love, when love was exactly what we both needed to ignite the months ahead. We didn't know how long Tim had to live. We expected longer than the eight months that he got; he deserved more than he got. But we got to fill those months with laughter, happiness, craziness and recklessness. We lay on the grass in the middle of the night outside his house, and laughed at each other and talked about the universe being a Rubik's Cube, that every single moment and thing was a tiny square, and we would never understand how it moved and changed and yet stayed so beautifully one. I still don't understand, and I miss him with my entire heart, but I know he is here, somewhere in the cube. He's alive in my mind, alive in my heart, as beautiful and spectacular as he ever was.

A few days before he died, we were talking about past loves on the bed. I told him about one of mine, about how he had a backpack always ready to go and a nomad spirit. He was smiling at me, and he said, 'I wonder how you will describe me one day.'

Well, Tim, you were something spectacular. And so, so, so much more. I still haven't found the words, but I'm getting there.

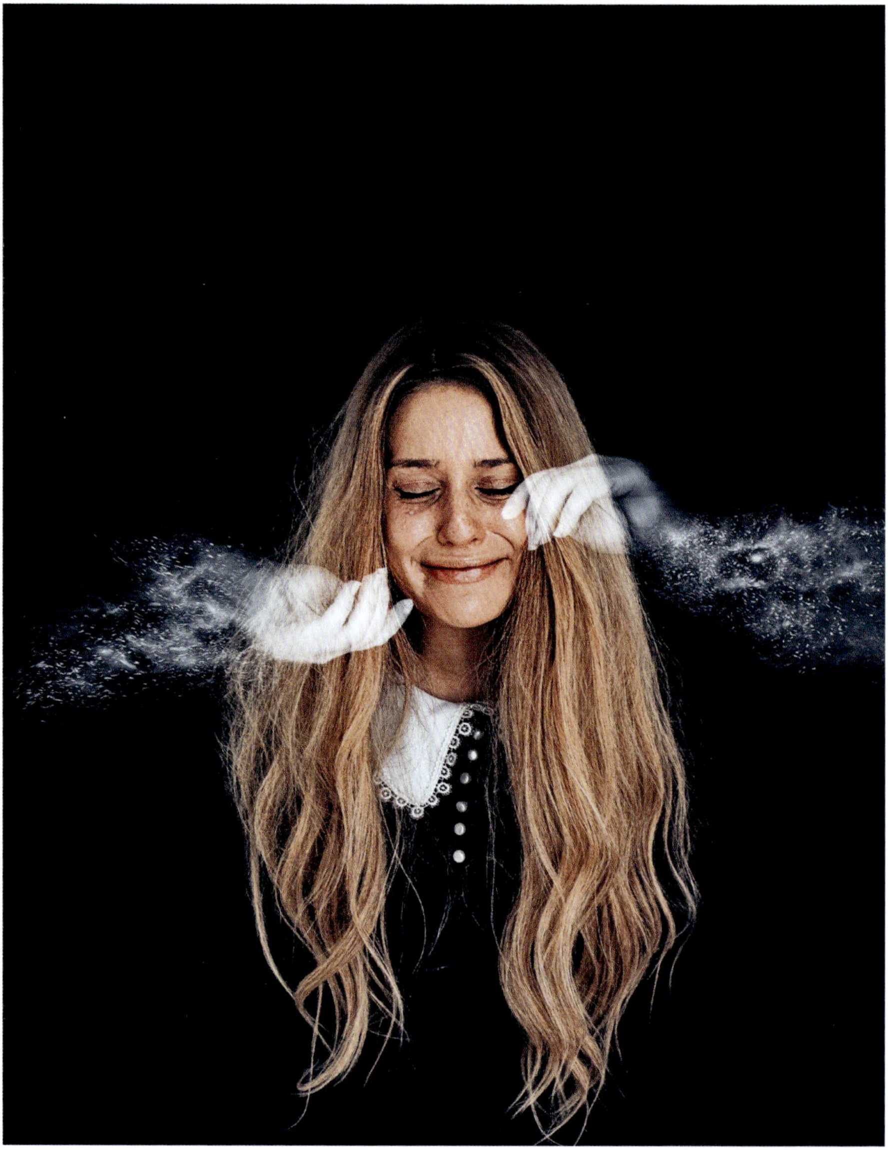

365 CHALLENGE — 74

THINGS I WOULD HAVE TOLD MYSELF THIS TIME LAST YEAR:

- Your naive and romantic view of love is silly, but pure and inspiring nonetheless. Keep it. Love laced in cynicism isn't anywhere near as sweet.
- Your ability to risk normality for heartachingly beautiful joy and the promise of uncertainty and pain is not stupid, it is brave.
- You are not someone built for shallow swimming and you know it. You also don't learn to swim by never getting in the water.
- You are going to cry a lot, but you are going to smile a lot, too. Sometimes, you'll smile then cry. Sometimes, you'll cry then smile. (It will be worth it.)
- When it all collapses, I will be here to remind you of all the wonderful things you have already built inside of yourself. I will remind you that life is an embroidery of joy and sorrow, which is made of more threads than love alone. You're going to want to punch me for being so bloody optimistic sometimes, and I'm going to want to punch you right back for being pathetic. So, we're equal.
- Have a wonderful night, enjoy it all. You'll wish you were able to do it all again this time next year, I promise :-).

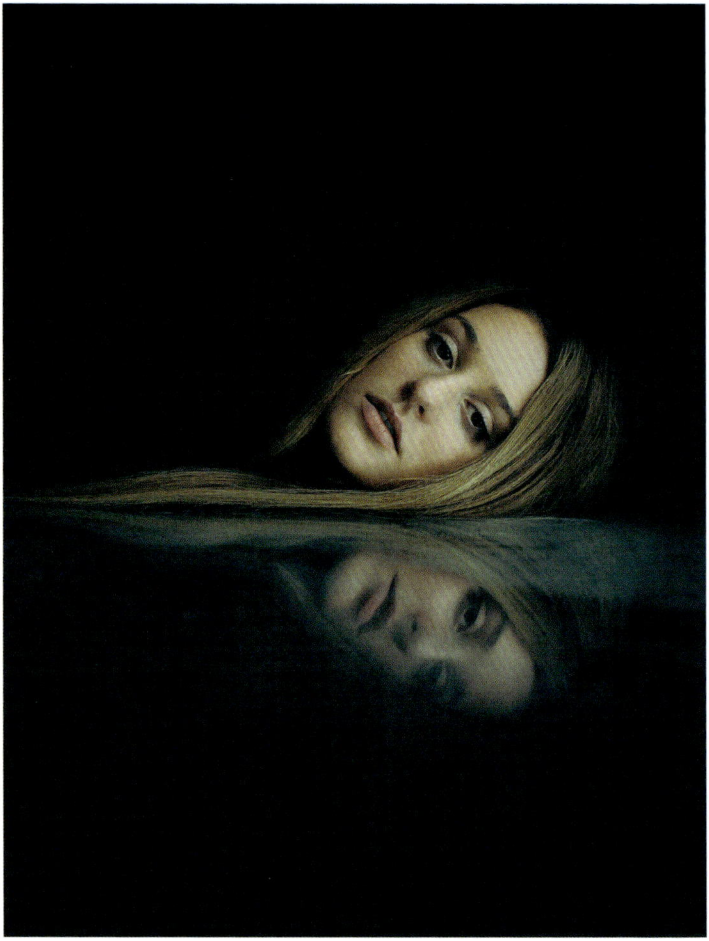

97/365

'So often loneliness comes from being out of touch with parts of oneself. We go searching for those parts in other people, but there's a difference between feeling separate from others, and separate from oneself.'
– Diane Ackerman
The Impossible Will Take a Little While: Perseverance and Hope in Troubled Times

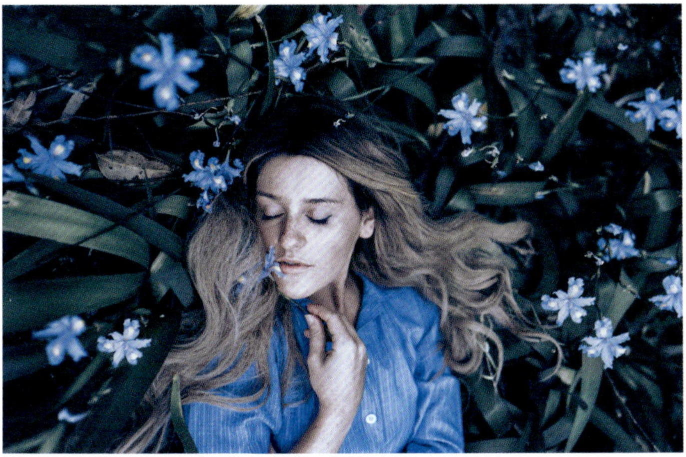

116/365

Last night, darkness came in and swallowed me up, and is lingering this morning like an unwanted hangover. Trying to prize its fingers from its nasty grip on my mind. Editing this picture soothed it somewhat. Today I'm staying inside. Didn't really want to write about this, would hate to dispel the myth that travelling heals a mushed-up heart, but hey, I'm not here to trade honesty for looking like I know what I'm doing...

Today, I feel angry at myself for my inability to function like a normal individual on holiday. Where has my eagerness to explore gone? I haven't had the motivation to explore the city by myself yet, I've been relying on other people to show me around, and I dislike myself for it. I dislike the way I rely on people in general, for their validation of my self-worth. I've had this highlighted especially hard this year with grief and needing other people's permission to do it on my own terms, and I hate myself for that, too. When did I become someone who was this weak? Or have I always been, and it's taken this year to reveal it to me? Why don't I care to change? It feels like such an uphill struggle, and surely changing to be more self-motivated is only there to benefit the person I am, which is of no benefit to anyone but me anyway, so why bother. I don't have anyone to impress, and I don't want anyone to impress. I want to tell the people I have made myself vulnerable for to stay the hell away from me.

These are the thoughts I'm trying to not let swallow me up today. The masochist in me wants to let them devour me anyway, just to see what happens. I'm very tired.

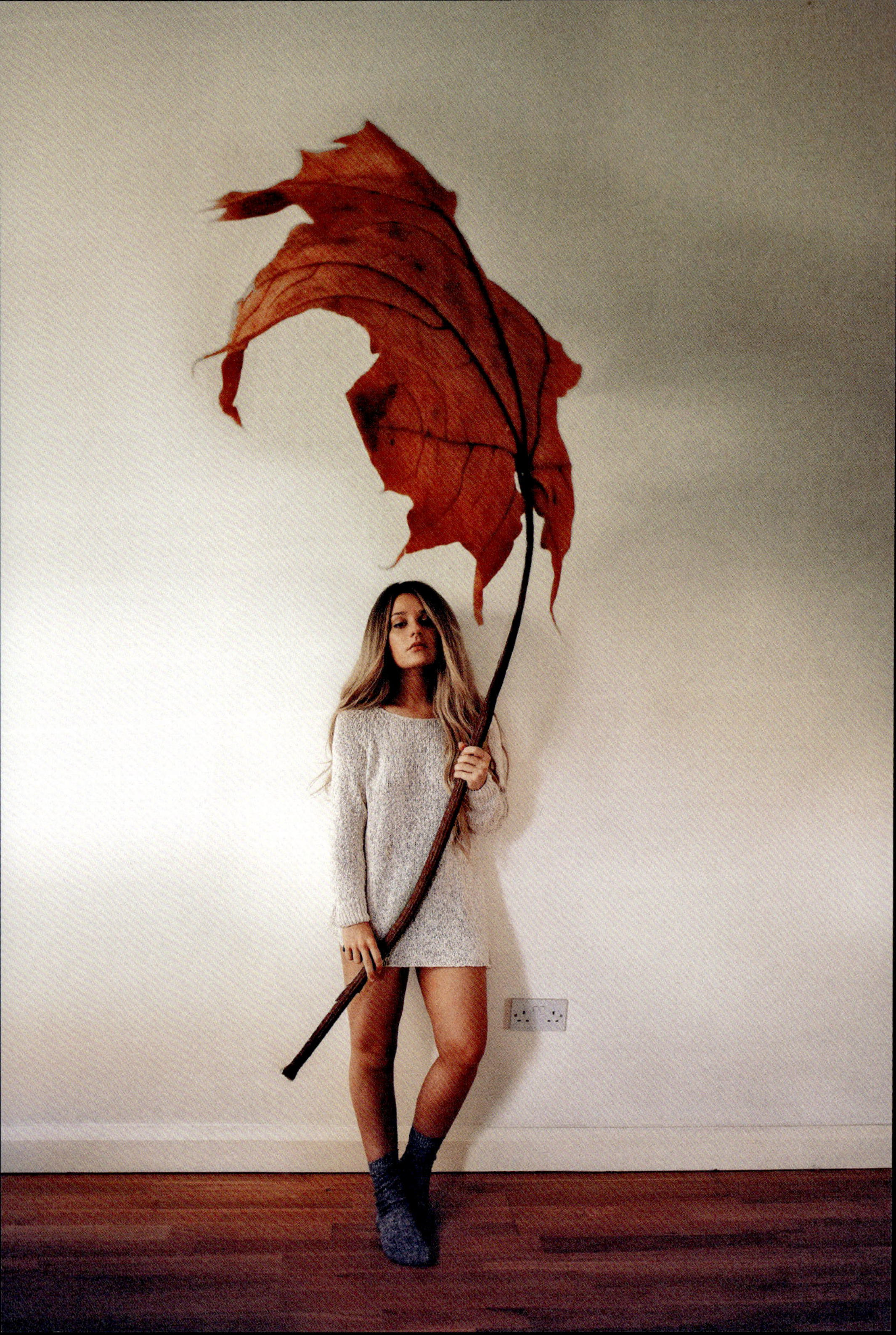

126/365

I'm going into hibernation today. Today is my annual bad-mood day. I have a cold, my phone won't stop buzzing at all hours, and my last roll of loo roll fell into the toilet when I flushed it earlier. Yep.

Being self-employed is damn hard work sometimes. I feel like I'm expected to be on call and reachable 24/7, expected to drop everything at all times, expected to place my business above all else simply because it's my business. But I don't roll that way, tried it for a couple of years, ended up hating life. I work on the presumption that if I am happy in my life, then a successful business will fall into place naturally, simply because I'll be up for being productive and putting the work in.

So, anyone waiting on emails: I'll be doing emails and editing when I get back to work next week, but today I'm switching my phone off and hiding under this giant leaf. And the rest of this week I will be making the most of my time out, enjoying all the autumn colours and catching up with friends. Thanks <3

update

My bad mood hurricane has downgraded to a category two storm. I'm now whispering 'fuck off' under my breath at nothing in particular, which is providing huge relief. And I even replied to a few emails.

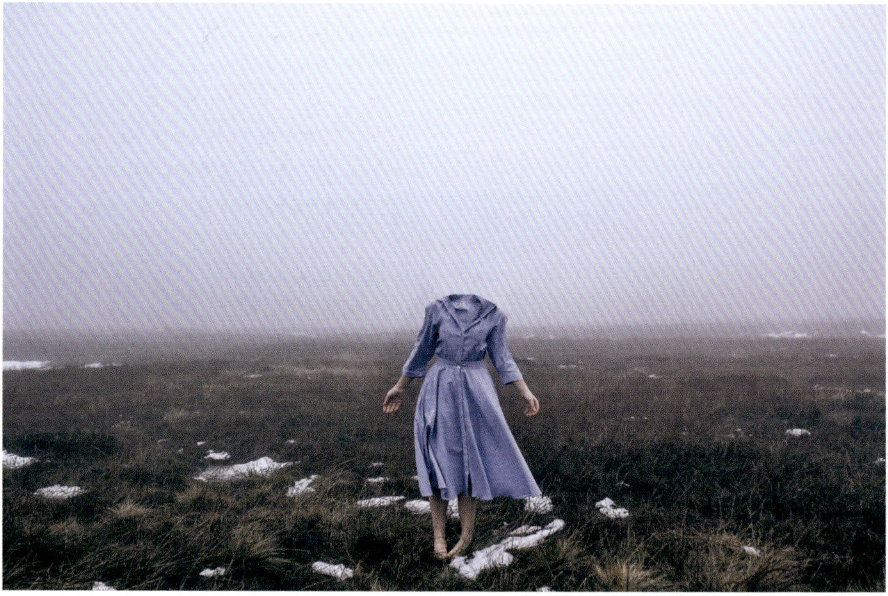

159/365

Don't lose your head, girl, or those stars
kept up inside
Remember how you climbed those ladders
with your mind to pluck them from the
skies?
Well, they're yours now.
Turn off the light, girl, let them show you
the way.
I know your head feels heavy
but heaviness isn't here
to stay – you know this.
Don't lose your head, girl, instead just get
some air
Let it all rise up and out, then go meet
yourself somewhere.
Just come back down inside that head
You know you'll need it soon
Your head contains your eyes to gaze
back at that lonely moon, and ears that if
were to fade away
They'd miss the music too, in fact, I'd be
inclined to say
that music would miss you
And don't forget about the scents and
smells of winter air,
and how it feels to run fast with wind's
fingers in your hair
Your tongue to taste the honey that hangs
from your fingertips,
Without your head, I have to say, the
world would not exist, so
sweetly, girl. Please do not forget,
There's a world that needs a girl like you,
with a magic, achy head.

My 365 today is for anyone who has ever longed to not be inside their own head... The last few days, the climate inside mine has been pretty awful, but today the skies are clear, and I managed to get some perspective and write a little poem. Shooting this was cold, but afterwards I blasted the heat in my car and sat there for song after song, for no reason other than the pure enjoyment of feeling the vibrations wrap me up inside their tiny musical arms. And I thought, the music probably equally enjoys having someone to wrap up, someone to feel it so much, just like the fields might enjoy having my bare feet taking soggy 365s... so maybe it's a give and take thing, and not so bad being in this head, after all. :-)

180/365

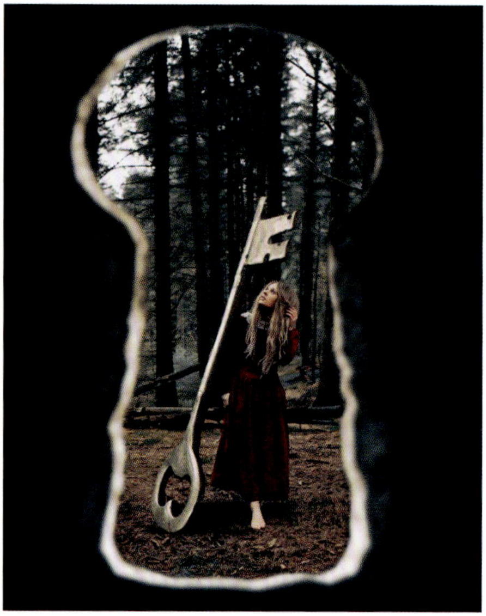

Uploading late again, sorry! I've decided to write different descriptions on Flickr to the ones on Instagram and Facebook. Sometimes, I feel a bit too influenced by the eyes of friends on there, I'd like to be able to be a bit more honest so Flickr seems like the place to do it!

So, I've had the roughest month since I lost Tim. I started dating a guy back in October, and was terrified, really. We clicked incredibly well, I joked that had Tim been alive and had he met him, he'd have been trying to set me up with him, we were that well matched. *Anyway*. After three weeks of me trying to resist developing feelings, he lured me into a safe place, lots of reassurance that he wasn't going to hurt me etc. We went to London, I met his friends, we went to open mic nights together and I read some of my poetry and he played his guitar. It was lovely. I soared. My happiness went sky high, not just the normal amount for having 'met' someone and felt a good connection, but way way higher because it was the first time I knew I could access the path to love again since Tim. I couldn't stop it, the entire time my mind was screaming 'Hey! Slooooooow down!' But my excitement got the better of me.

We got back from London and he ghosted me completely, disappeared off the face of the earth. I don't know who looks at someone who has been through losing a partner, and decides, 'Yeah, the way to break things off with them is to recreate that experience of sudden death, that's the way to handle this', but he did. I was in shock the first day. I went into survival mode, mentally jumping to peace before my body had time to adjust. The next two weeks were like an emotional nuclear bomb – it was like going through all the feelings of grief again but obviously nowhere near as terrible, but similar. And the entire time I guilted myself into feeling bad because dating a guy for three weeks wasn't a patch on my feelings for Tim, but it was hitting me so hard.

I then wondered what on earth was so wrong with me that this guy couldn't just be kind. I fell apart pretty much. Shooting 365s was half cathartic/half hell.

Then, after a few days of emotional hell, some wedding clients started throwing a wobbler. My apartment building flooded and the lift alarm was going off for three days straight, like the sound of an ambulance in my corridor. I couldn't think, I couldn't work, I couldn't handle it, and my head felt like it would explode. All the while I'm trying to maintain inner peace because I've done so much bloody thinking about inner peace the last few months. I thought I'd cracked it – clearly not!

And then, two weeks after this nightmare began unfolding, my best friend of the last couple of years took a metaphorical DNA stick to the foundations of our friendship.

The last month has wiped it out of me. I've felt lethargic, hopeless, like I couldn't even get out of bed. The times I did, I would watch people walk about the streets going about their days, and just wonder how on earth they were doing it.

Mentally, something has not felt right at all. So, I've taken this as a sign that I needed to take care of myself – I'm staying away from serious dating until my emotional reactions are less intense and therefore less turbulent. I really, really don't want to close myself off to life, but man it's a struggle sometimes. It's been hard to put so much effort into my emotional wellbeing after this year and have someone stamp all over it with big dirty inconsiderate feet. It's even harder to want to lay myself out again for more stamping. But I can't miss out on the good stuff for fear of the bad, so instead, I'm gonna just allow non-stamping good stuff, like kayaking, hiking, music, nice-smelling candles, friends, visiting new places, writing angry poems...

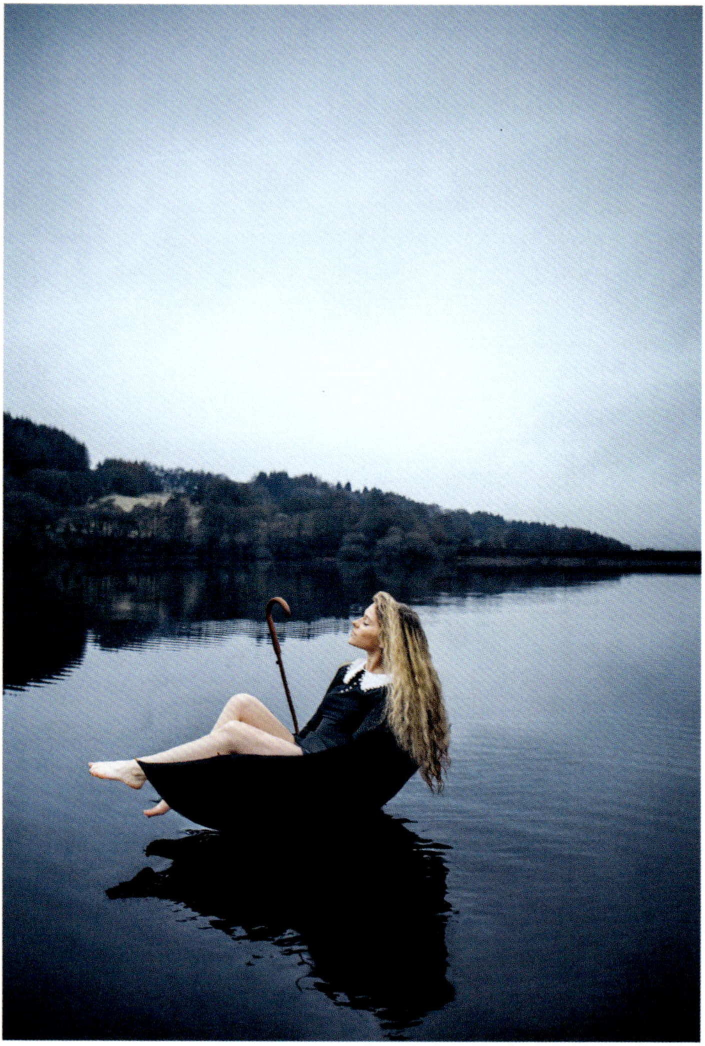

214/365

Tonight, I drove home, sat in my car after I parked up, and listened to 'Drift' by Kim Janssen. I felt so far away from all my previous troubles and sadnesses. I felt so peaceful in my head, like it would be disruptive to my peacefulness to even come up with a good analogy to how peaceful I felt. It was lovely.

So, today, just... drift.

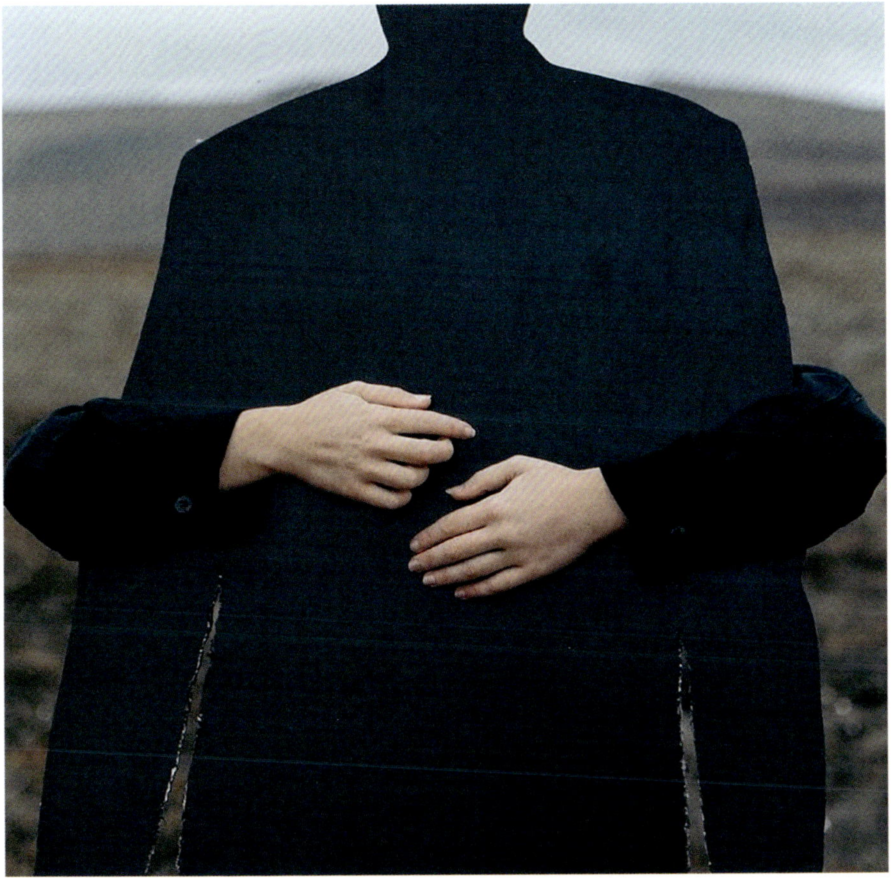

229/365

'There is a place in the heart that will never be filled / a space / and even during the best moment, and the greatest times / we will know it'
– Charles Bukowski, 'No help for that'

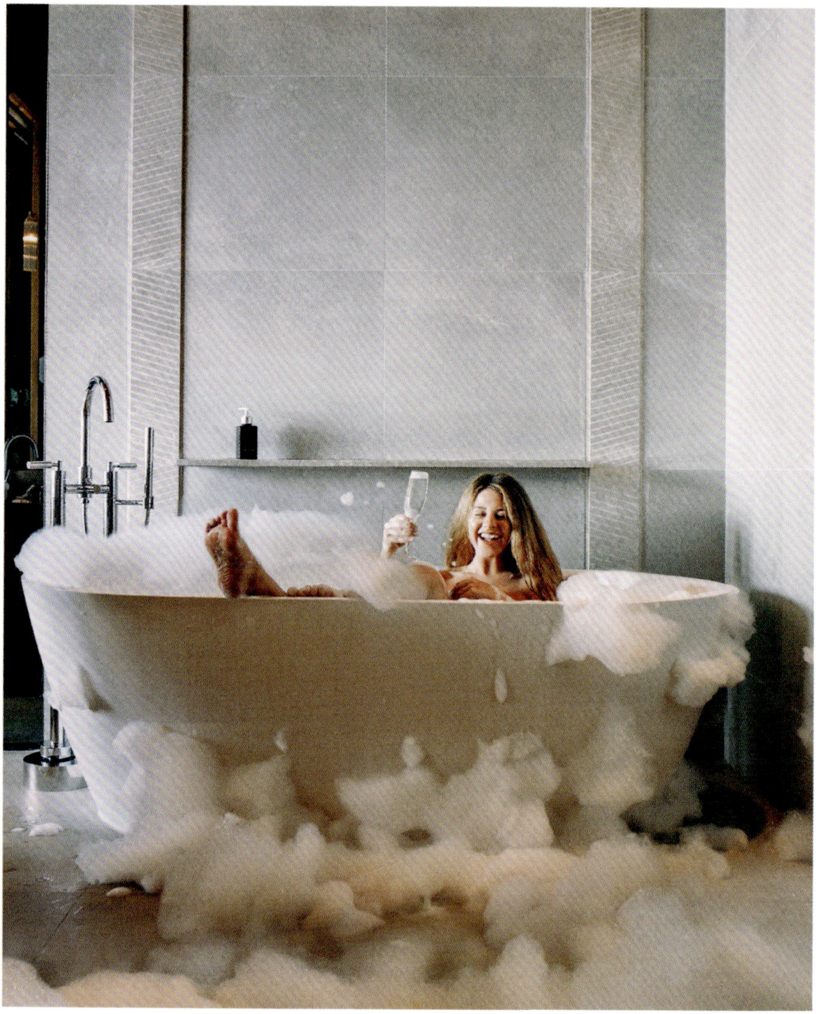

249/365

No, nope. *This* is the best way to cool off from the Thailand heat!

We're leaving for the airport in 30 minutes, Adam is going home and I'm heading North to Chiang Mai. I'm so sad to say goodbye to South Thailand. It's been a dream! So glad I got to squeeze in a week of holiday before a few days' work, and extra glad I got to share such a beautiful place with my wonderful best friend, Adam!

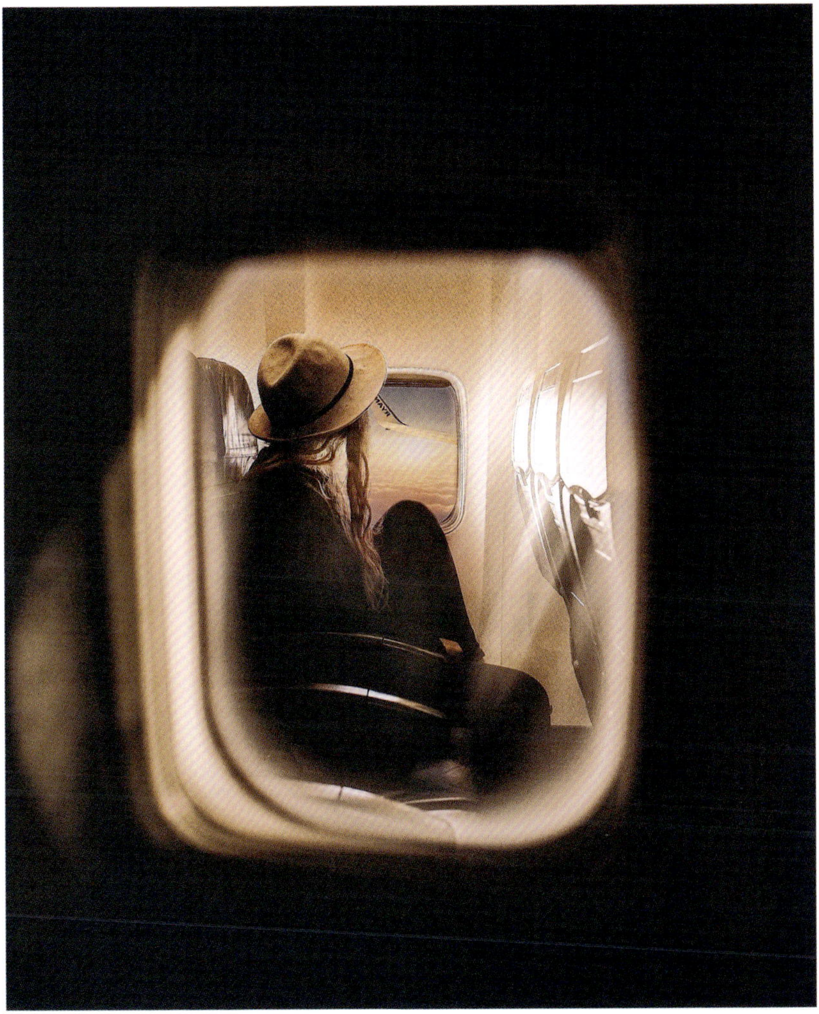

259/365

Homeward bound! Highest self-portrait I'll ever take! Setting up my tripod mid-flight was perhaps one of the stranger experiences I've had on a plane...

But I'm home, grounded for at least a couple months. Today is my Mum's birthday, so tonight is family night! I'm off to cuddle my cat for a bit. Hooray!

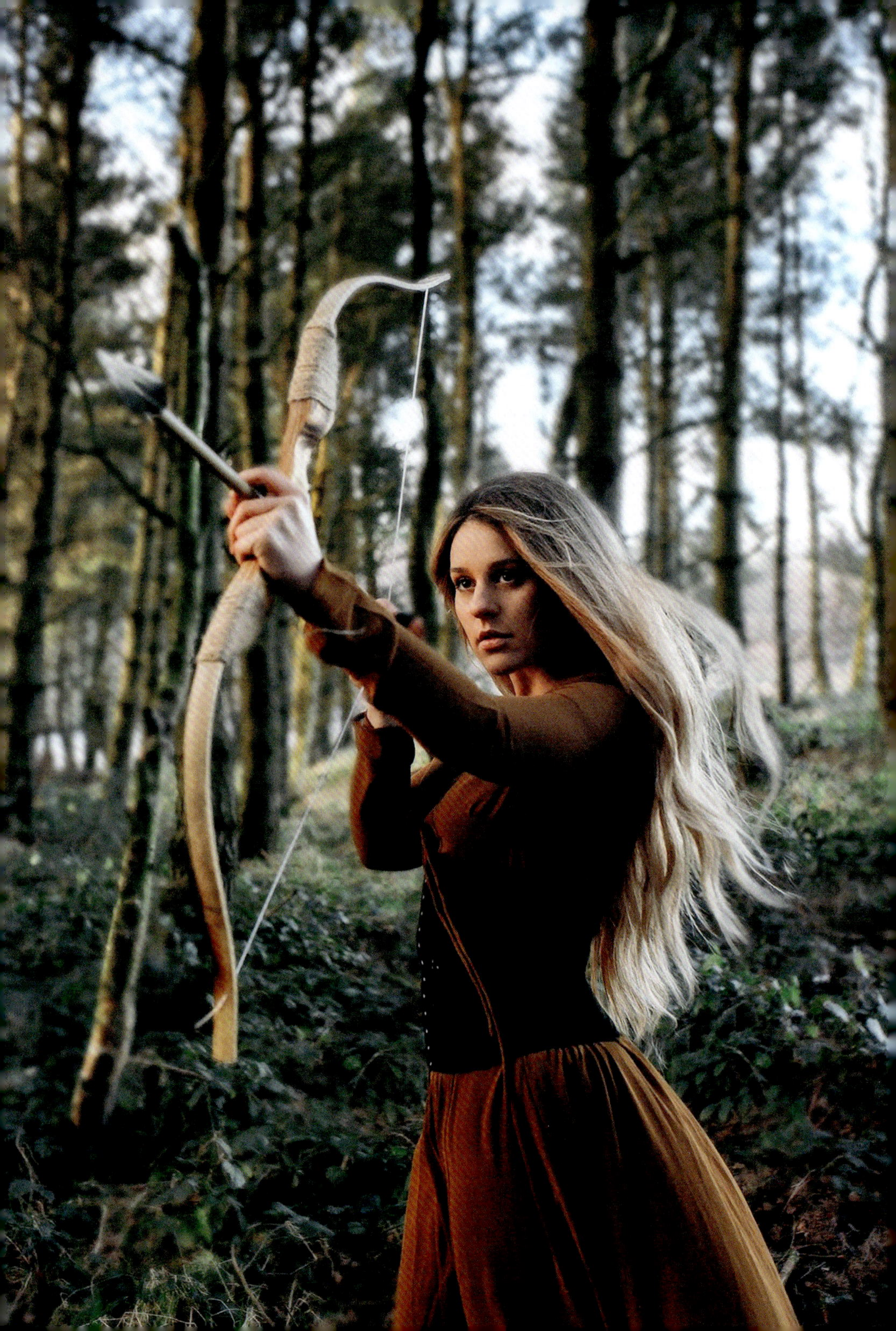

264/365

It's International Women's Day! And I woke up to lots of wonderful, inspiring words. But today, I felt like a massive let-down to the incredible ladies who have redefined what it means to be a woman – and continue to do so – so that people like me can reap those benefits everyday. I woke up in a foggy mix of grief, disappointment and frustration, and proceeded to distract myself from those feelings by binge-watching documentaries about Mr Bean all afternoon.

Eventually, the time came to do my 365 and instead, I threw myself on my cat and sobbed that I didn't want to be inspiring today. I didn't want to do anything today. I just wanted my person back, that old life back.

Nevertheless, I dragged myself out of bed and to my car, drove to these woods, cut my legs and tore my dress on a million brambles walking to this spot. But just as I started to shoot, the wind picked up, my dress started blowing, I took aim, and I felt like me again, just like that.

I thought to myself, 'This project really does force me to make something good out of the bad days,' and then I realized that actually, nope, I do. It's me, forcing myself. That little pea of determination is something that I planted, that I nourish alone, that I have to be proud of. Some days it's super duper small, but it's there.

So, here's my cheesy but important toast to IWD. (FYI, toast is always better when it's cheesy.)

Here's to the women that don't look like warriors, that don't feel like warriors, that don't even want to be warriors, but that are.

Here's to the women that take aim and hit their target. Here's to the women that take aim and miss, but try again and again.

Here's to the women here on good old Facebook/Instagram that inspired me enough to get out of bed today.

And here's to the ones that couldn't make it out – for whatever reason. I hope tomorrow is better.

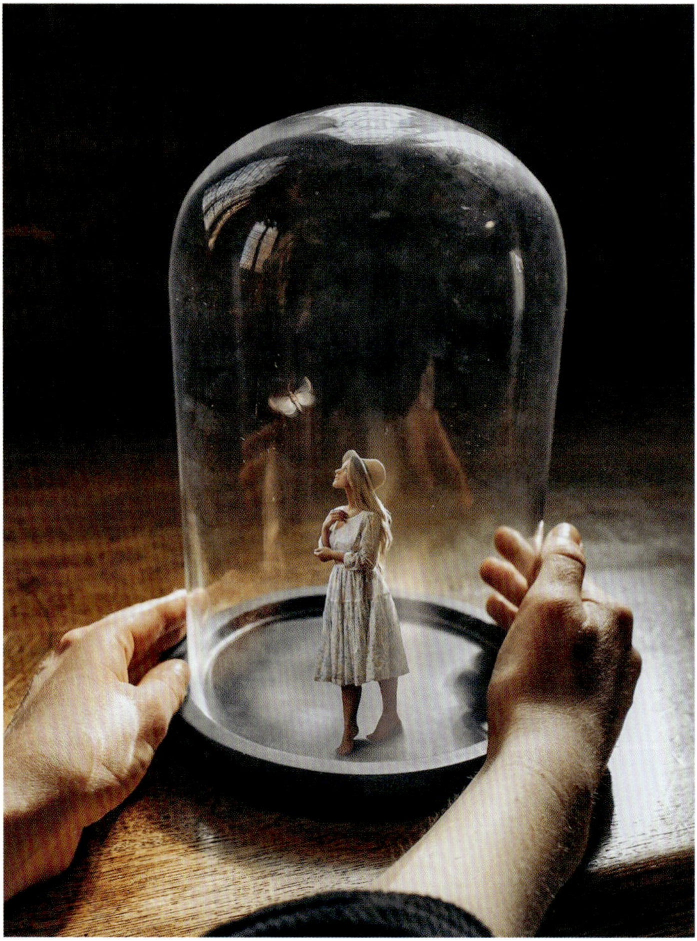

294/365

'You hold an absence / at your centre, / as if it were a life.'
– Richard Brostoff, 'Grief'

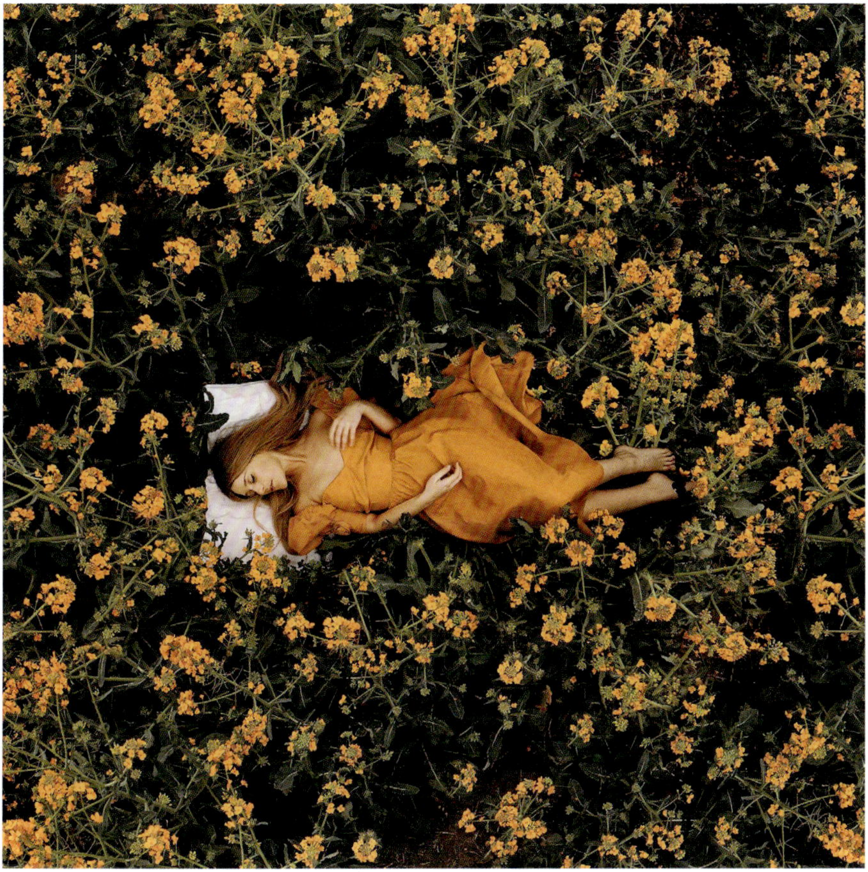

299/365

'I am learning peacefulness, lying by myself quietly
As the light lies on these white walls, this bed, these hands [...]
I didn't want any flowers, I only wanted
To lie with my hands turned up and be utterly empty.
How free it is, you have no idea how free...'
– Sylvia Plath, 'Tulips'

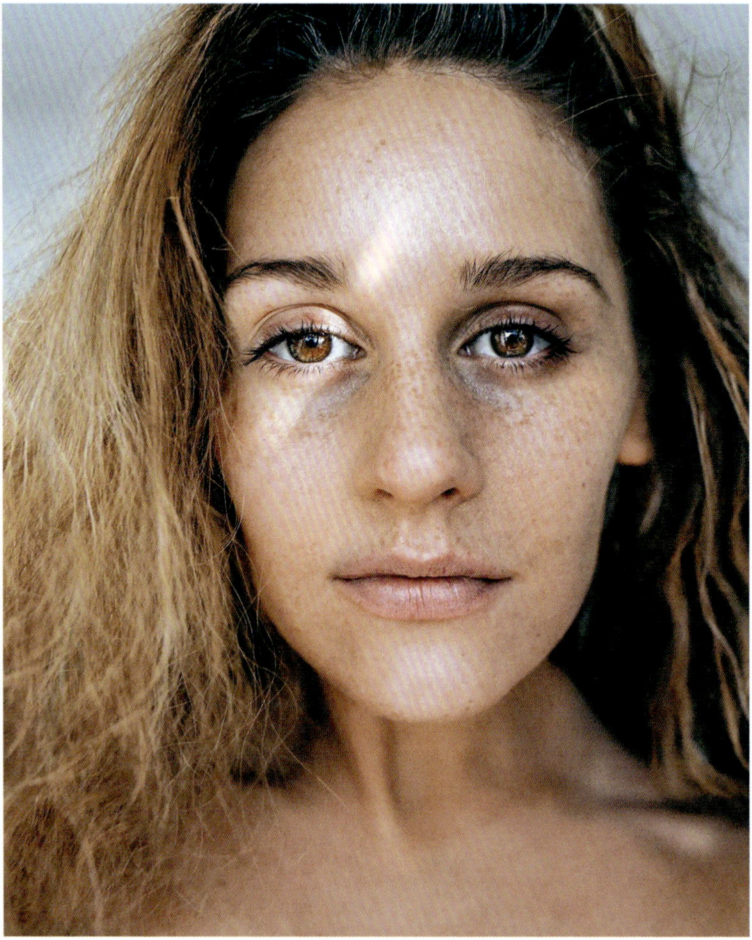

312/365

REFRACTION

Today was one of those days. I woke up to the sunlight in my eyes and decided I didn't want it.

This afternoon it started snowing, exactly like it did this week last year. The reason I remember this is because I was driving home, alone, through it – watching it, wondering if it would be the last snow we would ever see together. It was.

This whole week feels strange, I don't know what to make of it yet. I'm glad I have this project to keep me company through whatever unfolds. For now I think I'll go back to bed.

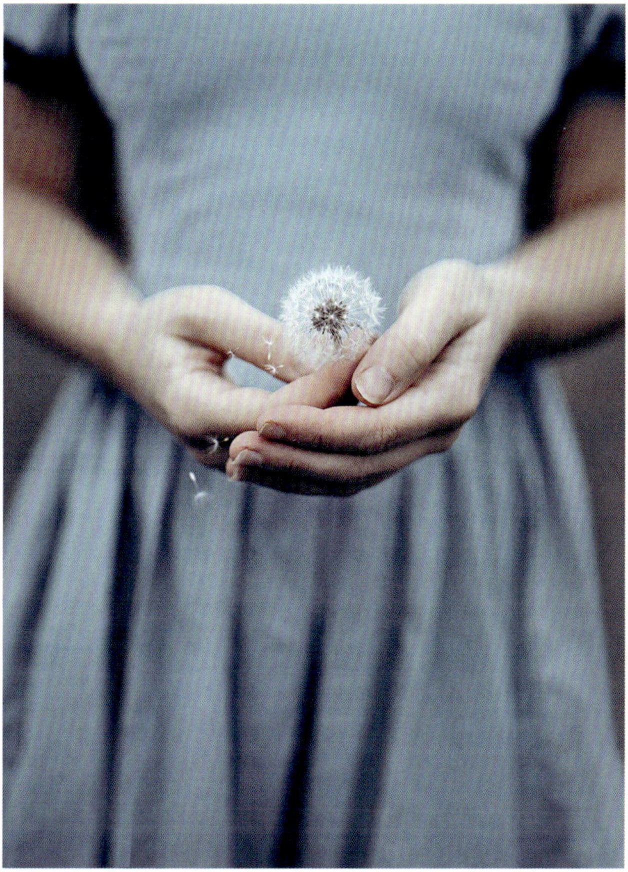

316/365

DELICATE

A year ago today I got the heart-shattering phone call to say my beautiful, spectacular boyfriend had passed away. This whole year has been a blur in some ways, and yet also held some of the most spectacular feelings of grief, loss and gratitude that I couldn't even begin to describe. I miss him every day, like everyone else who was lucky enough to cross paths with him. Loving him showed me what life in full colour looked like, losing him taught me the rest of the spectrum.

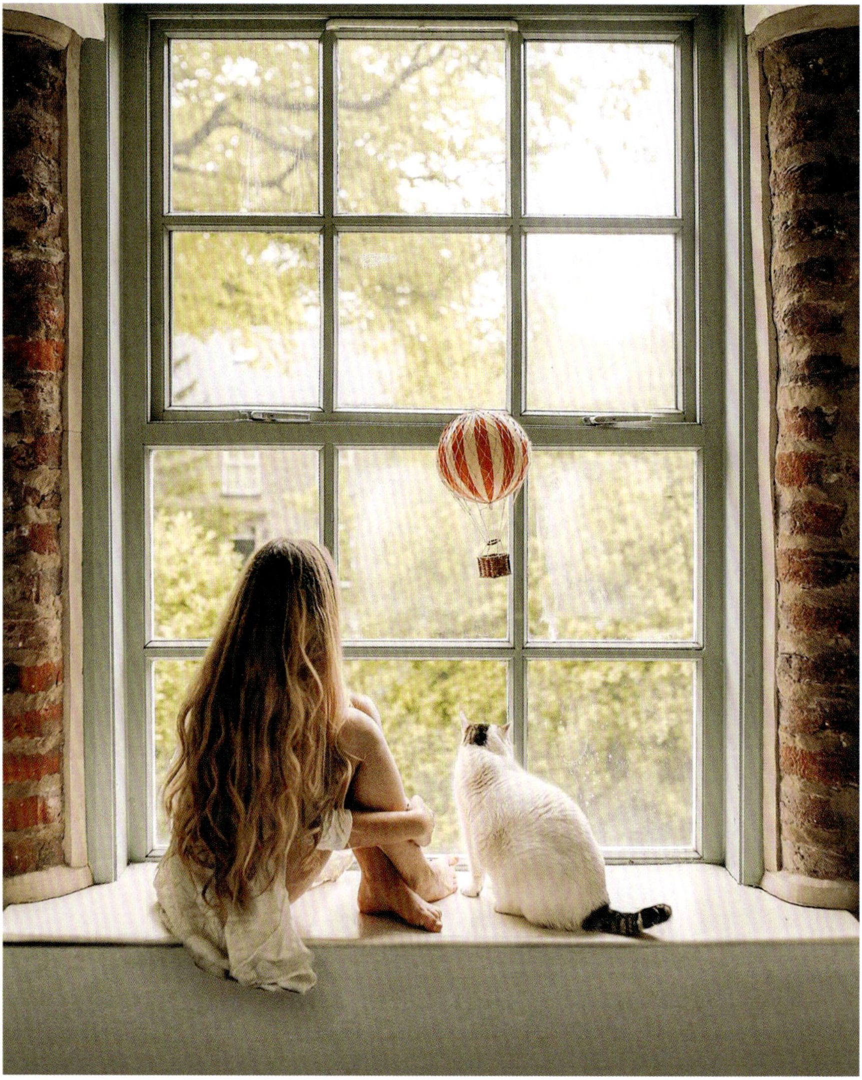

334/365

When you have an epic 365 concept planned and then it rains all day, so you spend the day inside dreaming with your kitty instead!

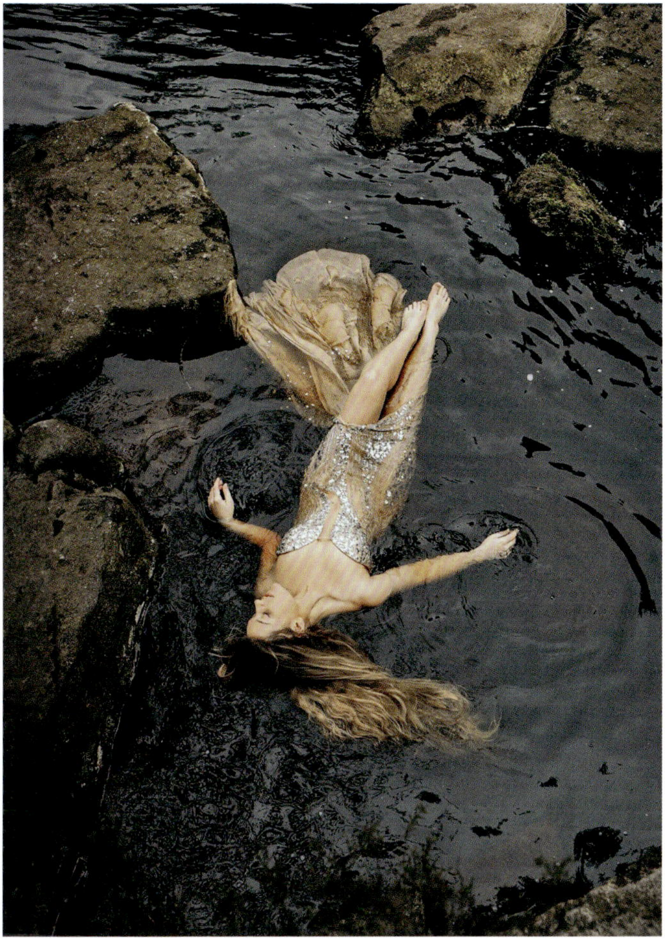

340/365

I sent him the poem 'What Can I Say?' by Mary Oliver the day he left the world, both of us none the wiser that it would be the day one of us carried on floating down the river alone. I had a little cry in the car tonight, it felt better afterwards.

I had a beautiful day today in nature with my friend Nina. We marvelled at how big the trees were, how the stones got there. We felt them and might have even been a bit naked in the waterfall at one point... It was lovely to feel part of it all today. Today my heart felt so full it might just have spilled over a bit.

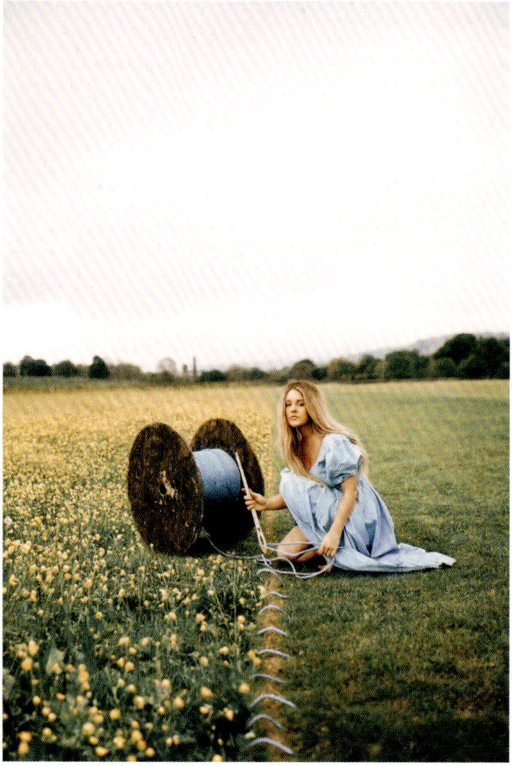

342/365

'Some nights, I will stay awake, and let the sorrows of the world tear me apart. But then, I must allow the joys of the world to put me back together – different from before, but whole once again.'
– Oriah Mountain Dreamer
'The Invitation'

A WORLD NEEDING REPAIR

I've not been able to stop thinking about the poor families involved in the Manchester Arena bombing tragedy all day. I've been remembering my own initial grief and the shock this time last year – every minute that passed felt like a lifetime in the wrong direction, towards a life that held no interest to me whatsoever. Hoping those people can find light in absolutely anything that brings them comfort.

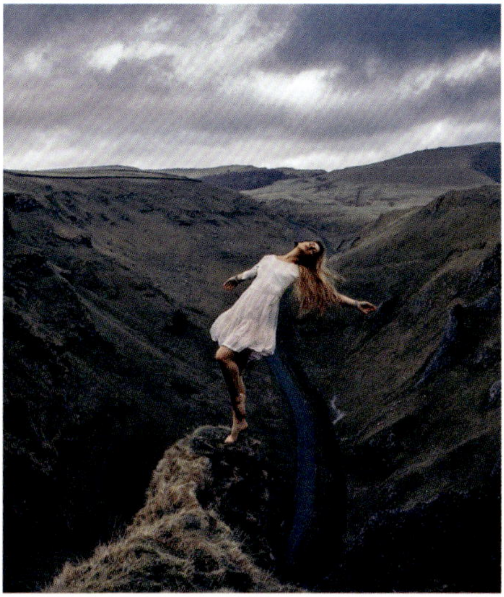

360/365

THE FALL

'That's the paradox: The time most people feel alive is when they're suffering, when something overwhelms their ordinary, careful armour, and the naked child is flung out onto the world. That's why the things that are worst to undergo are best to remember.

The only calibration that really counts is how much heart you invest, how much people ignore their fears of being hurt or caught out or humiliated. The only thing people regret is that they didn't live boldly enough, that they didn't invest enough heart, that they didn't love enough. Nothing else really counts at all.'

– Ted Hughes

Letters of Ted Hughes

Five days left of 365 to go! This shot was an absolute nightmare to get. I drove all the way to this cliff and hiked through nettles to get there (in a dress! A dress! My poor bare legs!), only to set up at the top and see 'No Card' flash up on my camera screen. Ha! Back home I went! I guess this was my 365's way of making sure I don't miss it...

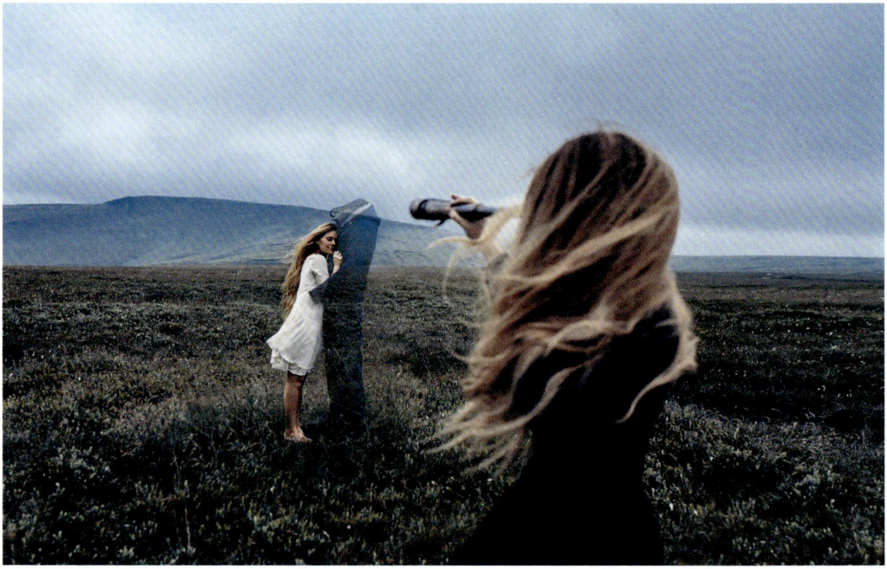

365/365

A YEAR OF OBSERVATION

I started this project on 15 June 2016. It's now 15 June 2017, and today's a big one for me.

I wanted to work this 365 into the same shot I took on Day One.

I was six weeks deep into an all-consuming grief I never knew existed, trying to fathom making a way through it, trying to fathom never seeing you again.

The way I took to grief was to try and see it as an aid – a human process – nothing to be ashamed of, nothing to hide. Grief was going to get me through your loss. The poems, songs, articles and quotes I read about others' experiences with loss gave me so much comfort, but I realized the only reason I was able to read them, and feel that comfort in the first place, was because these people had the courage to openly share their incredibly complex, raw and personal times with the world.

Today, I observe and share myself again, and I look at where I am.

It turns out, 365 days hasn't stopped me missing you one jot. Turns out, I talk to you every single day, I smile and reminisce every single day. I comb through all the things you ever told me and all the conclusions we ever drew about the world, and I think about them. I think about how it would feel to hug you, how it felt to hug you. I think about all the beautiful things I see and feel, and I wish you were here to share it – as a lover, as a friend, or as what could have been just two strangers passing through each other's lives in a costume shop one day.

Moving forward from a relationship like ours is a challenge. I've realized when you grieve for someone, it's your own little way of keeping them breathing inside you. Grieving romantically and moving on from the loss (like you would with a breakup) and keeping someone alive inside you are completely opposing concepts, and it's been a struggle to get my head around that, but having such a wonderful base of friendship has helped.

So, Day 365.

I miss you and I would like a hug.

And I would like them for the rest of the days that I get, even if they're only ever in my head.

That is all.

04.

PLANNING

LOCATIONS AND HOW TO FIND THEM

When it comes to questions about my work, one of the most common I get asked is 'How do you find your locations?'.

I'm happy to say that location scouting is one of the most fun parts of my job, and I'm excited to share all the secrets to finding amazing locations here for you.

1. HAVE AN IDEA OF WHAT KIND OF LOCATION YOU WANT – OR DON'T!

There are two ways to put a photoshoot together, and in my lifetime I've used both techniques equally. The first is to plan, research and compare your options rigorously. The second is to head out with a camera and a tripod, and see where your feet take you.

The latter is self-explanatory, and can often result in better stories, pictures that capture your inner feelings a little more, and equally, more frustration and failures.

But let's talk about the planning side of things.

You can categorize locations into different genres. Here are some of the types of location that feature heavily in my style of work:

- Castle/fairytale/folly
- Woodlands/forest
- Moors/desolate landscape
- Long grass fields/hills/mountains
- Lakes/reservoirs
- The ocean/rocks/sea
- Flowers/bushes
- Crops/wheat/rapeseed/lavender
- Industrial (old style/mills/ cobbled streets)
- Industrial (modern/architectural/ clean)
- Indoor locations/manor houses/ photo studios/abandoned places

Once you've chosen your location style, you then want to find areas that project that ambience.

The lavender fields at Cotswold Lavender create a great backdrop for a purple explosion.

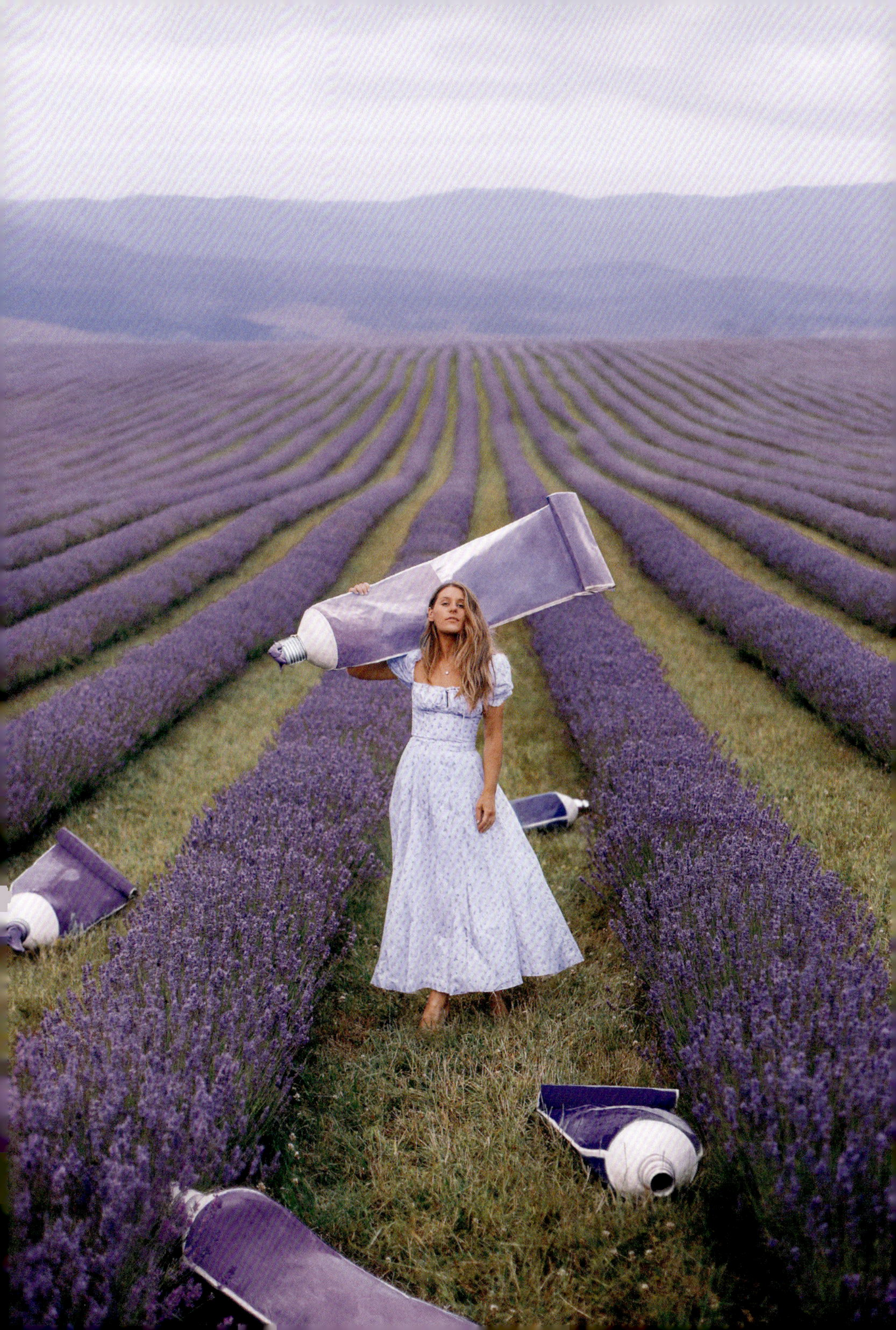

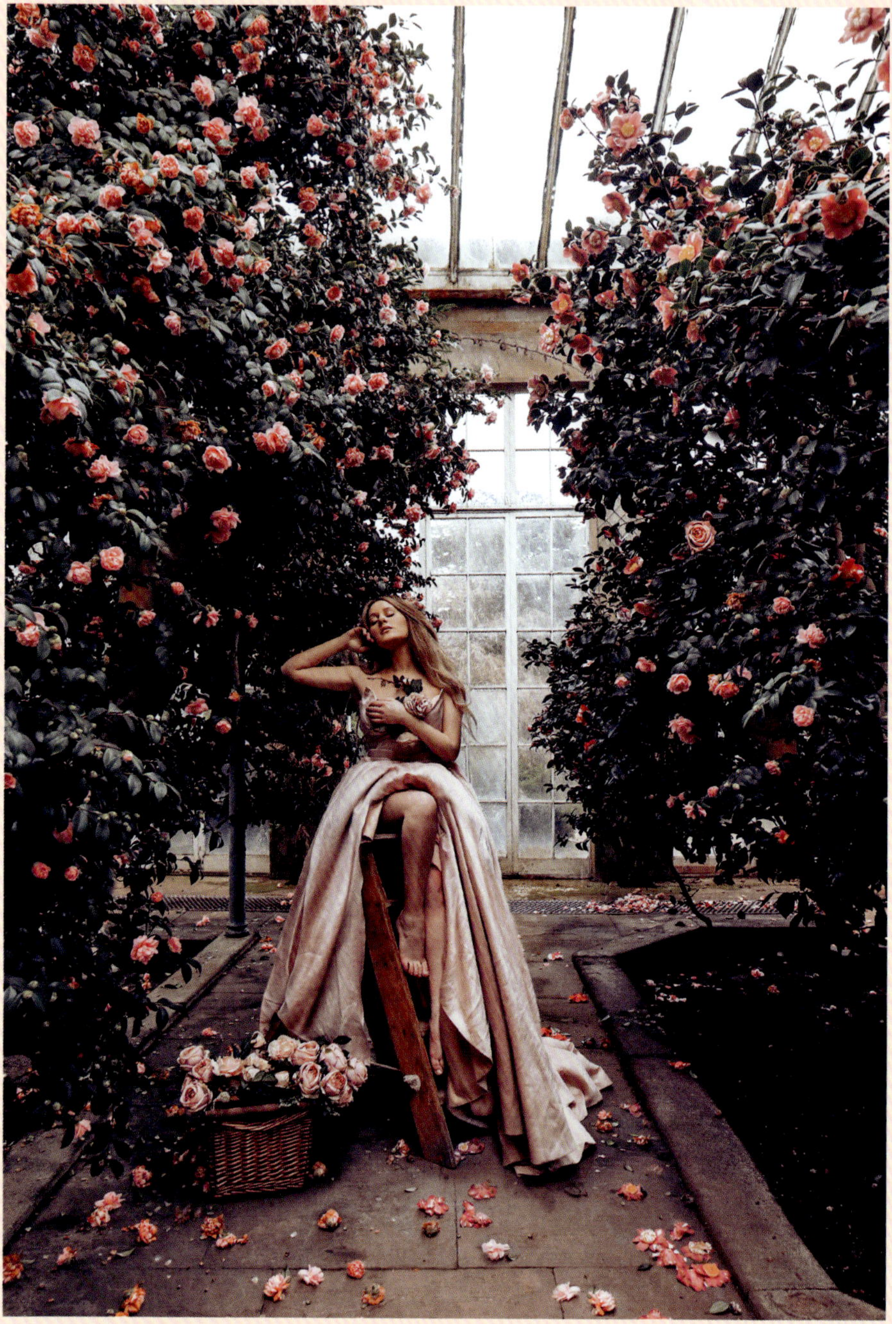

The Yorkshire Sculpture Park's 'Camelia House' makes for a perfectly romantic pink backdrop even in the depths of winter.

2. LOCATION DEEP DIVE

To do this, you want to engage in what I call a 'Location Deep Dive'. For me, this includes the following things:

- Typing in keywords into Google (such as folly, castle, fairytale).
- Using Google Maps to find locations that might include those words in their name (for example, flower farm, folly, tower, manor, hall, castle, estate).
- Search the name of your find on Instagram, then hit the 'Places' filter. (This will give you the option of seeing the most recent images that have been taken there so you can see the way the location looks at that particular time of year.)
- You can then contact the venue/ location if possible or necessary, and check that they allow photography.

3. WHAT ARE THE LAWS?

In the United Kingdom, the laws surrounding photoshoots on public and private land are primarily governed by the Copyright, Designs, and Patents Act 1988 (CDPA) and various privacy laws. Let's get into the official details:

PHOTOSHOOTS ON PUBLIC LAND:
Because public spaces (streets, parks, or other publicly accessible areas) are considered to have limited privacy expectations, you generally have the right to take pictures without obtaining explicit permission from anyone, and there's no need to seek any kind of permit.

However, there are a few important considerations to keep in mind:

- **PRIVACY:** Although you can generally take photos of people in public places without their consent, there might be limitations if you invade their privacy. This, of course, is not an issue when shooting self-portraiture. That said, if someone has a reasonable expectation of privacy in a particular situation (such as being in the background of one of your images – say, swimming in a lake), it would be illegal to photograph them without their consent.

- **COMMERCIAL USE:** If you plan to use the photographs taken on public land for commercial purposes, such as selling them, or using them in advertising work for a brand, you might need additional permissions from any people featured in the images, particularly if they are recognizable.

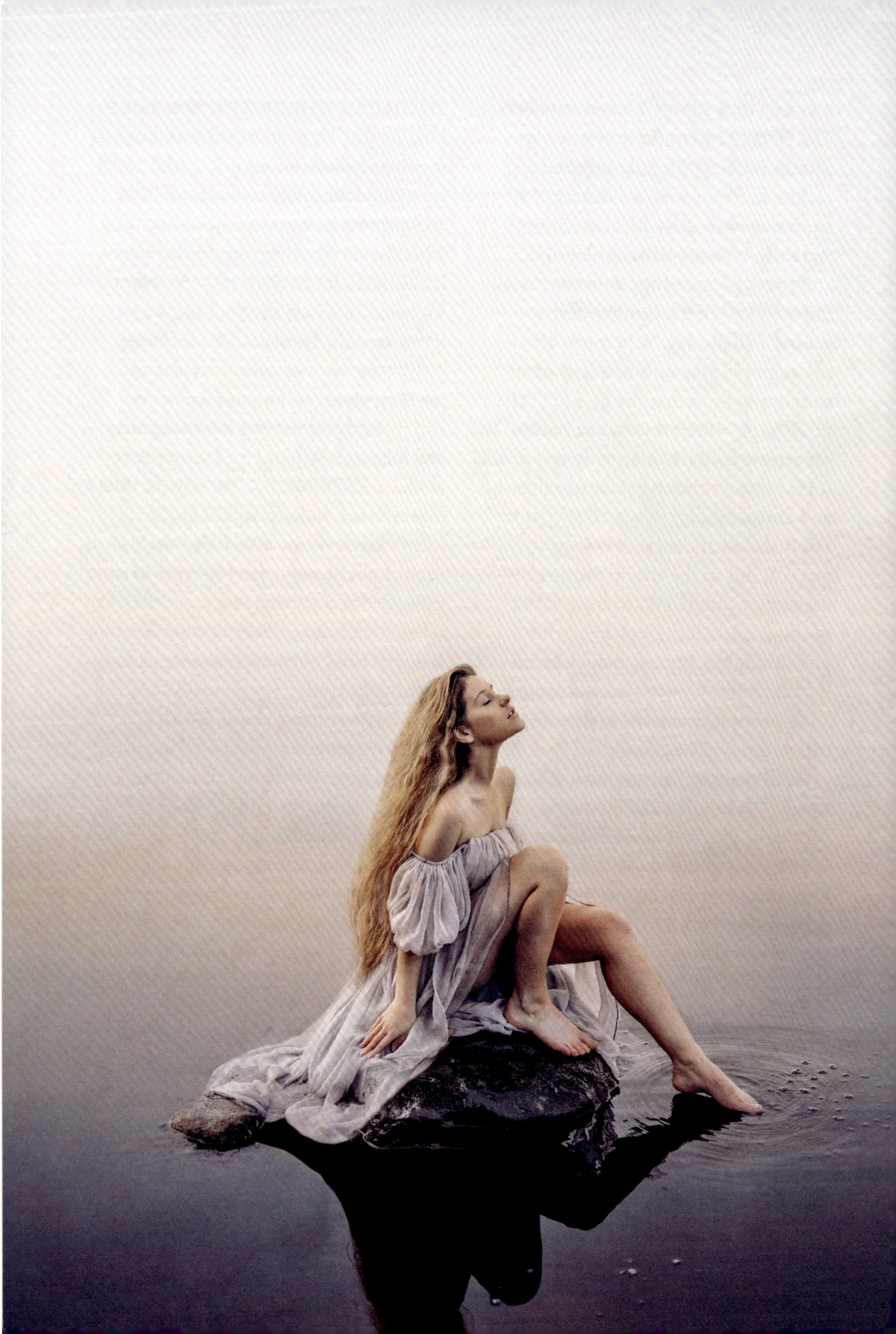

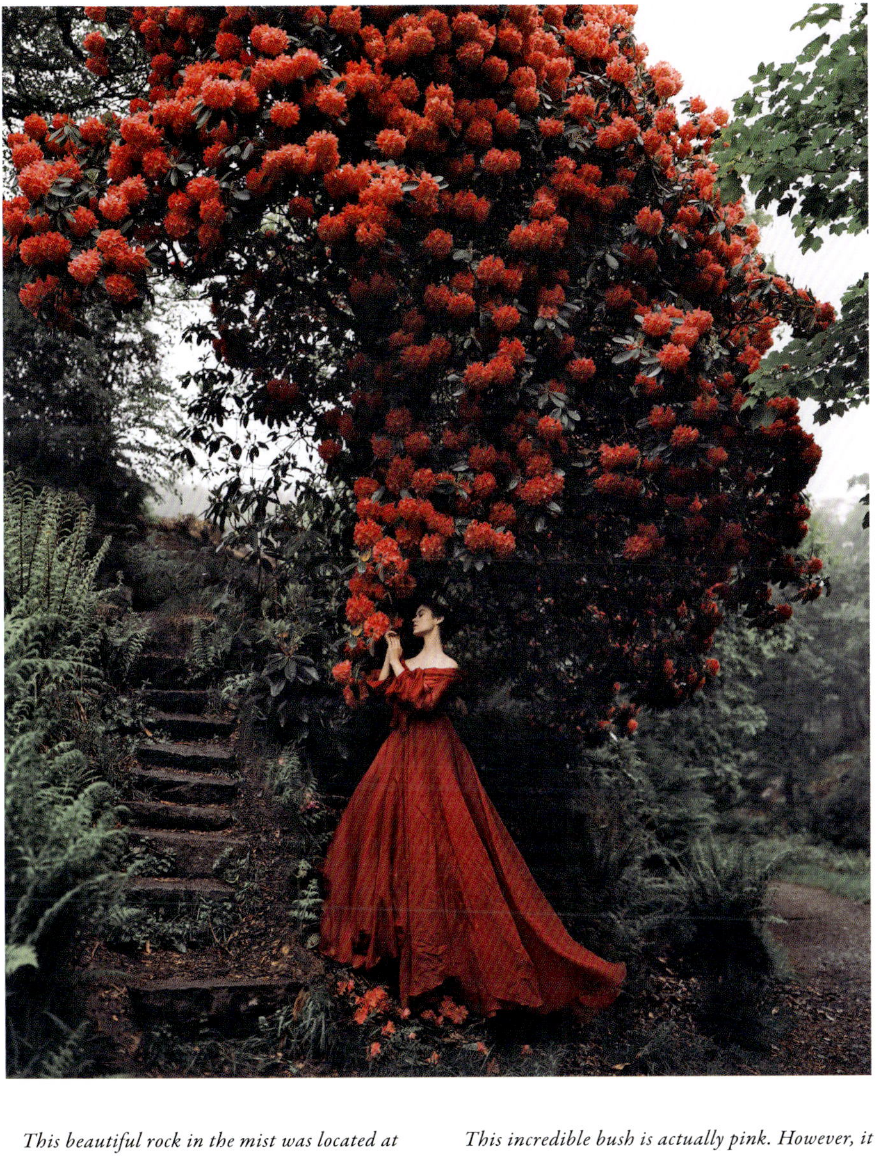

This beautiful rock in the mist was located at Torside Reservoir, which I discovered driving home one day. I made sure to check the wind speed was below three miles per hour on the day of the shoot, to ensure still, glass-like water on the lake.

This incredible bush is actually pink. However, it does grow in this beautiful shape. It's located near the ruins of Errwood Hall in the Goyt Valley in the Peak District, and flowers for ten days each year in May.

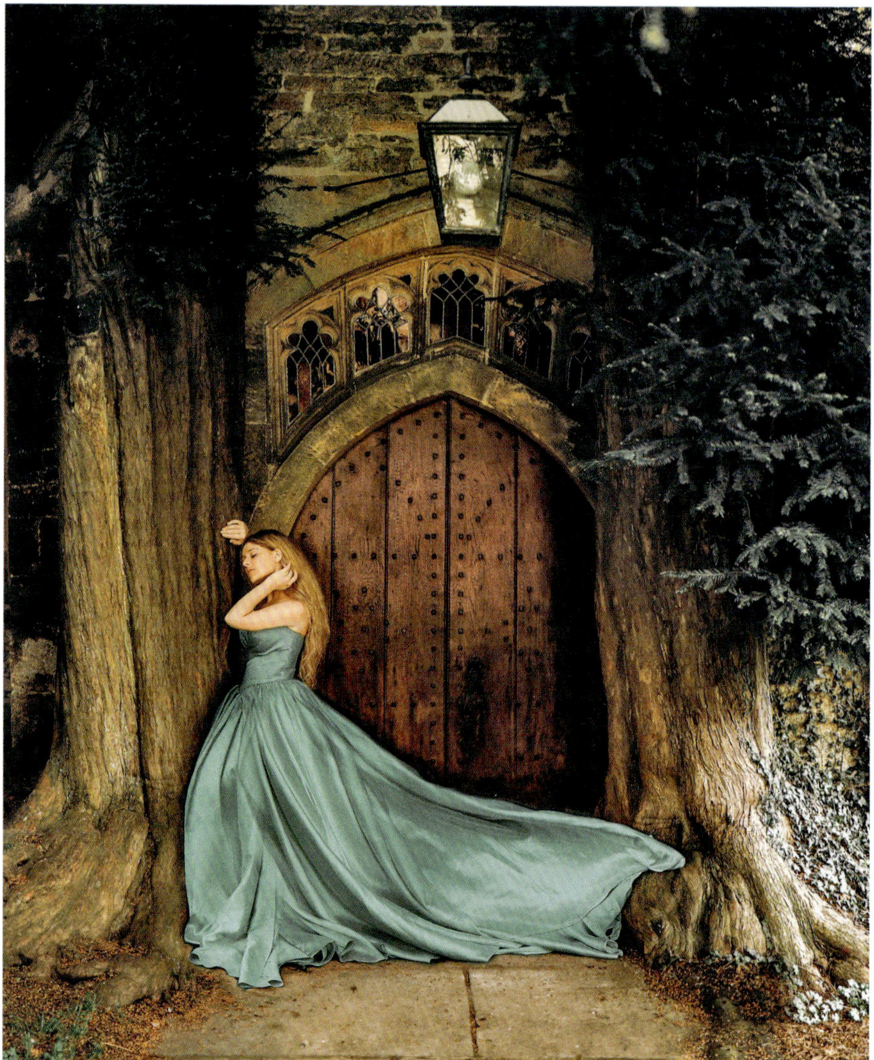

This amazing door surrounded by trees is found in a small churchyard in Stow-on-the-Wold.

Using your own house as a backdrop also works well – find any plain wall and edit away!

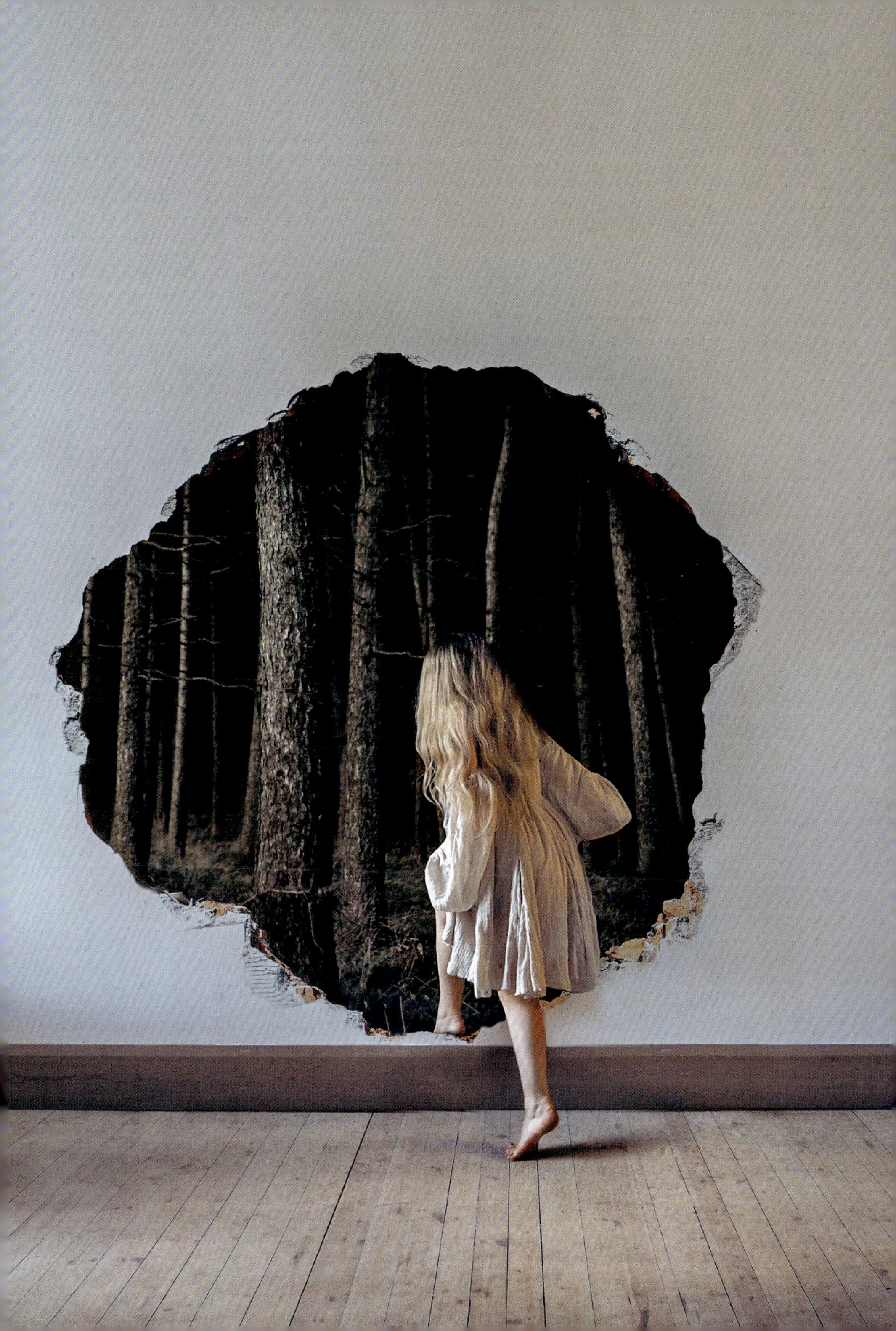

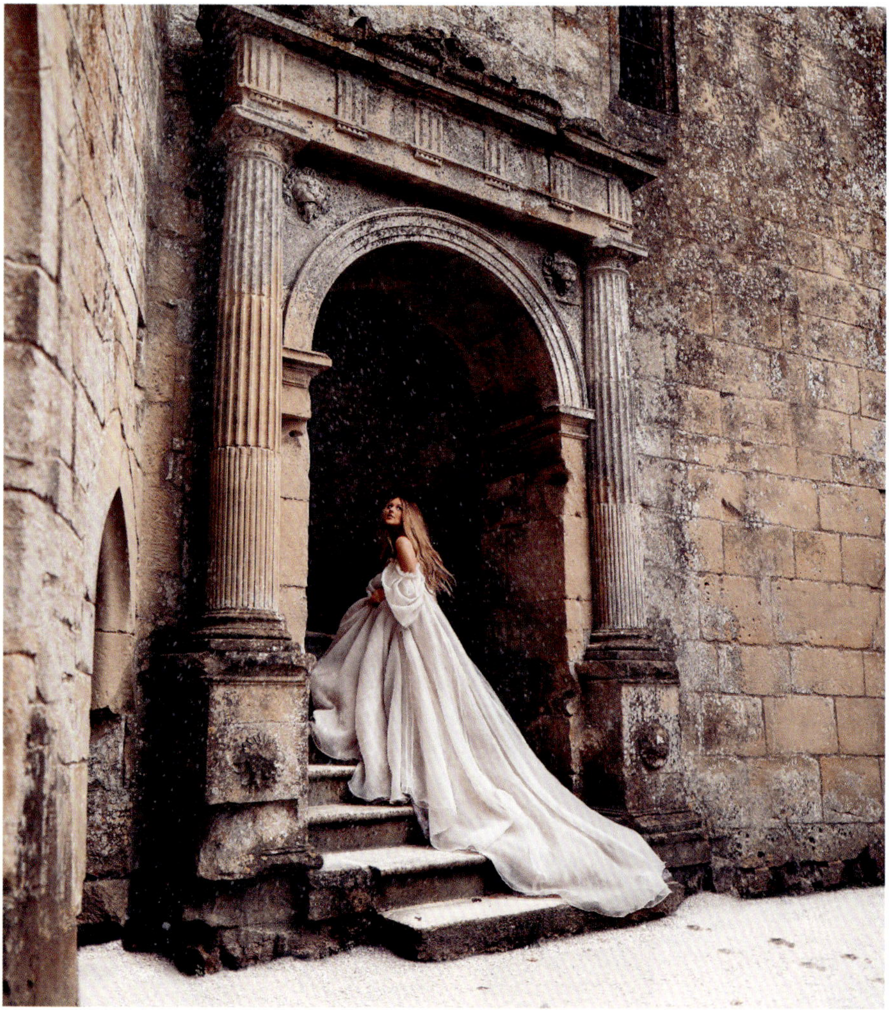

Old Wardour Castle in Wiltshire was the perfect backdrop for this princess-inspired shot. I added the snow in edit to create a mythical feel.

SHOOTING IN PUBLIC

Leading on from locations, for most people, a much scarier thought is the idea of having the general public walking past as you stand in front of your tripod. Trust me, this is as horrendous as you're picturing it to be, and the awkwardness and anxiety still hasn't left me, even though I've been shooting in public for over 15 years.

Here are my tips to making it 'slightly' easier:

1. CHOOSE TO SHOOT AT A QUIET TIME OF DAY

Or at least a quiet day of the week. This means trying your best to avoid weekends, 3.30–4 p.m. on a school day, and bank holidays. If you can, shooting at sunrise or sunset will give you the added benefit of beautiful, (hopefully golden or misty) cinematic lighting.

2. TAKE A FRIEND ALONG WITH YOU

There's nothing that eases the look of self-portraiture insanity more than having someone else standing next to you, at best, to distract you and at worst, to commiserate with you over the embarrassment of shooting in public. Having a photo friend is also helpful in other ways – they can watch your kit while you shoot, check the focus for you and generally keep your mood upbeat.

3. BEFRIEND AND INTERACT WITH THE PEOPLE AROUND YOU

By far the most effective tactic in my experience is to talk to the people walking by who are interested (or concerned) by what you are doing. It's a great way to spread the word of your work, have them check up to see how the picture turned out later, and make yourself feel more welcomed in the space you're shooting in.

I've actually formed many friendships/client relationships with people who have been passing by as I shot in public, and if you remain friendly and open while you shoot, you can actually form some pretty nice new connections.

Shooting in public may feel awful, but it is part of the process. Don't be tempted to rush your shoot, throw the towel in or tone yourself down to fit into the crowd. If people don't like it, they can leave. One of my first shoots in my first 365 involved me standing on a ladder on a hill, pretending to paint a rainbow in the sky. I'll never forget the cruel words a group of boys shouted at me while I posed for each shot. Yet I ended up selling that image as a book cover, so I'm very glad they didn't push me into giving up.

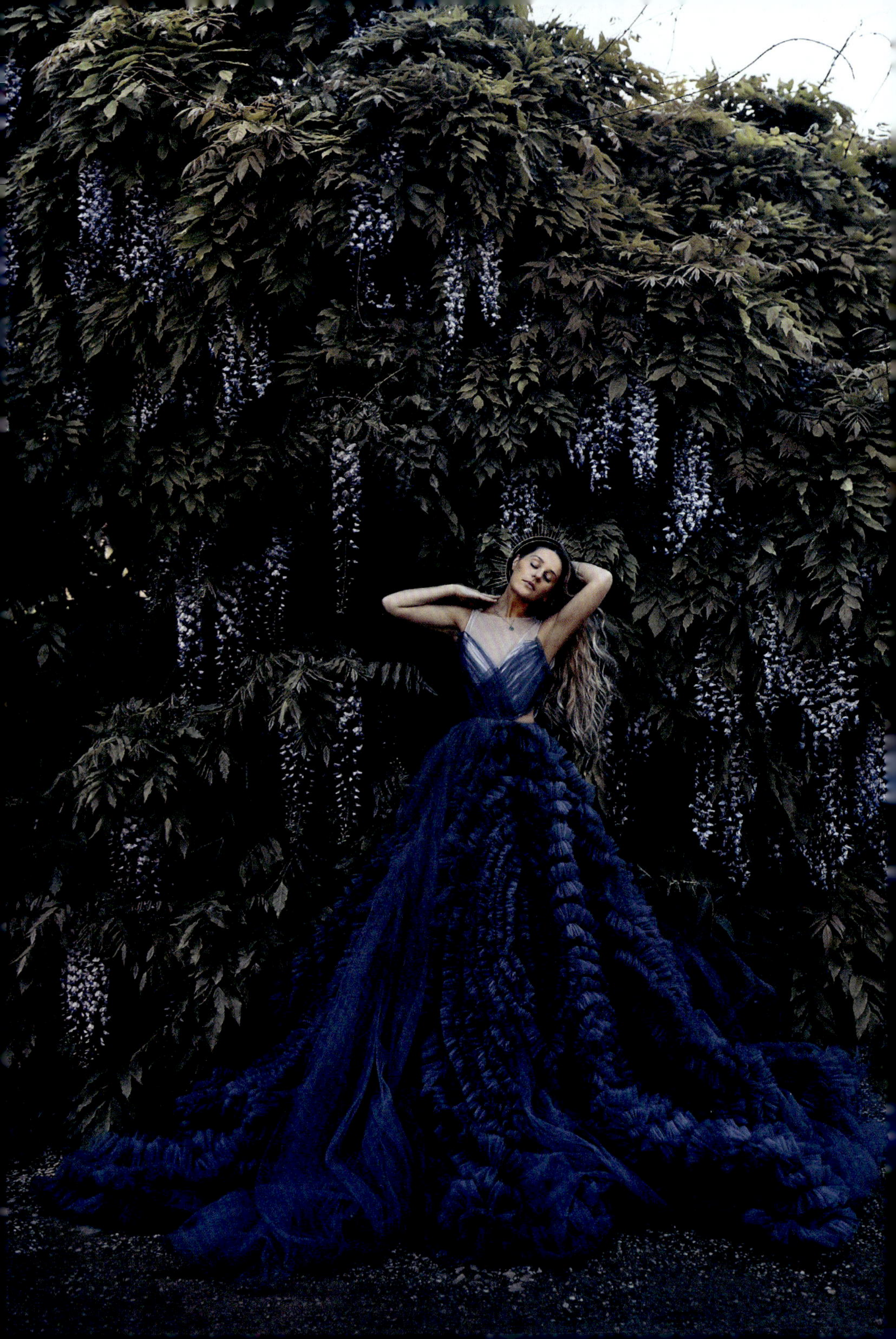

Shooting in the wisteria at Hidcote Manor Gardens in Gloucestershire. This was done in front of about 20 people, including a gardener...

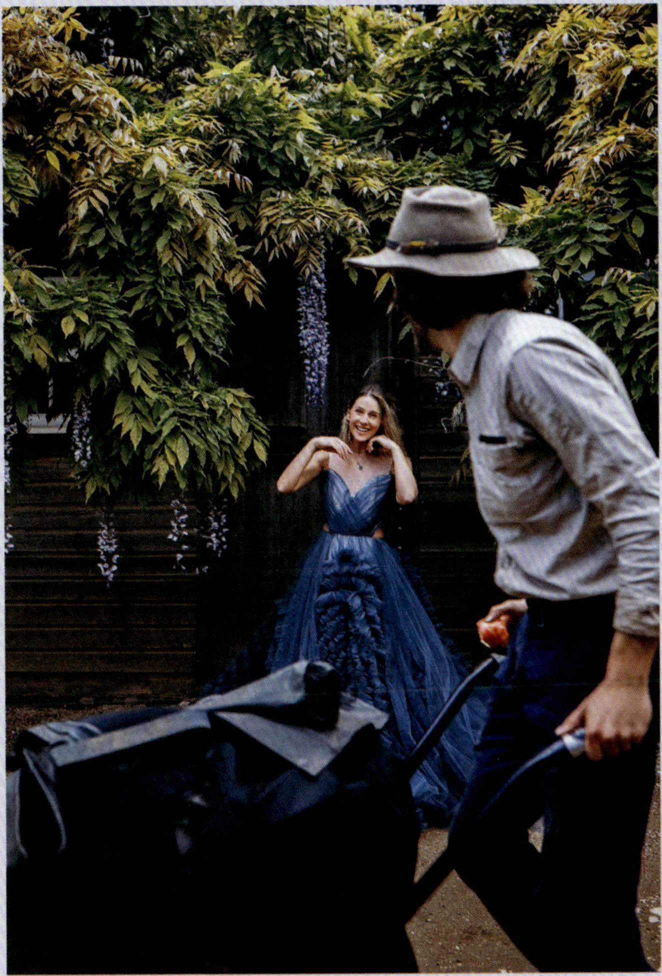

Luckily, everyone was incredibly friendly and found the whole shoot very entertaining!

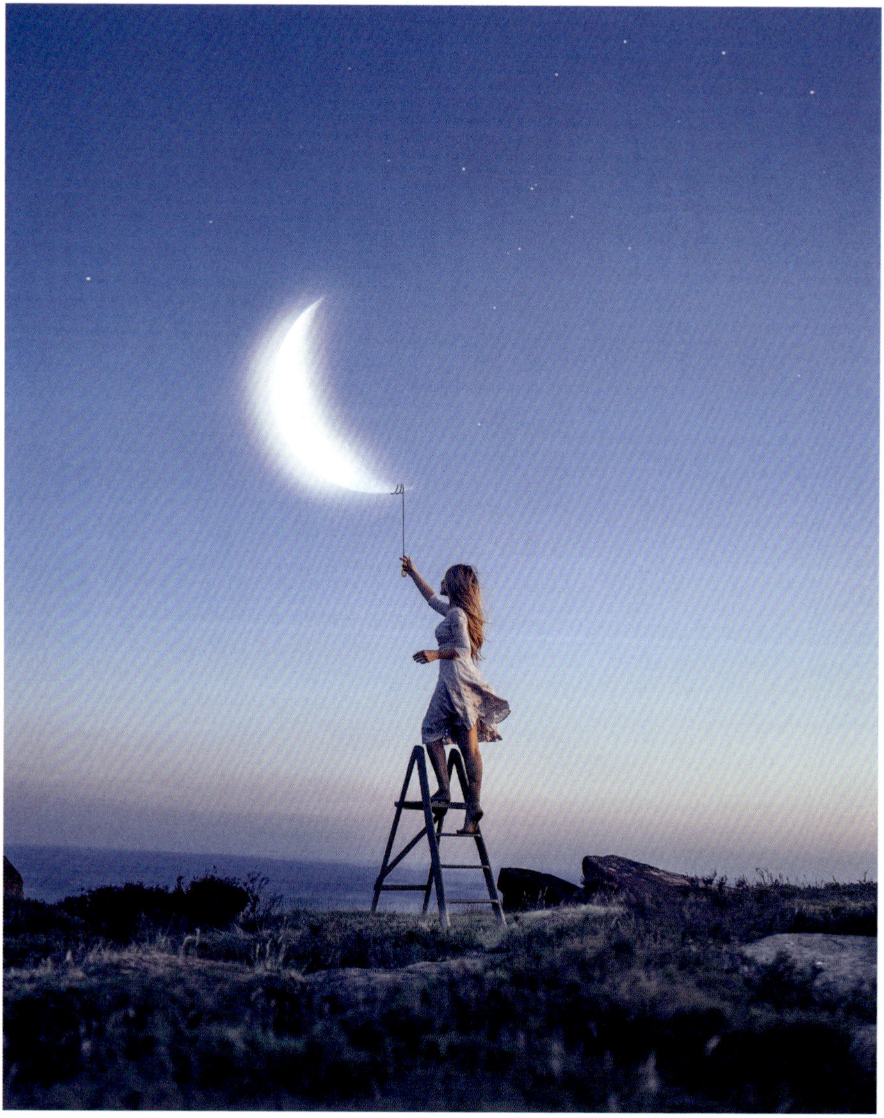

Shooting a self-portrait at the public beauty spot known as 'The Roaches' in the Peak District.

PROPS AND CONCEPTS

Once you have shooting in different locations under your belt, you can always crank your work up a level by shooting with different props and costumes. In this chapter, I'm going to share my methods and tips for getting the most out of each of these areas, suiting all budgets, and how you can use props and costumes to tell stories via visual concepts within your work.

PROPS

Sourcing props for photography is an exciting and creative process, and probably my next favourite thing to shooting and editing the picture itself. Using props allows photographers to enhance their work and tell compelling visual stories. There are various avenues for finding your props, ranging from online platforms like eBay and Facebook Marketplace, to DIY projects and prop warehouses. Let's explore these options in more detail.

ONLINE PLATFORMS: Websites like eBay and Facebook Marketplace provide photographers with a super-wide range of options to find props for their work. These platforms allow users to buy or bid on second-hand items, vintage pieces or unique objects that can add character and interest to a photoshoot. Photographers can search for specific items, browse through categories and even negotiate prices directly with sellers. The amount of hours I've spent searching 'giant prop' on eBay must be in the hundreds! Here are some of my favourite images with props I've sourced from various outlets.

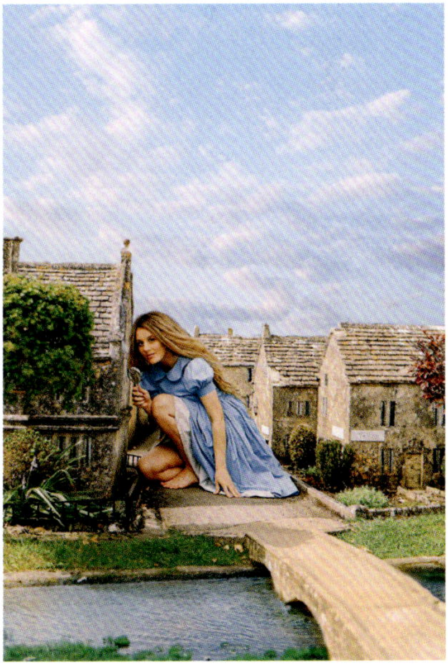

This magnifying glass was found at my local antique shop – perfect when combined with a miniature Cotswold village!

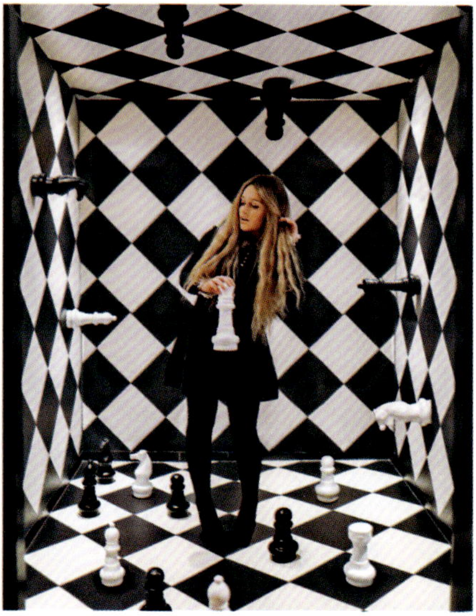

These chess pieces were bought on eBay and stuffed into my suitcase for a flight to Amsterdam. I came across a bathroom in a hotel designed like this! I edited the toilet out, held each chess piece to a different part of the wall, stitched it together and... voila!

DIY PROJECTS: Creating your own props can be a more cost-effective and personalized approach. Platforms like YouTube offer a wealth of tutorials and DIY videos that provide step-by-step instructions on making props. Whether it's crafting handmade backdrops, building simple sets or creating unique accessories, DIY projects enable photographers to add a unique touch to our work as well as giving another creative itch a good scratch.

PROP WAREHOUSES: For photographers with higher budgets (or if you're working on higher-scale productions), prop warehouses are another fantastic resource. These amazing places offer a wide selection of props, furniture, set pieces and decor items for various themes and styles. eventprophire.com is one of my favourite prop warehouses, as well as the RSC Prop Warehouse in Stratford-upon-Avon. Photographers can browse through an extensive inventory and rent items for their photoshoots or events at a fraction of the cost of buying more extreme and high-quality props. Prop warehouses provide convenience and access to professional-grade props that can significantly elevate the visual impact of a shoot.

CHARITY SHOPS AND ANTIQUE SHOPS: Thrift stores and flea markets are treasure troves for photographers seeking unique and vintage props. These places often offer a diverse range of items at affordable prices. By exploring these venues, photographers can discover one-of-a-kind pieces that bring character and nostalgia to their compositions. Think vintage suitcases, a weird old hat, antique books and magnifying glasses, for example.

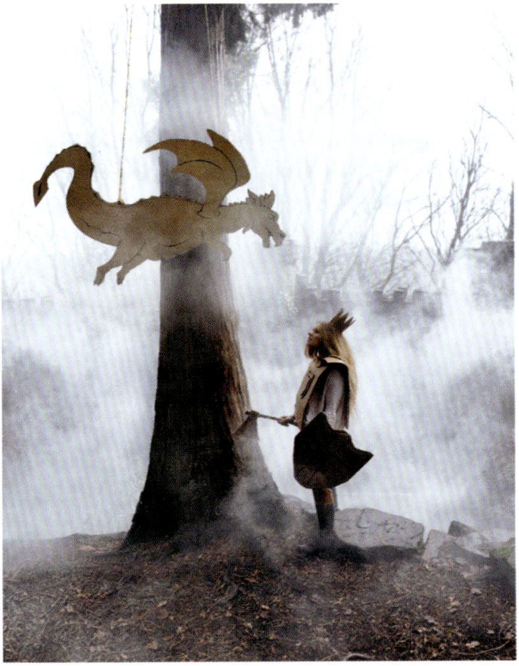

Instead of throwing away my used cardboard,
I created this cardboard armour set for
a childhood-inspired war scene.

BORROWING AND COLLABORATION: Another option is to reach out to friends, family or local artists for prop borrowing or collaboration. Someone may have interesting objects or furniture that align with the desired aesthetic of a shoot. Collaborating with other creative individuals, such as stylists or designers, can also open doors to unique prop opportunities and shared resources, as well as great new friendship connections.

THE TIP SHOP:
Check with your local tip to see if there's an onsite tip shop – a wonderful, magical place where people leave their unwanted items in good condition. Usually, you can purchase items at a ridiculously low cost.

THE ROLE OF PROPS IN PHOTOGRAPHY

Personally, I adore the use of props in photography. They help to set the scene, evoke emotions and create storytelling. Here are a few ways props can contribute to the narrative of your photograph:

CONTEXT AND SETTING: Props provide visual cues that establish the environment and setting of the photograph. They help transport viewers to a specific time, place or theme, allowing photographers to create immersive and engaging visual narratives. I love using props that people relate to easily, and using them in a playful way to ignite people's minds. A giant tea cup, an oversized apple missing a bite, a mysterious door in the middle of a lake... Props invite the viewer to take part in the story, using their own interpretations and feelings towards the items they see used.

SYMBOLISM AND METAPHOR: Props can also be used to convey symbolic meanings or metaphors within an image. By carefully selecting and placing objects, you can evoke emotions, suggest narratives to your viewer or communicate abstract ideas in a visual and impactful manner. You can see an example of this in the image opposite.

ENHANCING COMPOSITION: Props can be used to enhance the overall composition of a photograph. They add depth, layers and visual interest to the frame, creating a more dynamic and visually appealing image.

ADDING STORYTELLING ELEMENTS: I prefer to use props that act as part of a storytelling narrative. I like to use them to help create more of a background to a character, or a feeling, or a place. Props provide context, indicate a person's interests or occupation, or act as a visual metaphor for the story being told.

CREATING MOOD AND ATMOSPHERE: Finally, props can also contribute to the mood and atmosphere of a photograph. They really can evoke emotions, set the tone or create a specific ambiance that enhances the overall impact of the image.

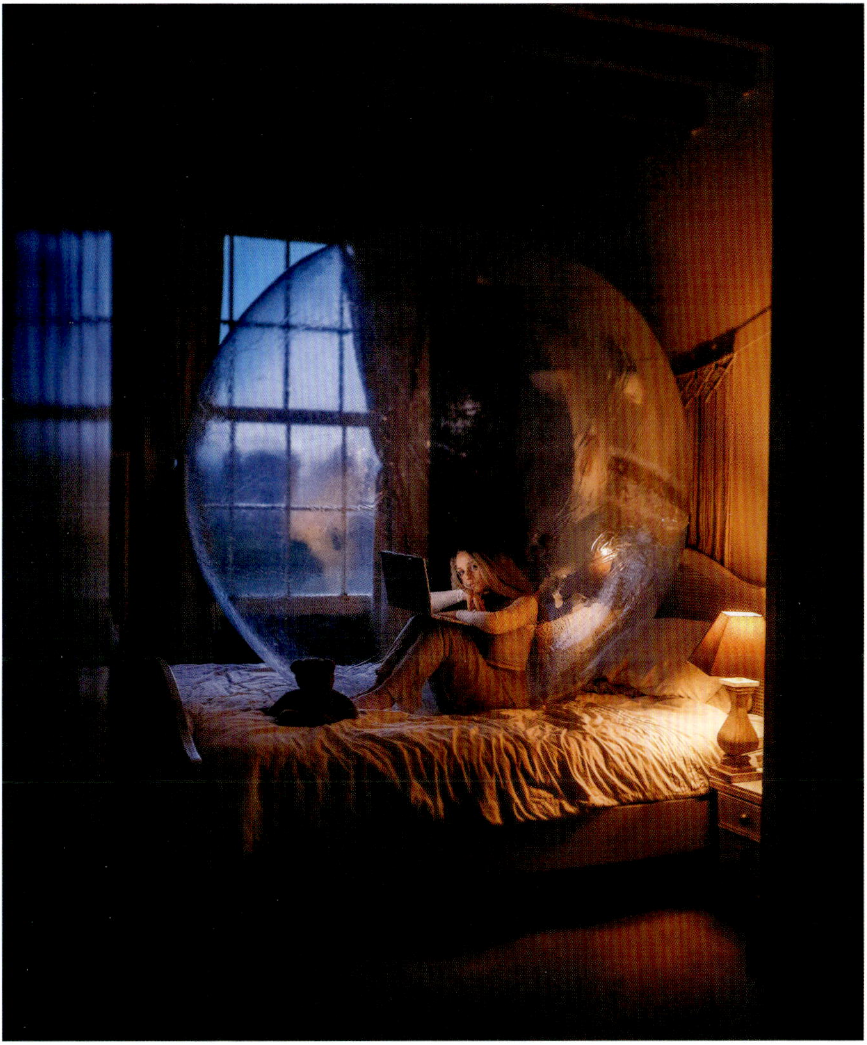

The giant zorb ball was my last purchase before the Covid-19 lockdown restrictions hit. Using a giant bubble helped symbolize the isolation I felt during the first lockdown.

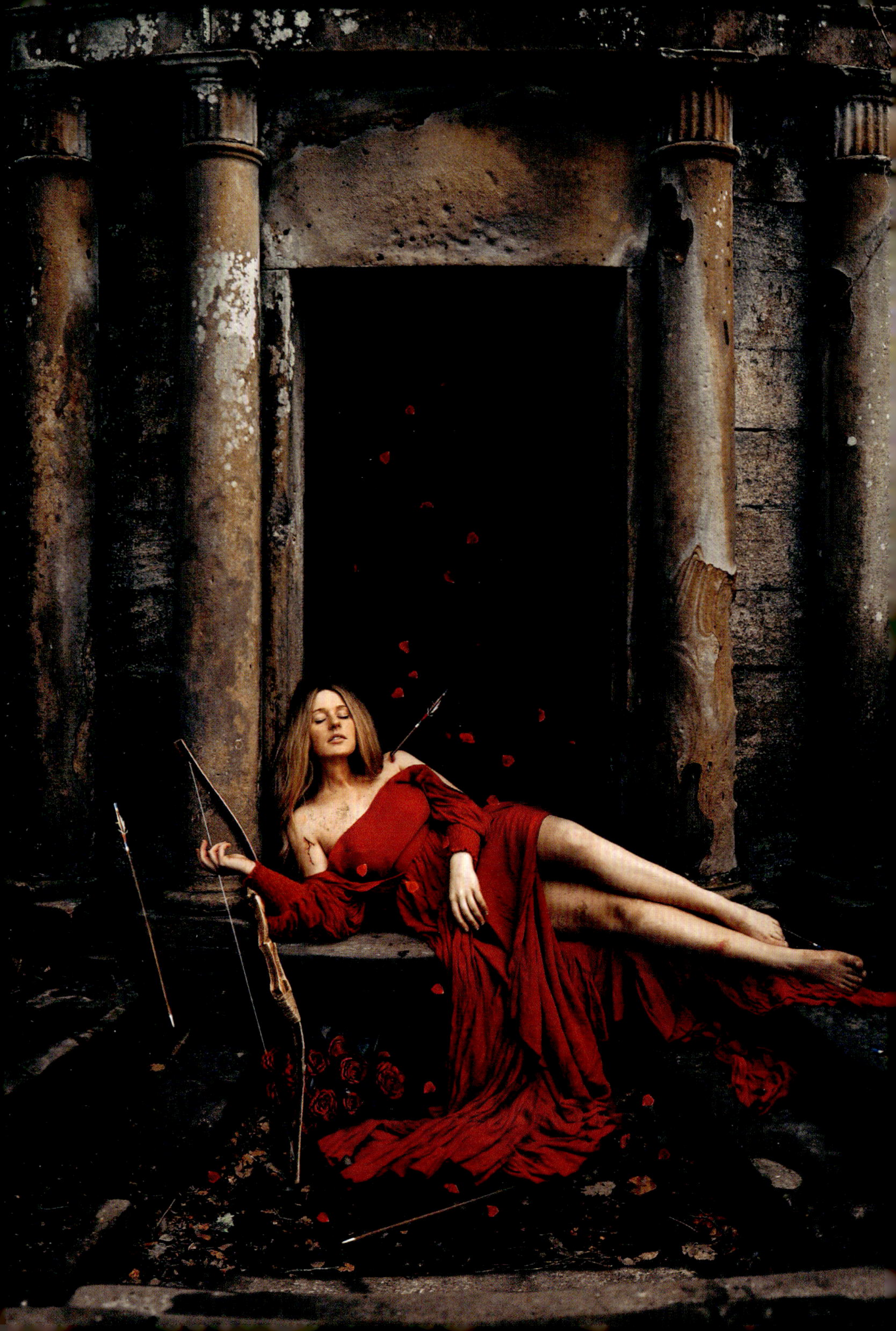

STUDIO LIGHTING

If shooting outdoors doesn't appeal to your sense of style, another type of photography to consider for your self-portraits is the enigma that is studio shooting. It was about three years into my photography journey before I finally ventured into a photo studio, and while it wouldn't be my go-to location choice, I know photographers who create mind-blowing work with artificial lighting in a studio. There are a variety of reasons that photographers might choose to shoot inside a photography studio, the lowest on the list being the risk of rain!

Studio photography provides ultimate control over lighting conditions and all external variables, as well as eliminating external distractions such as the general public and the weather, and allows for precise manipulation of your environment to achieve desired effects.

Let's explore the different types of lighting equipment most commonly used in studios, and how they can be used to create various moods within your work.

CONTINUOUS LIGHTING

Continuous lighting refers to lighting equipment that remains on during the entire photoshoot. It provides a constant light source, allowing photographers to see how the lighting falls on the subject in real time. Common types of continuous lighting include:

1. SOFTBOXES

Softboxes are square or rectangular light modifiers that create a soft and diffused light by using a translucent fabric or material to cover the light source. They produce even, flattering light with gentle shadows, making them suitable for various genres like portraits, fashion and product photography.

2. UMBRELLAS

Umbrellas are affordable and versatile lighting tools. They can be used to diffuse or bounce light, creating a soft and even illumination. The silver or white reflective surface of the umbrella can help control the intensity and direction of the light.

I used a bow, arrows and falling rose petals to create the feeling of bleeding, grief and death against this archway folly. Using the colour red helps bring the idea of war and blood to the forefront of the viewer's mind.

3. LED PANELS

LED panels are flat, rectangular light sources consisting of multiple small LED bulbs. They provide consistent and adjustable lighting, allowing photographers to fine-tune the intensity and colour temperature. LED panels are often used for video shoots and product photography, and I actually love to use them when shooting at night.

STROBES/STROBE LIGHTING

Strobe lighting, also known as flash photography, involves using powerful bursts of light to illuminate your subject. Strobe lights are typically more intense than continuous lighting, and they provide a higher level of control over the lighting environment. Common types of strobe lighting equipment include:

1. STUDIO FLASH UNITS

Studio flash units are powerful lights that are synchronized with the camera to fire a burst of light at the moment of exposure. They can be adjusted to control the light output, and various modifiers such as softboxes, octaboxes and beauty dishes can be attached to shape and diffuse the light.

2. OCTABOXES

Octaboxes are octagonal-shaped softboxes that produce soft and even lighting with a circular catchlight in the subject's eyes. The larger the octabox, the softer the light it produces. Octaboxes are commonly used for portraits, fashion and beauty photography.

3. BEAUTY DISHES

Beauty dishes are shallow, bowl-shaped reflectors with a central light source. They provide a combination of soft and hard light, creating defined shadows and a distinct catchlight. Beauty dishes are often used in fashion and beauty photography to highlight facial features. Alternatively, you can use a mix of all three.

This image was shot with a large softbox to my front left. The diffused light helped create a soft, romantic feel.

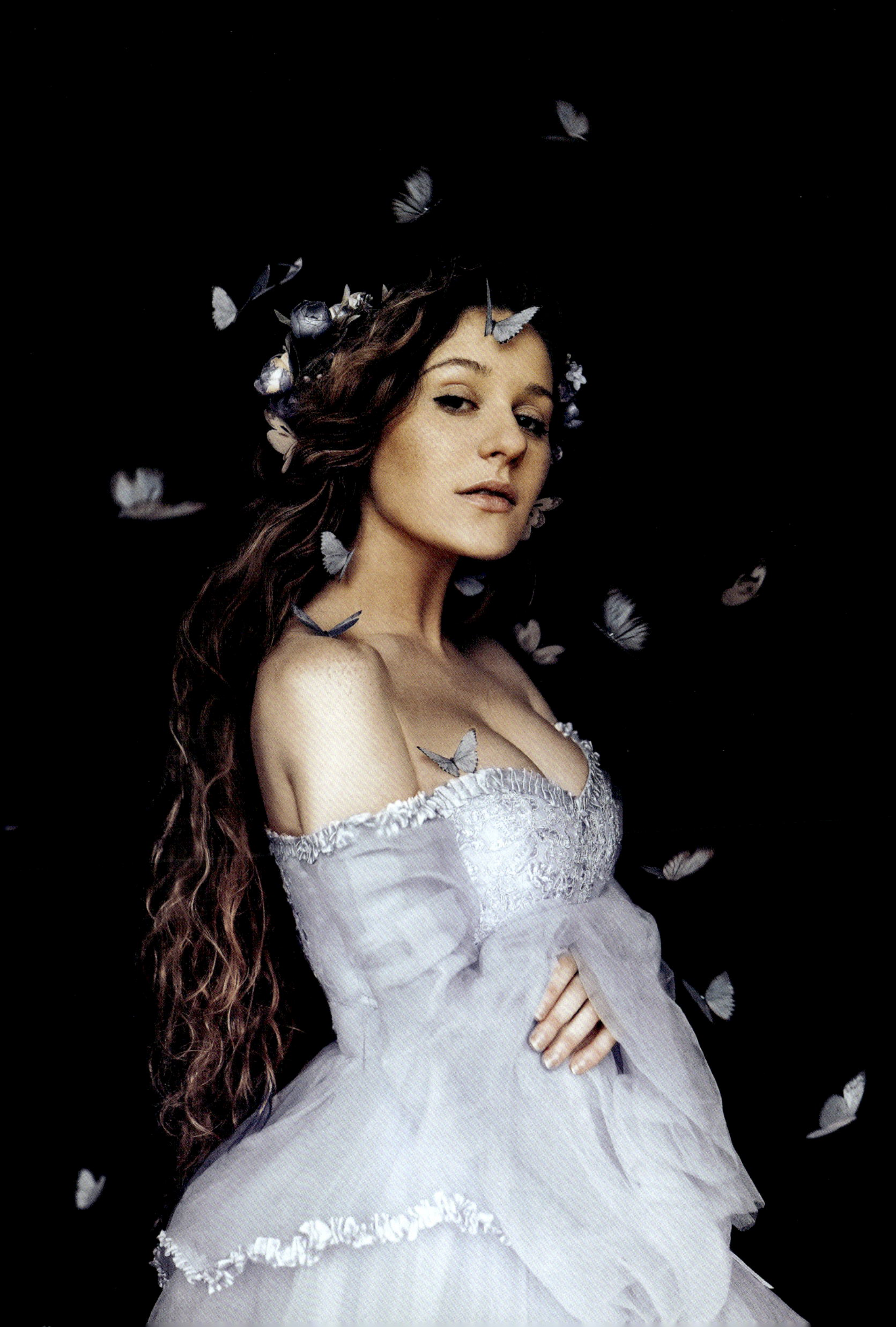

LIGHTING FOR DIFFERENT MOODS AND STORIES

The way lighting is used in a studio environment can dramatically alter the mood and narrative of a photograph. Here are a few examples:

1. SOFT LIGHTING

Soft lighting, achieved through the use of diffused light sources like softboxes or umbrellas, creates a gentle and flattering illumination. It minimizes harsh shadows and is often associated with a sense of beauty, serenity and warmth. Soft lighting is commonly used in portrait photography, newborn photography or any scenario where a soft and comforting atmosphere is what you're aiming for.

2. DRAMATIC LIGHTING

By using harder light sources, or controlling the direction and intensity of the light, photographers can create a more dramatic image. This can involve creating strong contrasts, deep shadows and intense highlights. Dramatic lighting is often used in fashion, conceptual or fine art photography to evoke emotions, add intrigue or create a sense of mystery. So be brave and throw the softbox away!

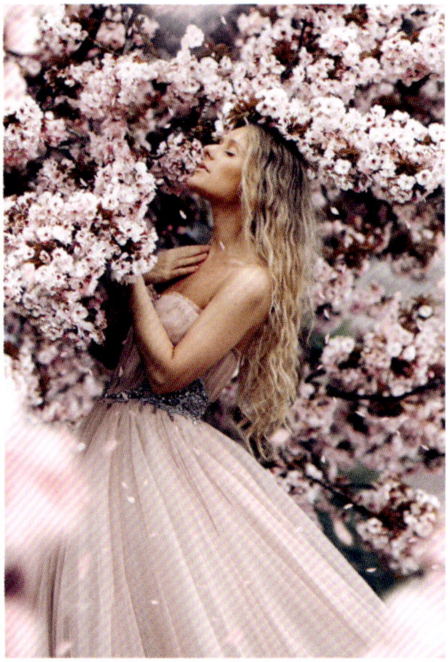

Using natural overcast lighting helped this image stay soft and feminine, in line with the theme of pretty cherry blossom.

3. REMBRANDT LIGHTING

Rembrandt lighting is a technique that creates a triangular patch of light on the subject's cheek opposite the light source, with the rest of the face partially illuminated. It adds depth, dimension and a classic aesthetic to portraits. This lighting style is achieved by placing the light source at a specific angle, usually above and to the side of the subject.

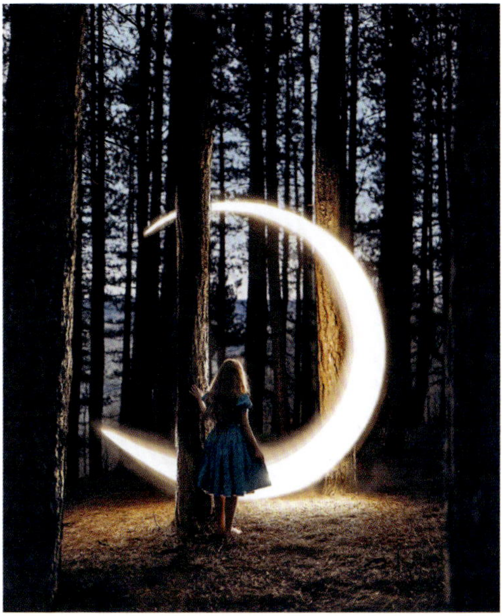

I used strobes to mimic the light of a giant moon behind me, lighting my hair, legs, arms and hand separately, and then stitched them all together in post. I lit the floor where the moon would be, created the moon shape in edit too, and layered it all together into one final shot.

4. HIGH-KEY AND LOW-KEY LIGHTING

High-key lighting involves using bright, evenly distributed lighting to create a predominantly white or light background. It creates a cheerful and airy atmosphere, often used in fashion, beauty and commercial photography. In contrast, low-key lighting involves using darker tones, with strong contrasts and minimal lighting on the subject. It adds a sense of mystery, drama and intensity to the photograph.

These are just a few examples of how different lighting set-ups and techniques in a studio environment can influence the mood, atmosphere, and storytelling in a photograph. By understanding the characteristics and effects of various lighting equipment, photographers can shape the visual narrative and evoke specific emotions to convey their intended story.

05.

PUTTING YOU IN THE PICTURE

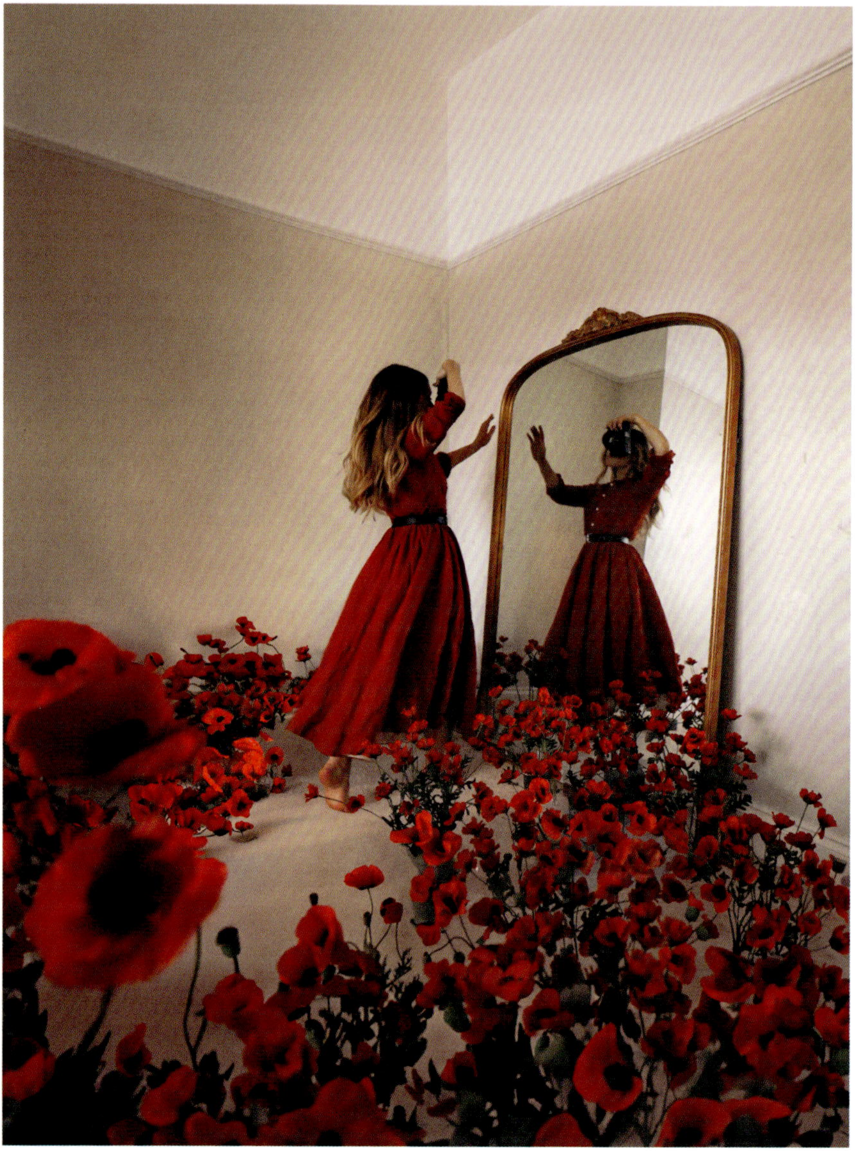

'Nothing ever ends poetically. It ends and we turn it into poetry. All that blood was never once beautiful. It was just red.'
– Kait Rokowski

BODY IMAGE AND SELF-REFLECTION

When it comes to shooting self-portraiture, one thing that might be holding you back is the idea of looking at hundreds of photographs of yourself.

Certainly, as a 15-year-old girl with alopecia and a history of eating disorders, my sense of self-esteem was strikingly low. The reality of seeing myself up close, raw and in all kinds of unflattering lighting, was both a blessing and curse in my journey with body image.

When I use the term 'body image', I'm referring to a person's perception, thoughts and feelings about their own body. In today's image-driven society, where beauty standards are often unrealistic and unattainable, many individuals struggle with negative body image, regardless of gender. As a teenager, I personally felt this was exacerbated by the constant exposure to carefully curated images on social media and in adverts, and the toxic commentary on women's bodies in magazines and online. It's very difficult to see a fixed visual of yourself staring back at you through the camera and not feel a small sense of panic somewhere... 'Is that what I really look like?'

Over the years, I've become increasingly interested in the way self-portraits can have a positive and negative effect on our own sense of identity and body image, and I wanted to dedicate a chapter to explore this in more detail. I've experienced both the dark side and lighter side, and always think it's better to be prepared for this aspect of self-portraiture.

When we see numerous images of ourselves, whether in photographs or videos, it can unknowingly lead to heightened self-scrutiny. We may become more critical of our appearance, comparing ourselves to edited and filtered images that are prevalent in the media. We can also compare ourselves to people who are just, simply put, genetically different to us. Society favours a certain aesthetic and it can be difficult to be faced with our own fixed, physical form. This constant comparison can contribute to body dissatisfaction, low self-esteem and, eventually, the development of body image issues such as body dysmorphia, eating disorders and depression.

As someone who was already in the pit of eating disorder hell, I figured my body image probably couldn't get much worse by shooting self-portraits. And in some ways, that was true. I learned that I could control how I looked in imagery and in real life. That by standing in flattering lighting, I automatically looked 'prettier'. That the harsh afternoon sun would indeed make my cellulite dimples jump out a lot more, whereas shade would smooth them. While self-portraiture didn't slow my racing, constant thoughts about my body, it did make me become more of an observer of myself, and I felt more separate to my body (in a good way).

I learned that what I thought was an awful, scary, fixed body was actually one that was quite malleable and adjustable, given the right or wrong lighting and poses. And I learned that this was true of just about everybody – that we all look worse with a spotlight under our chins, and hard light casting shadows over our eyes. That everyone has flaws when you zoom up close in high definition, and that actually it doesn't matter at all.

The connection I felt from other people was what made things shift. These people leaving kind comments on my work didn't seem to care about my side profile or the size of my thighs, they seemed more interested in the content of my brain and my heart. It's absolutely cheesy and very cliche, but it's true – it's what's on the inside that counts.

I began thinking more. I had such little control over the body I was born into – the way the DNA combined from my parents and ancestors, all culminating in a very short stature, that shows a 5lb gain like most people show a 15lb gain. I realized it was actually quite silly to think that the way I looked externally meant anything about me at all – whether or not I was kind, able to forgive, able to overcome. The shape of my toes tells you nothing about me. It's just a body. I'd become so attached to the idea that it was the keeper of my worth, and it took losing my hair to realize that you just can't pin your self-worth on something that will eventually enter into entropy, wither away and die.

So, without further ado, here are the ways my body image issues were affected by self-portraiture and ways yours might be, too.

SELF-AWARENESS AND ACCEPTANCE

Through self-portraiture, we engage in a process of self-exploration. By studying our own features, body shapes and expressions, we gain a deeper understanding of our unique identity. This self-awareness for me eventually led to a softer self-acceptance, and a more positive body image, by focusing on my individuality, rather than conforming to societal beauty ideals.

CONTROL OVER SELF-REPRESENTATION

Self-portraiture provided me with agency over how I presented myself visually. I could choose poses, lighting and angles that made me feel comfortable and confident. This control allowed me to showcase what I felt were my better qualities, and quieted the voice in my head that told me I couldn't be myself. I got to create myself, in a world where everyone else tells you who to be.

'Not Going Anywhere' – 2020.

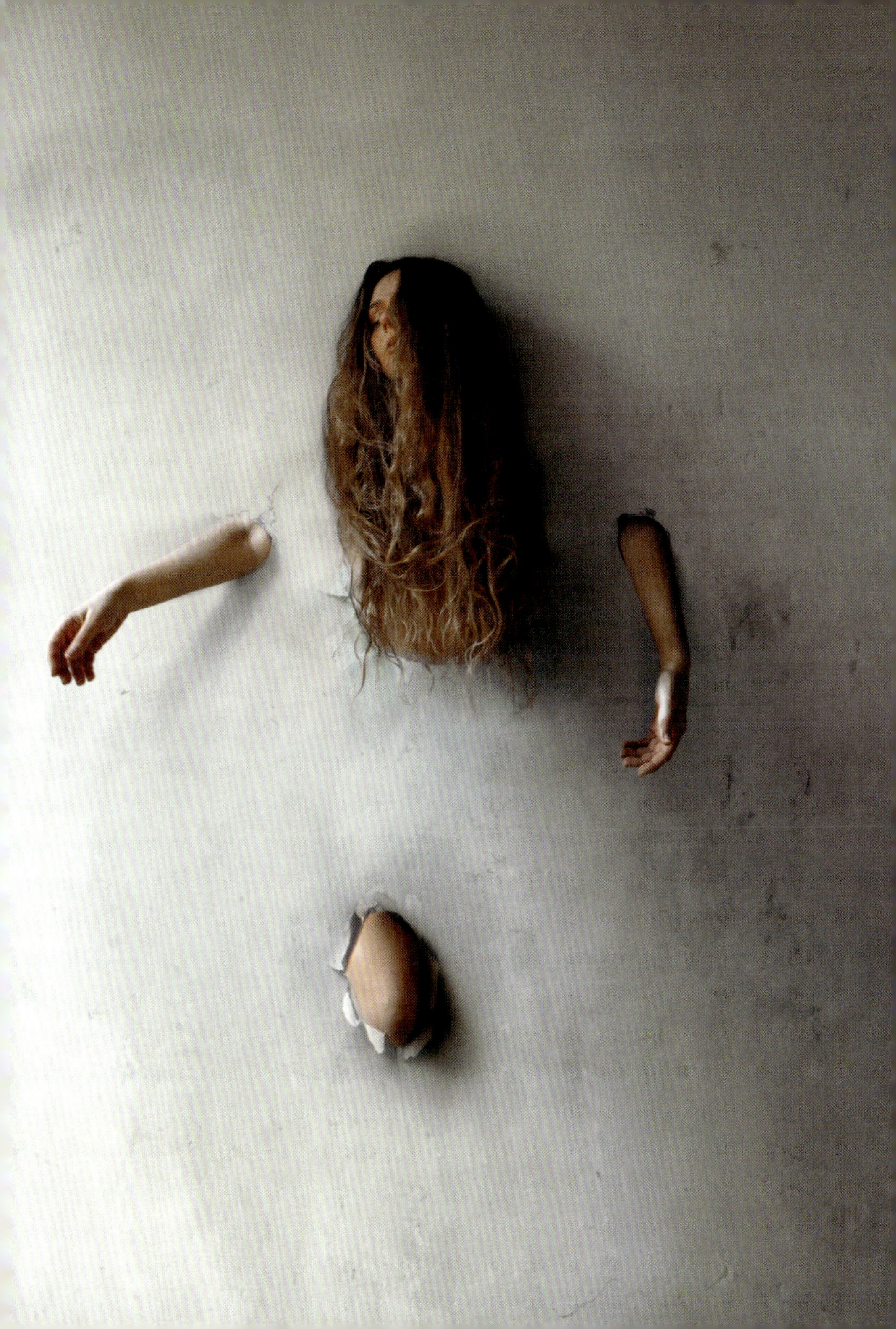

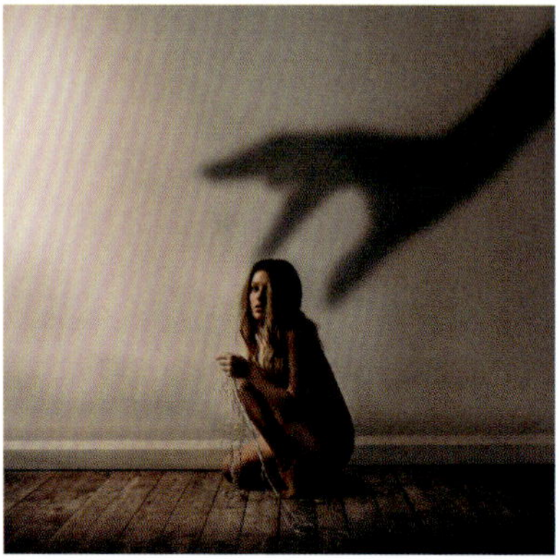

'Cutting the Strings' – 2017.

ARTISTIC EXPRESSION AND EMPOWERMENT

Engaging in self-portraiture that had deep, conceptual meaning as a form of artistic expression boosted my self-confidence. By creating authentic representations of my heart and mind, I felt like I could communicate who I really was inside – my thoughts, emotions and experiences. This act of self-expression built resilience, encouraged my own self-acceptance and empowered me. Even now, I walk into tough situations with a sense of confidence knowing honestly that I will be able to manage any difficult feelings, simply by evicting them from my body and turning them into art.

REDEFINING BEAUTY STANDARDS

Self-portraiture has always had the potential to challenge and redefine the traditional beauty standards of its time. By capturing diverse body types, ethnicities, genders and abilities, we show others that we are worthy of being seen. We can contribute to a more inclusive and representative visual culture, making our body types, nose shapes and belly button sizes included, rather than invisible. Seeing a broader range of self-portraits can positively influence not only the creator, but also those who view the work, which promotes body positivity and self-acceptance on a much broader scale.

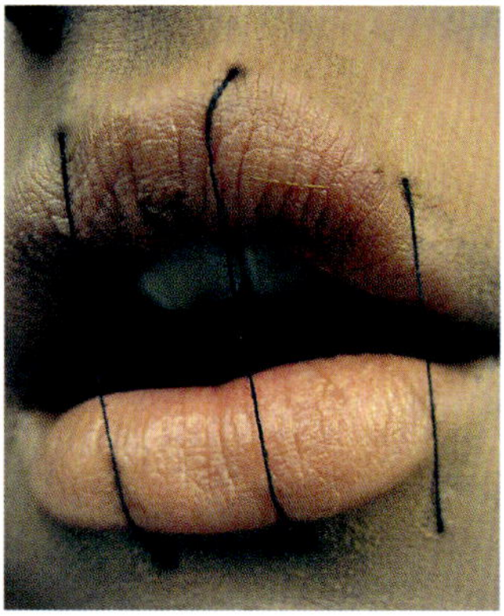

One of my first ever self-portraits. I was about 15 years old, and super-glued some thread over my mouth to symbolize my struggles with my eating disorder.

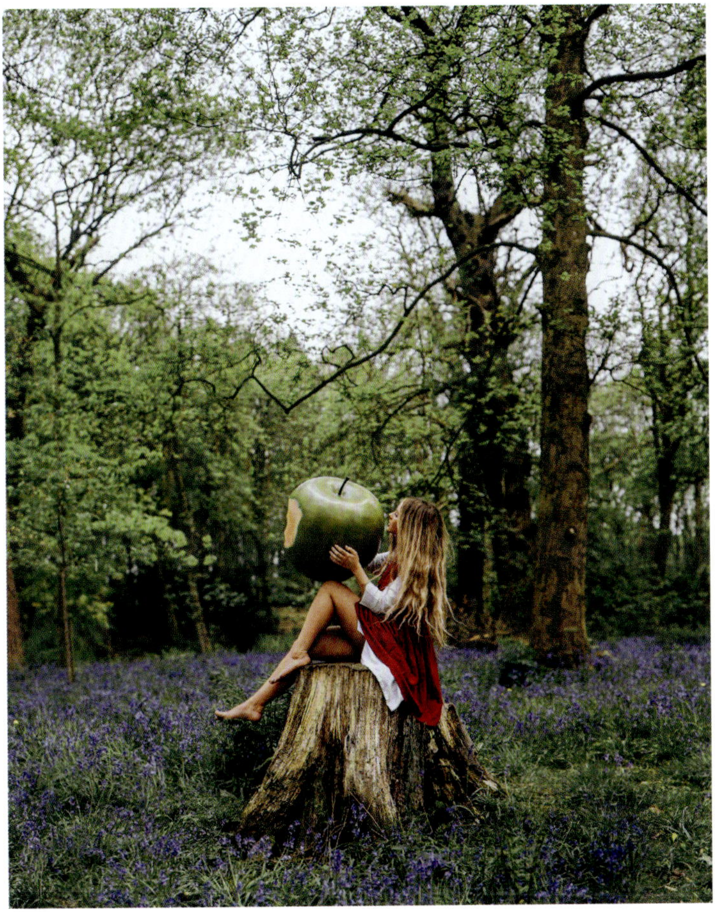

'Take a Bite...' – Self-portrait shot in 2019, giant apple prop located on eBay!

The relationship between our body image and self-portraiture is complex. While a proliferation of images can in some ways contribute to (or exacerbate) a negative body image, self-portraiture, when approached with gentle intention and self-reflection, can serve as a powerful tool to improve self-confidence, foster self-acceptance and challenge societal beauty standards. It allows us to redefine our own perception of beauty, and create empowering representations of ourselves, promoting a more positive body image and an overall much, much healthier sense of self.

06.

STORYTELLING

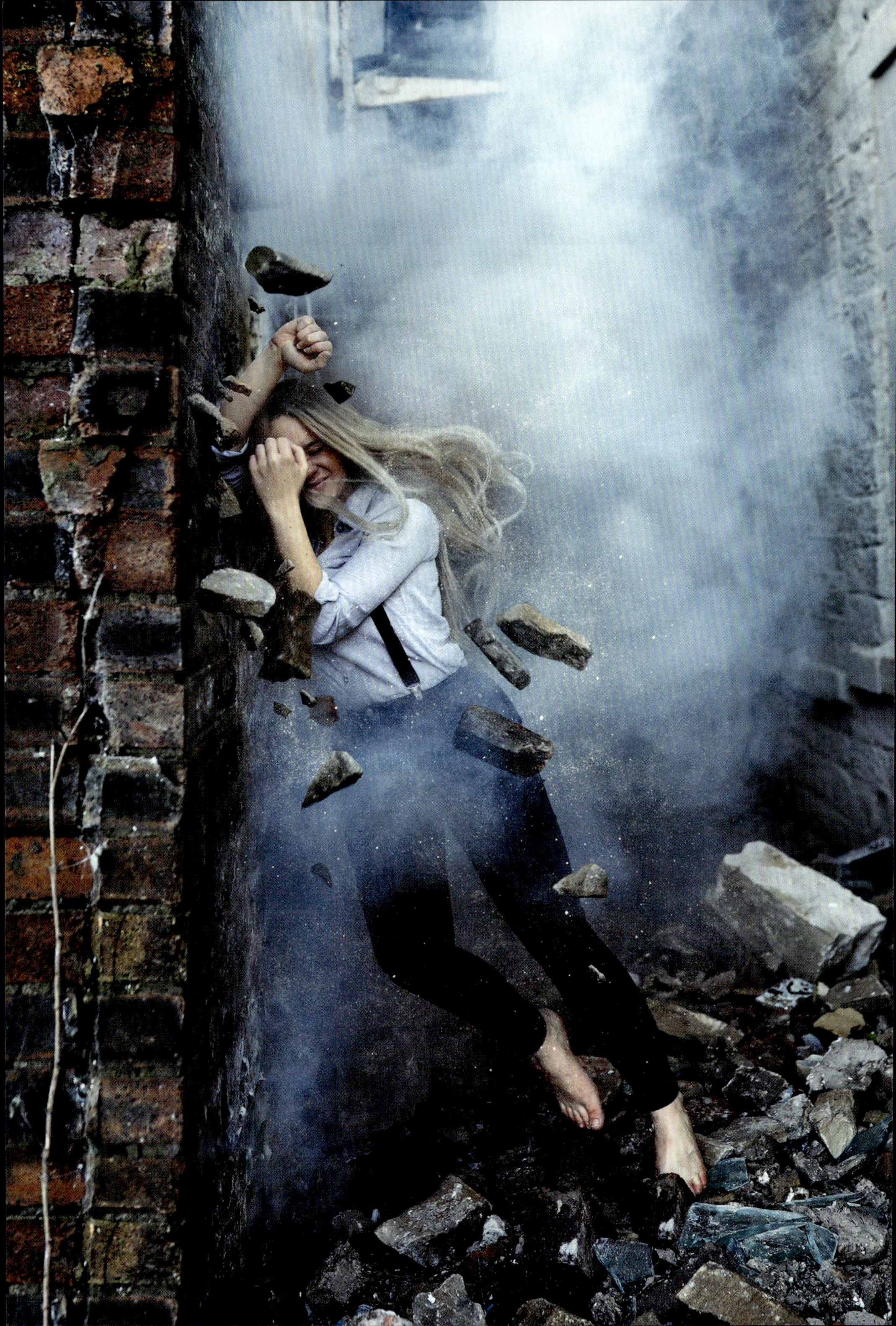

FINDING A DEEPER MEANING

When I look back over the years I've spent shooting, and the community that found my work and stuck with me, I think I can credit it all to some accidental storytelling.

Stories are the DNA of connection when it comes to being human. Before books, we told stories. We sang them into song, so the next generation would remember the words. We pass on our ideas, our morals, our traditions and our heavily learned lessons through them – and we listen to other people tell theirs.

Fundamentally, I believe that all connection is built on the stories of our shared experiences, and if we really want to connect through art, then storytelling is the way to do that. Pretty pictures are lovely, but curating imagery that isn't much more than models in expensive clothes (and good lighting) very rarely leads to anything greater than setting even more unrealistic standards of living and beauty. The work that stands out in my mind, that I've seen through my life, is work that holds a deeper meaning. Something that made me feel understood, interpreted, seen. Or at least, an image that made me feel *something.*

'Hitting the Wall' – A piece I created when I had zero artistic drive and motivation.

'Poetry is a life-cherishing force. For stories are not just words, after all, but fires for the cold, ropes let down to the lost, something as necessary as bread in the pockets of the hungry.'
– Mary Oliver, *A Poetry Handbook*

When it comes to storytelling in your own self-portraiture, there are three key components of storytelling to focus on: emotion, character and viewer engagement. Let's explore each of these in more detail:

EMOTION AND FEELING

Emotion is the star of the show when it comes to storytelling. It can be evoked by creating a specific mood, sentiment or atmosphere that resonates with the viewer (and, of course, yourself). To evoke emotion effectively, we need to utilize the various techniques that we covered in the earlier chapters of this book – things like composition, lighting, colour and, more importantly, the subject matter. More on this in the next topic.

For example, using warm colours, soft lighting and serene landscapes can evoke feelings of tranquillity or peace. Or, for a stark contrast, using harsh lighting and dark shadows may elicit a sense of tension or melancholy in your work. By harnessing these elements, we can learn to really infuse our images with an emotional resonance, enhancing the overall narrative.

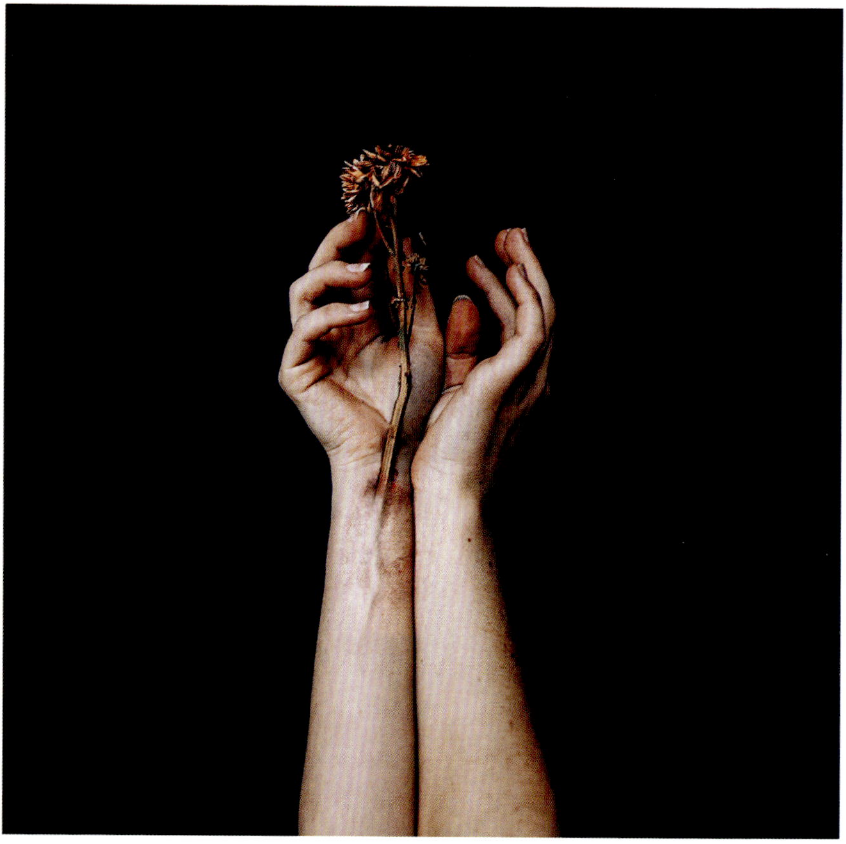

You don't even need to shoot your face to show emotion – fragility and vulnerability can be portrayed by veins, delicate hand position and freckles.

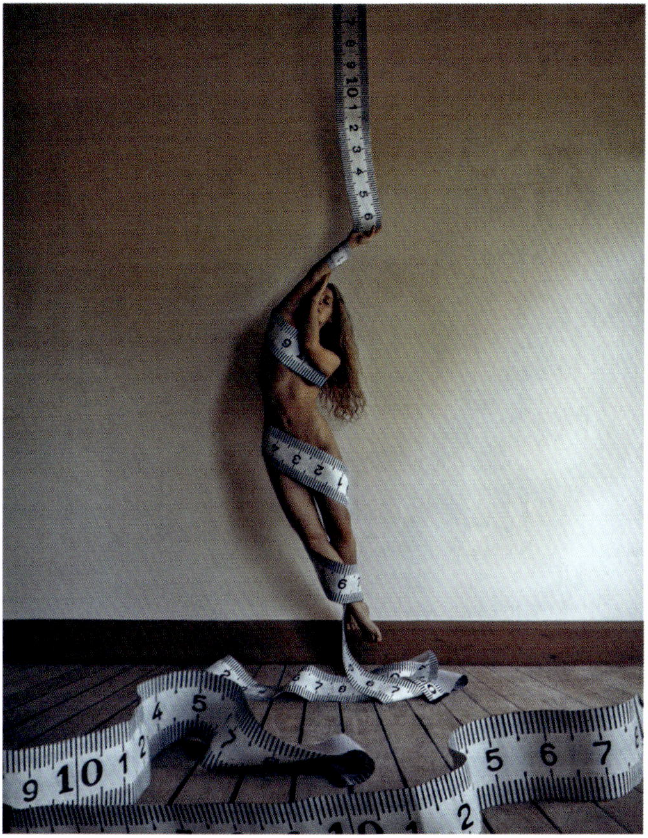

BUILDING A CHARACTER AND SUBJECT MATTER

Even though I'm shooting a self-portrait, I always try to see myself as a character within the image. It may look like me, but really I'm playing someone else – a princess on the steps of a castle, a wounded wild girl in the woods, a small child. Using characters in our photographs establishes a visual narrative. We can also use the props, costumes and locations to further detail more of the characters we play.

For example, in this photo, using a giant-sized tape measure, I created a feeling of being wound up and constrained. The tape measure implies weighing/measuring myself, and being naked establishes a feeling of vulnerability. By floating a little in the image, it also adds a narrative of overcoming, rising above something. A plain canvas location (the wall in my living room) tells the story of opening up inside my private space. The combination of these elements evokes

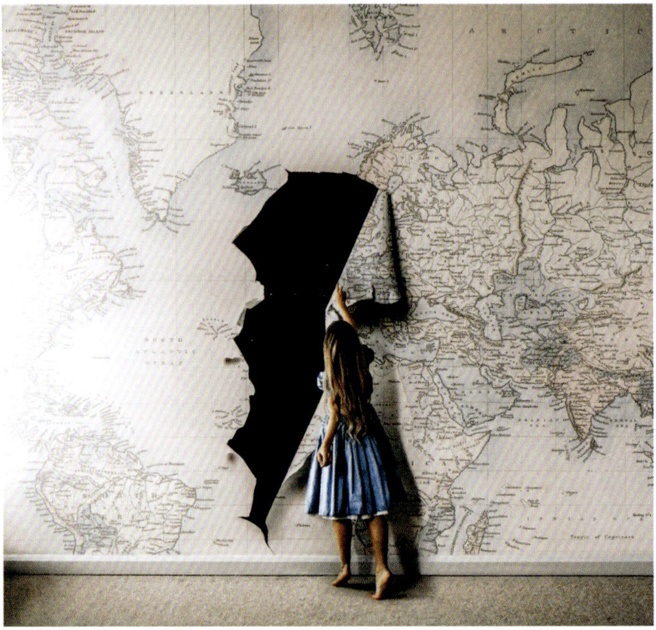

'Should I stay or should I go?' – 2016.

the story of someone who has struggled with body image, and is learning to overcome it. The composition catches the eye of the viewer, and I've made sure there is interest throughout the entire image – swirling the tape measure at the bottom of the image keeps the eye scanning around for more details.

A photographer has ultimate control over all the factors to construct these characters and stories. I try to teach people to see putting together an image much like baking a cake – and storytelling is a combination of all of the ingredients. What's also true is that any of the ingredients being measured incorrectly, or replaced with a poorer alternative, will have a negative effect on the image.

For example, the more realistic and detailed your props are, the more likely it is that your image will look surreal and interesting to viewers. Costumes, locations, lighting, mood and colours are all ingredients that heavily influence your final result. Each of these elements contributes to shaping the character's identity and role within the story. The choices made by the photographer in constructing a character help to convey specific messages, personalities or even cultural and political contexts.

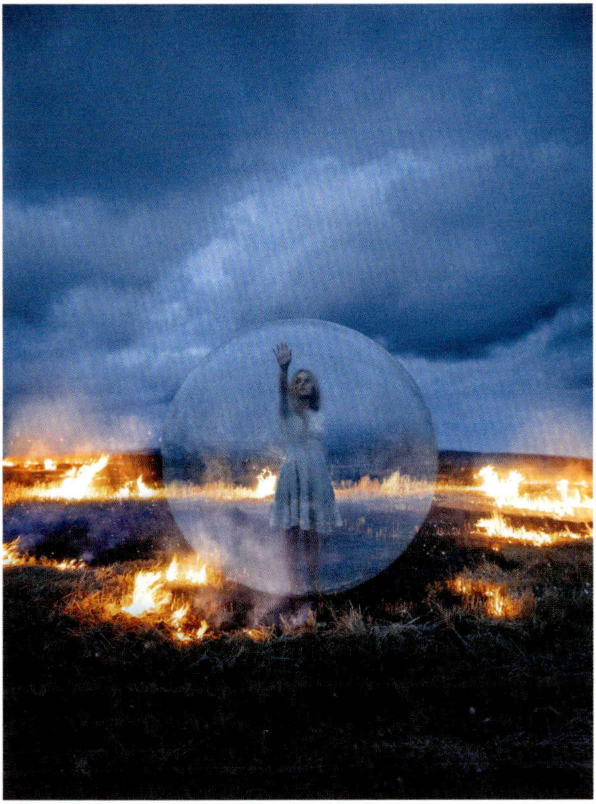

'White Privilege' – Shot during the Black Lives Matter protests in 2020.

Opposite is an image I took on the day Brexit came to be. The character I've created is one of innocence – a blue childhood-style dress, barefoot. A little reminiscent of Alice in Wonderland, and as such a reminder of youth for many. I chose to combine this wholesome character with the contrast of a huge tear down the map of the EU. This was to represent the division Brexit had caused, the split down the middle that was happening across the country. I also posed in a way that evokes a sense of curiosity – standing on my tip toes and peeling back the tear to look inside, as if to try to better understand the situation, or to search for hope. It's the combination of all of these things that come together to not only create a striking image, but to tell a real story and invite the viewer to take part.

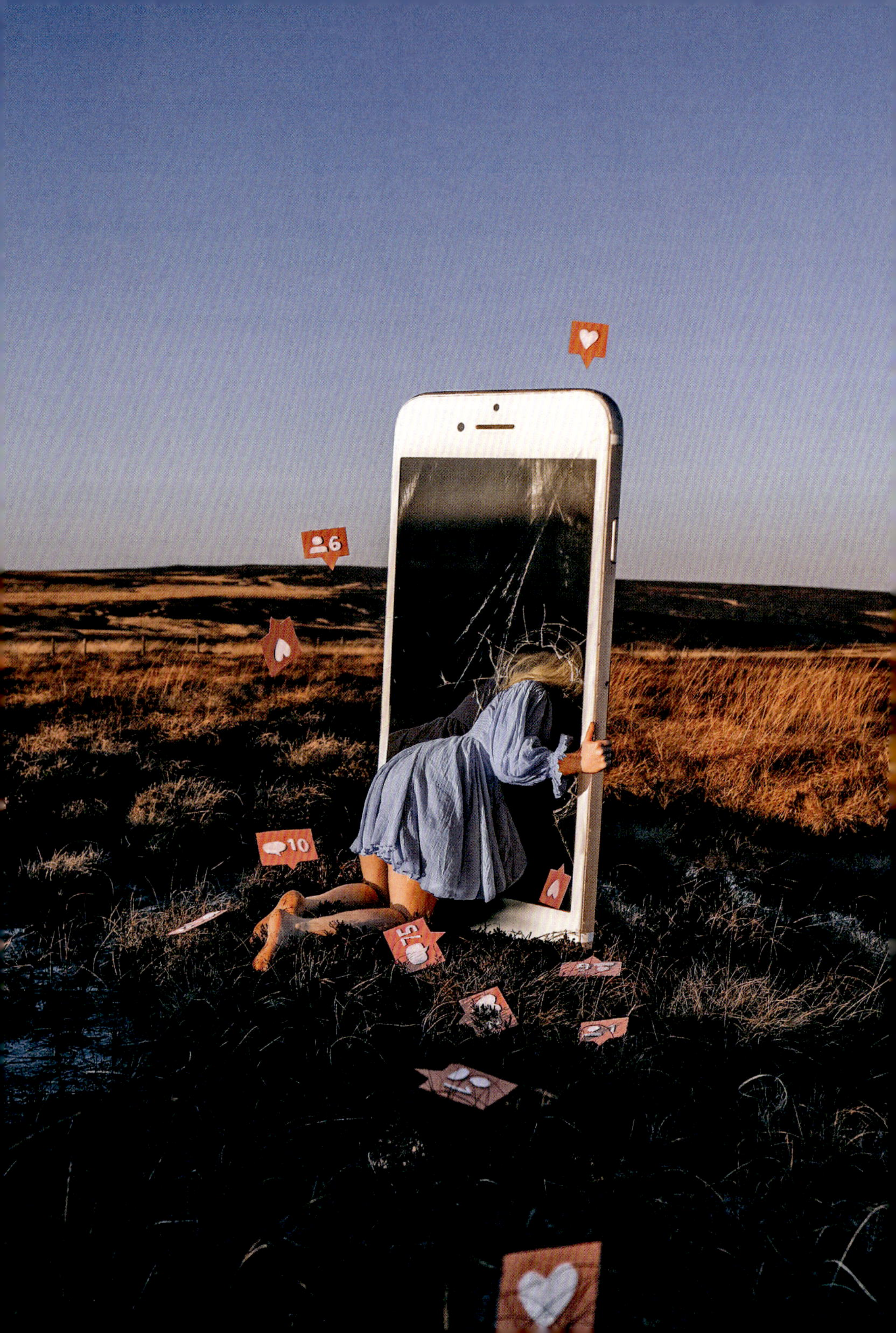

6
10
75

VIEWER ENGAGEMENT AND QUESTIONS

Photography, as a storytelling medium, is often used to prompt viewers to engage with the image, and when done well, hopefully sparks their curiosity or imagination. We photographers aim to evoke a response from the audience by raising questions or inviting interpretation. By leaving certain aspects open to interpretation, we can encourage our viewers to explore and connect with the story we are telling on a personal level. The questions you want the audience to ask might vary (depending on the intended message), but they often encourage deeper reflection, introspection or an emotional response.

On the facing page is an example of an image I created with the purpose of igniting discussion. I titled it 'The Search for Validation'.

With this image, I wanted to explore the way that our generation uses social media to validate ourselves and our worth, and to find meaning and connection through small, usually low-value interactions. I included my own personal feelings in the caption, discussing my internal conflict with conflating how good my images were with the amount of likes on Instagram they received. How it was putting me off creating work, in case they didn't perform well online.

'The Search for Validation' – 2020.

When I deconstruct this image, you can see how each of the ingredients comes together to tell the story.

LOCATION: Choosing an empty, undistracting landscape keeps the focus on the subject in the image.

PROP: I edited a picture of me climbing into an empty frame, and combined it with an image I took of an iPhone.

DETAIL: I added the detail of not only the crack within the glass of the phone, but another layer of prop detail in the 'likes' floating about the image. This added another recognizable feature – our eyes are trained to enjoy the heart symbol associated with Instagram, so I knew people would be instantly drawn to the image.

COSTUME: Knowing that my face wouldn't be on show, but my body would, I wanted something that was a balance between showing human limbs (another thing we humans like to look at) and not being too naked – I didn't want to sexualize the image and detract from the serious meaning.

COLOUR: Choosing bright colours like a blue dress complemented the bright pink 'likes', and shooting at sunset meant the moors were more colourful than they would have been on an overcast, misty day. I knew the phone would be mainly black, so I wanted colour surrounding it to balance the overall look of the image.

It can also be good to use ambiguity or mystery in an image. For as much as storytelling can be used in an obvious way, it's also equally possible to intrigue your viewers and inspire them to fill in the narrative, by shooting in a more subtle way. This allows the viewer to bring their own experiences and perspectives to the photograph.

Here's an example where I used less obvious storytelling in my work, while still maintaining interest for the viewer. The image opposite was shot while I was travelling in Australia. I had a bird's-eye view shot of me on a boat in my head, but I wasn't sure how I was going to achieve it.

I didn't have a drone, so had a friend dangle my heavily duct-taped camera/tripod combo over a bridge on the river we'd been rowing in. My other friend, Kiara, was trying to keep the boat still and sat near the back – I edited her (and the oars) out later! I then overlaid a different stock image of water underneath the boat, as well as some light reflections.

Let's break down the ingredients of the shot:

LOCATION: Choosing an unusual angle of something like water evokes a sense of tranquillity – the lake looks still and calm. I wanted to make people feel as though they were floating when they looked at the shot.

PROP: In this case it's the boat itself! Most people associate boats and sailing with a feeling or emotion in some sense.

DETAIL: Adding light reflections to the water gave the image more interest – a black, detail-less water would have lost the viewer's interest more quickly.

COSTUME: This is a more ambiguous costume – it's very neutral, if a little sad looking. The black dress and the Peter Pan collar combo is mostly reminiscent of Wednesday Addams, from the Addams Family. It often evokes the feeling of being an outcast, having dark thoughts and being a bit of a goth.

COLOUR: Again, I wanted to keep this shot neutral and not overpowering. I wanted a feeling of drifting, without direction. Using subtle, neutral colours combined with darker areas in the image adds to the ambiguity of the shot.

The viewer is then able to project their own meaning onto the story. It asks questions. Where is the girl floating to? Why is she alone? Is she scared or is she at peace with the risk of floating away alone on a boat? This ambiguity gives

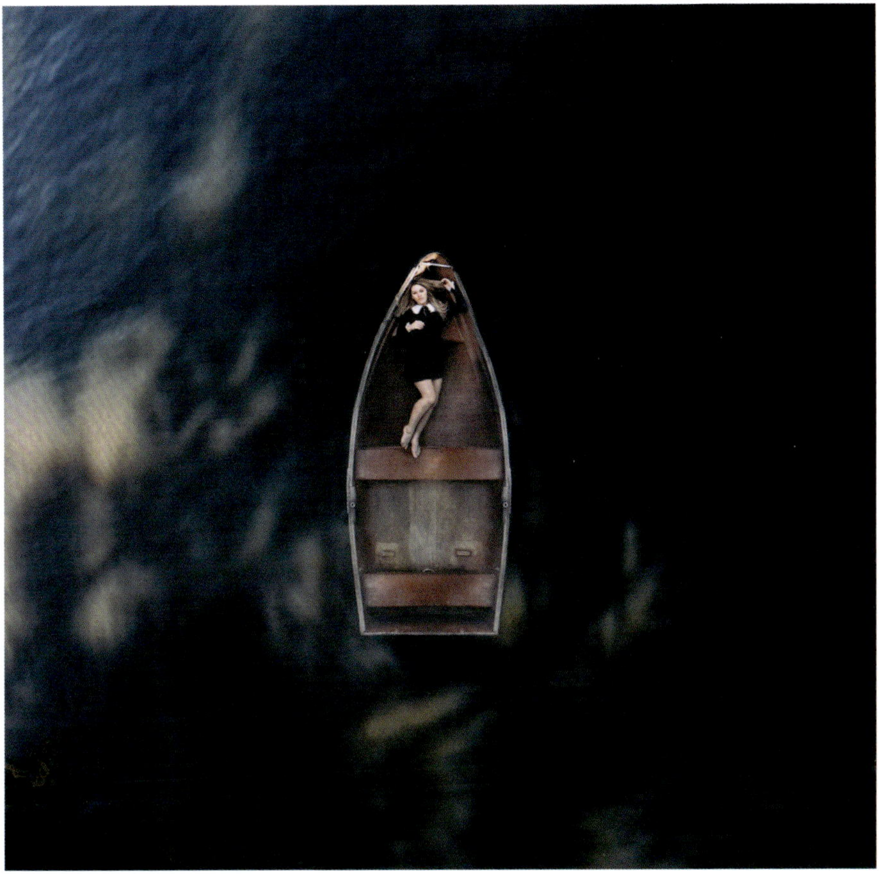

'Everywhere to go but Nowhere' – 2016.

room for the audience to connect with the image in their own way.

To summarize, the three components of storytelling in photography encompass the emotional impact of an image, the creation and portrayal of characters within the frame, and the viewer's engagement through questions and interpretation. By carefully considering and integrating these components, we can craft compelling visual narratives that resonate with our audience and convey a rich and meaningful story.

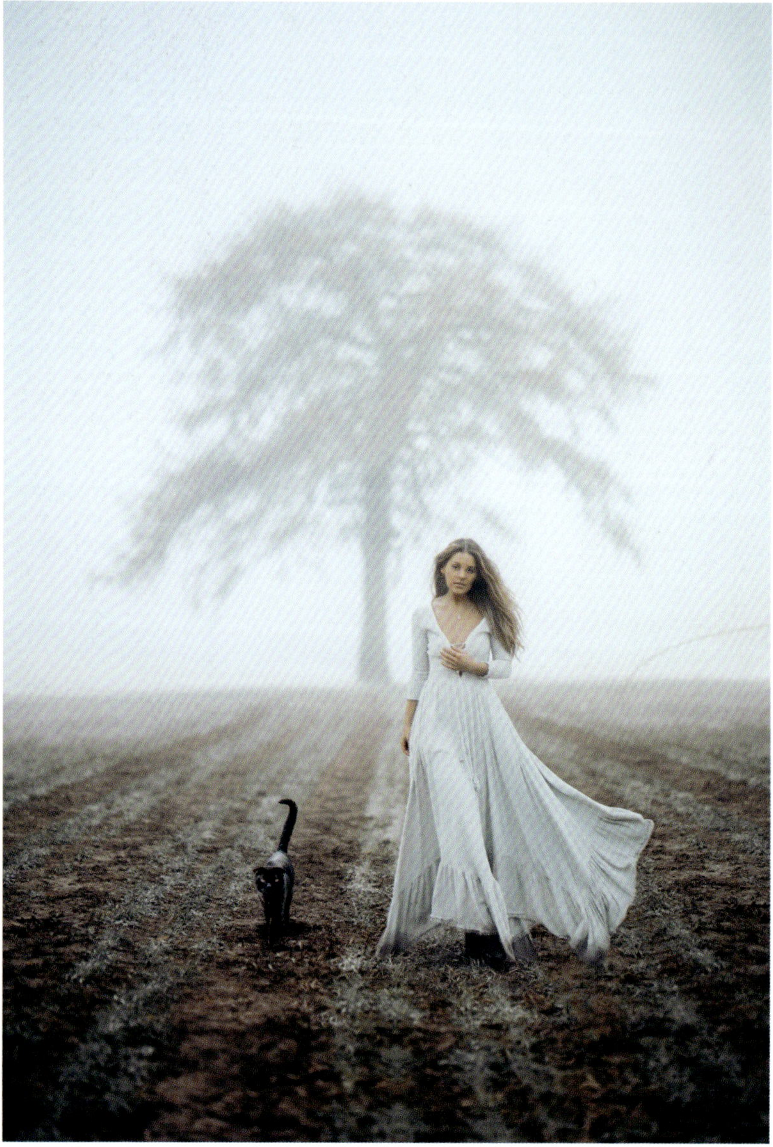

Newly single after a bad breakup, and entering my witch era!
Meet my new kitty, Juno.

HEALING VIA STORYTELLING

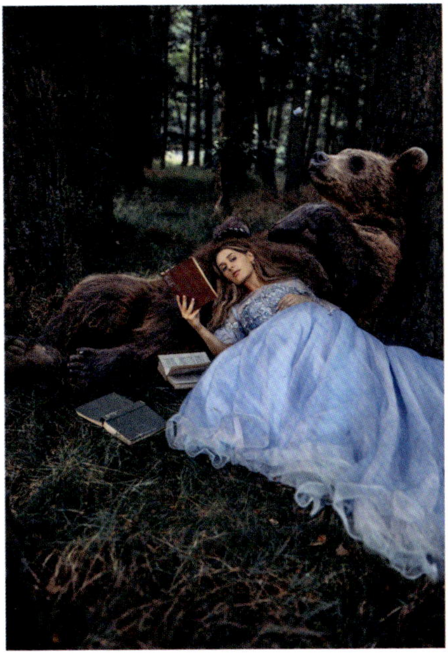

Using stock photography of animals helps me play with the theme of connection.

Another side effect of storytelling your own experiences in self-portraiture is the accidental healing that can take place when you express your truth.

'Perhaps some day I'll crawl back home, beaten, defeated. But not as long as I can make stories out of my heartbreak, beauty out of sorrow.'
– Sylvia Plath
The Unabridged Journals of Sylvia Plath

As I mentioned previously a few chapters ago, authentically I am an external processor and an external expressor. This means that I unburden myself of anxiety, stress and other negative emotions by talking with others about my inner feelings, creating from my pain, sharing and connecting. A byproduct of this is being a horrible over-sharer, and having very little time for small talk when meeting new people.

Other people might be internal processors – those who need to sit with their thoughts and unpick them alone before they express (internally or externally). Sometimes people feel better and safer this way – they know themselves well and don't require the bounce-back of others' input when Figuring Stuff Out. There's no right or wrong, just whatever is true to yourself.

When it comes to unravelling the storm of thoughts that occasionally gather in my mind, I then turn to photography and self-portraiture to release it. There's something about taking the feeling and turning it into a real-life visual thing that feels like a ceremony to me. Or perhaps an exorcism might be a better word for it!

Expressing yourself puts you at risk of vulnerability. It opens the door for people to laugh at you, shame you, exile you, send hate mail, and make a wound (that already hurts) bleed even more.

But the benefits of expressing

yourself honestly and openly are boundless, and well summarized by Brené Brown, a wonderful researcher and storyteller.

'Many think vulnerability is weakness, but it is not. Those who refuse to be vulnerable lose the ability to understand others who are, and their fear and discomfort quickly turn into judgement and criticism.
When we stop caring about what people think, we lose our capacity for connection. When we become defined by what people think, we lose our willingness to be vulnerable.
Owning our story can be hard but not nearly as difficult as spending our lives running from it. Embracing our vulnerabilities is risky but not nearly as dangerous as giving up on love and belonging and joy – the experiences that make us the most vulnerable. Only when we are brave enough to explore the darkness will we discover the infinite power of our light.'
– Brené Brown
Daring Greatly

When I look back to my dark early days overspilling with grief, I think of what got me through. I remember poring over quotes, books, YouTube talks and articles that wrote about grief. I fell into the arms of poems that depicted exactly how I felt, and let them hold me. I listened to sad song after sad song, and let the chords mop up what felt like endless tears.

While these were and are beautiful pieces of art, these were also resources that helped me understand my own grief, my own soul. They were a compass in a tornado and the only reason I had access to them in the first place was because people chose to be vulnerable with their own pain, and openly share their own private experiences.

It's the appreciation of this that continues to give me courage to share my own private thoughts and feelings in my art and with the world. It's adding my voice to the millions of others who allow nothing to be lost in their own hearts – joy and loss equally. And it's the human connection with others who feel and have felt the same things that gives my life purpose and meaning.

Sharing the pain and joy of life, and everything in between, isn't easy. But to me, it's the path to healing.

'I told you I wanted to live in a world in which the antidote to shame is not honour, but honesty.'
– Maggie Nelson
The Argonauts

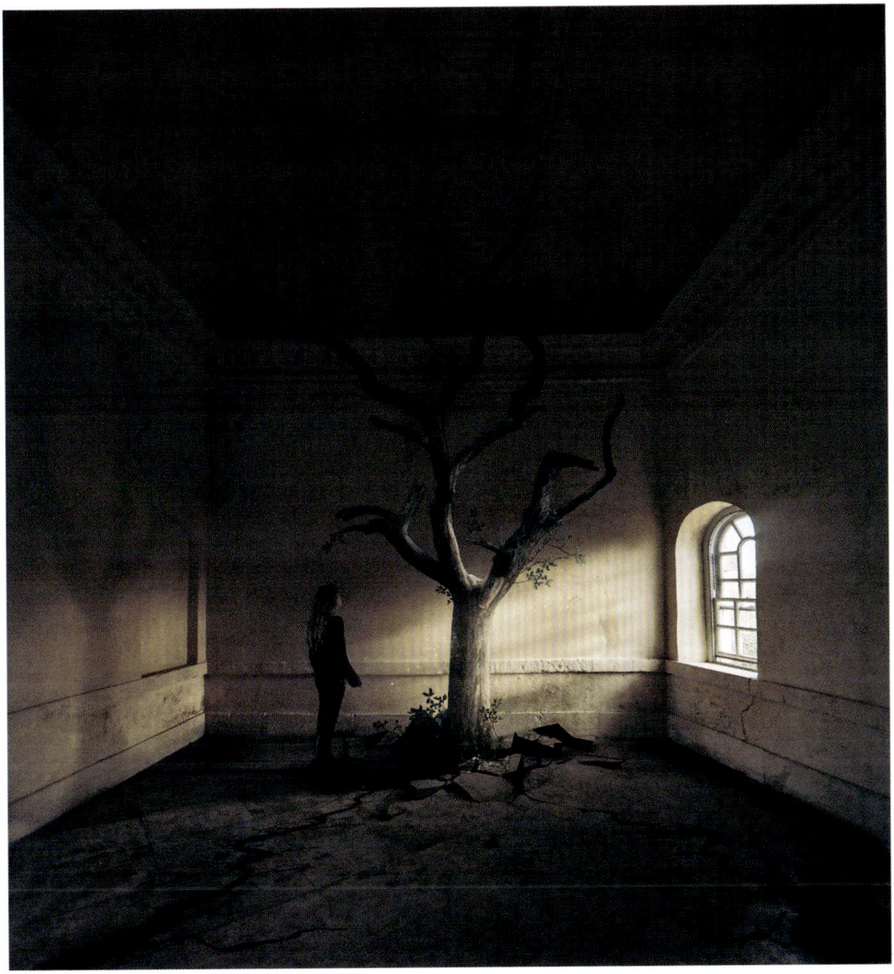

'Inner Growth' – 2022.

07.

EDITING

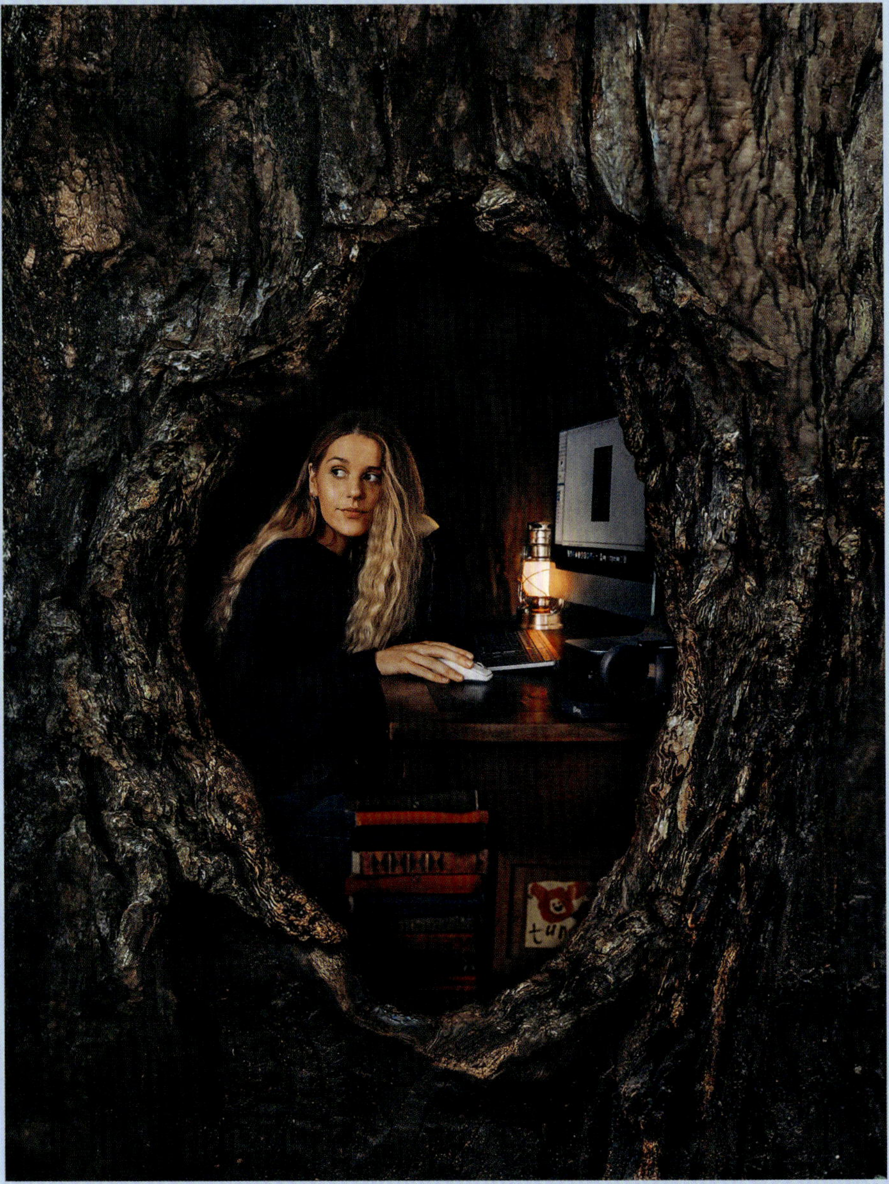

'Workspace' – A series commissioned by Logitech, 2021.

TRICKS OF THE TRADE
and a history of photo editing

As you may have realized while looking at the images I've included in this book, most of them wouldn't be possible without the use of editing software. Photo-manipulation is a huge part of my own work, but has played a role in the medium of photography pretty much since it began. In this chapter, we are going to explore the history of photo-editing, as well as some available softwares you may wish to try out and how to use them. I'm also going to show some of my befores and afters of my work, and explain how I use certain techniques in photo-manipulation to elevate the final image. I'll also show you some simple yet effective photo-editing methods, like the trick to levitating!

In the pre-digital era, photo manipulation was primarily achieved in the ever mysterious darkroom. Photographers used various techniques such as dodging and burning (lightening and darkening different areas of the image), multiple exposures, and retouching with specialized darkroom tools to alter and enhance their images.

For example, a popular trend in late 19th-century photography was 'spirit photography'. Photographers learned how to manipulate images to include photographs of dead relatives, and they were layered and masked into the final shot. Adding a 'ghost' effect to an image using darkroom techniques involves multiple steps and careful manipulation of the photographic materials. Here's a short explanation of the process:

CAPTURE THE BASE IMAGE: Start by taking a photograph of the scene or subject where you want to add the ghostly effect. Ensure proper exposure and composition as you would for any other photograph.

PREPARE MULTIPLE EXPOSURES: Set up your camera on a tripod to keep the frame consistent for all exposures. To create the ghost effect, you will need at least two exposures of the same scene. One exposure should have the ghost element, and the other should have the scene without the 'ghost'.

DARKEN THE DARKROOM: Set up the darkroom for developing and printing the photographs. Make sure it is completely dark – any light leaks could ruin the prints and lead to very disappointed customers!

DEVELOP THE FILM: Develop the film as per the manufacturer's instructions, ensuring proper development time and temperature.

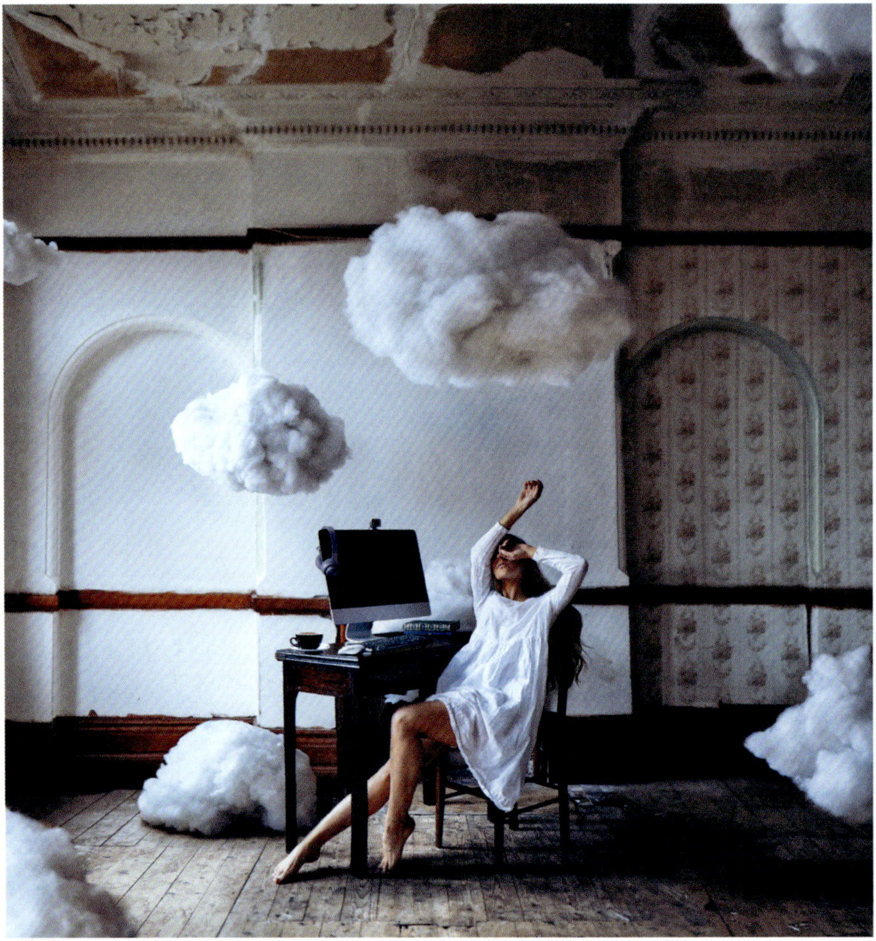

'Workspace' – A series commissioned by Logitech, 2021.

MAKE A CONTACT SHEET: Create a contact sheet by placing the developed film strip on a sheet of photographic paper and exposing it to light. This will give you a preview of the different exposures on the film.

SELECT THE GHOST EXPOSURE: Take the frame with the ghost element that you want to incorporate into the final image. Mark it on the contact sheet for reference.

MASKING: Now it's time for the fun part! To create a mask to control the exposure of the ghost element, use a darkroom-safe material, such as cardboard, and cut out a stencil or mask in the shape of the ghost figure. Make sure it fits precisely over the area where the ghost will appear.

PRINT THE BASE IMAGE: Place the selected negative (without the ghost) in the enlarger and project the image onto a sheet of photographic paper. Adjust the enlarger settings for proper exposure and focus. Place the mask you created over the area where the ghost will be.

PRINT THE GHOST IMAGE: Place the negative with the ghost element in the enlarger and project the image onto the same sheet of photographic paper. Make sure the mask is in place over the ghost area. This exposure will be much shorter than the base image exposure, to create the semi-transparent ghost effect.

INSPECT AND DEVELOP THE PRINT: Once the exposure is complete, carefully remove the mask and develop the print using standard darkroom techniques. Follow the recommended development time and fix the print to make it permanent. Voila!

Of course, photo-manipulation has come a long, long way since the 19th century. We're now looking at technologies that edit in a single click (Photoshop's Generative Fill AI tool is set to transform editing as we know it), and there are many, much easier ways of adjusting digital imagery to transform the final picture.

The advent of digital photography and powerful image-editing software has completely revolutionized the field of photo-manipulation. With the rise of our own personal computers, smartphones and the availability of software tools, photographers and the general public alike have gained unprecedented control over their images. Most people with a smartphone will have a host of photo-editing apps at their disposal, and you may already be familiar with your own favourites.

Here are some of the main software options favoured by me and other photographers – once you get to know your main tools, all of them are user-friendly, and a real rabbit hole of creativity to explore.

ADOBE PHOTOSHOP: Adobe Photoshop is arguably the most well-known and widely used image-editing software. It was first developed by Thomas Knoll and John Knoll in 1987 and has since become the industry standard for photo-manipulation. Photoshop offers a vast array of features, including layers, filters, retouching tools and advanced selection techniques. I began using Photoshop in October 2022, after years of using GIMP (see below). I like to think this proves that you don't necessarily need to pay for the best software or kit to create wonderful, realistic imagery – you just need to understand the techniques.

GIMP (GNU IMAGE MANIPULATION PROGRAM): GIMP is a completely free and open-source image-editing program that provides many of the features found in commercial software like Photoshop. It offers a comprehensive set of tools for photo-manipulation, including layers, masks, filters and customizable brushes. For 12 years, I used GIMP on every single one of my images, and was able to achieve every effect I wanted to. However, since upgrading to Photoshop, I can confirm that GIMP definitely took me longer! That said, it will always hold a place in my heart and I will always recommend it to anyone looking to use free, incredible software.

ADOBE LIGHTROOM: Adobe Lightroom is a popular software specifically designed for photographers. It provides powerful editing and organization tools, making it ideal for managing large collections of photographs. I edit all my wedding work in Lightroom and use it to adjust my colours, tones, shadows and highlights for my self-portraiture. Lightroom offers non-destructive editing, allowing photographers to experiment with adjustments without altering the original image.

CAPTURE ONE: Capture One is another professional-grade photo-editing software that caters to the needs of photographers. It offers excellent Raw file processing capabilities, advanced colour grading tools and precise control over image adjustments. Capture One is known for its exceptional image quality, as well as its tethered shooting capabilities – great if you're on set and want the images to pop up on a laptop as you shoot.

AFFINITY PHOTO: Affinity Photo is a relatively new player in the image-editing software market, but has gained a loyal following. It provides a wide range of features, including advanced retouching tools, layer-based editing and support for Photoshop file formats. Affinity Photo offers a more affordable alternative to Photoshop without compromising on functionality.

These are just a few examples of the numerous software options available for photo-manipulation. You can download them on your phones or to your computer/laptop, making photo-editing easy to access, wherever you are. Each program has its own strengths and weaknesses, and the choice depends on personal preference, budget and specific editing requirements. It's important to note that learning how to use these software tools effectively requires practice and experimentation, trial and error, success and failure. Photo-editing is a skill that develops over time, and is an artform in itself.

MY TOP TEN FAVOURITE PHOTOSHOP TOOLS AND TECHNIQUES

Across the board, these are my most commonly used tools when I edit. Here I'll explain what they look like and where to find them on Photoshop, and, of course, how to get the most out of them.

1. FREESTYLE LASSO TOOL

The Freestyle Lasso tool in Photoshop allows you to make freehand selections by drawing around the desired area. It enables you to manually select irregular shapes or objects in an image. This is my go-to tool for selecting parts of an image that I want to remove, use the Generative Fill tool with, or make adjustments to without affecting the entire image. You can also 'feather' your lasso selections if you want them to blend in with the image. I prefer to create a layer/use the eraser though, which I cover on the next page.

2. OBJECT SELECTION TOOL

An alternative to the Lasso tool is the Object Selection tool. This is designed to automatically select objects or subjects within an image, meaning you can easily select objects, people and items within your image without manually and painstakingly drawing around them. It uses Adobe Sensei's AI technology to detect and outline the objects, which makes it easier to separate them from the background. It also means you need to spend a little less time on blending when adding anything into your shot.

3. ERASER TOOL (FOR BLENDING)

The Eraser tool in Photoshop allows you to erase pixels from an image or layer. When used for blending purposes, it enables you to gradually erase or soften edges, creating smooth transitions between different elements, helping things that have been added in or moved look natural and seamless.

4. LAYERS

In Photoshop, layers are used to separate different elements of an image or design. By creating multiple layers, you can work on specific parts independently, making adjustments or edits without affecting the rest of the image. Copying and pasting elements onto new layers enables non-destructive editing and flexibility. Since I grew up using a version of GIMP that wasn't layer friendly, I prefer to flatten my layers once I'm happy with them. This means I treat my image more like a painting. Much as a painter adds paint over any flaws, I add layers on layers. Many photographers prefer an open approach to their layers, and like being able to move them around and adjust them as the image comes together.

5. GENERATIVE FILL (PHOTOSHOP BETA) AND CONTENT-AWARE FILL

Generative Fill is a new Photoshop feature that utilizes Adobe Sensei's machine-learning capabilities to automatically generate image content based on the surrounding pixels. It can be used to fill in areas with realistic and contextually appropriate content, and is completely mindblowing.

Content-Aware Fill is a powerful tool in Photoshop that intelligently fills in selected areas of an image with content that blends seamlessly with the surrounding pixels. It can be used to remove unwanted objects, fill in gaps or extend backgrounds by analyzing the image and generating plausible content.

6. DODGE AND BURN

The Dodge and Burn tools are used for selectively lightening (dodging) or darkening (burning) areas of an image. They simulate traditional darkroom techniques where photographers manipulate exposure during the printing process. Dodge helps brighten specific areas, while Burn adds shadows or increases contrast. This is a nifty little tool for helping do things like brighten eyes, add highlights or shadows to a shot, or help blend in stock imagery that wasn't shot in the same lighting by adjusting the highlights and shadows to match your own image.

7. CURVES

The Curves tool in Photoshop allows you to adjust the tonal range of an image by manipulating the brightness and contrast of specific tones. By plotting points on a graph representing the tonal range, you can fine-tune the highlights, midtones and shadows to achieve the desired look, as well as adjusting the tonal colour range using the red/green, yellow/blue and green/pink curves.

8. DISTORT AND LIQUIFY TOOLS

The Distort tool in Photoshop enables you to transform and reshape selected areas of an image. I use this a lot. It provides various options to stretch, warp or reshape parts of the image to correct perspective, change the shape of objects or create artistic effects. I use this to do things like stretch out the bottom of ball gowns to create more voluminous shapes to the dresses I use. I also use the Liquify tool to warp parts of the image. Most frequently, this tool is used in retouching; it's famous for making people slimmer – and leaving behind wobbly walls and door frames in its wake! But the Liquify tool can be used brilliantly, and I often use it to tighten up the edges of fuzzy layers, as well as warping different objects.

9. CLONE TOOL

The Clone tool in Photoshop enables you to duplicate or 'clone' pixels from one part of an image to another. It allows you to sample a specific area and then paint with that sample elsewhere, effectively covering up or removing unwanted elements. This tool is useful for removing blemishes, retouching imperfections and duplicating parts of an image. I also use it for taking out unwanted objects or expanding my image when using something that has little detail, like a plain wall.

10. FLOOD 2 PLUG-IN

The Flood 2 Plug-In is a third-party plug-in for Photoshop that adds realistic water effects to images. It allows you to simulate water reflections, ripples and other water-related distortions, providing a creative tool for enhancing or transforming images with water elements. It's a really fun tool that can help you experiment with a whole new aspect of shooting, without the risk of getting your camera wet.

BEFORE AND AFTER

Here are some examples of before/after in my work – see the real imagery behind the magic!

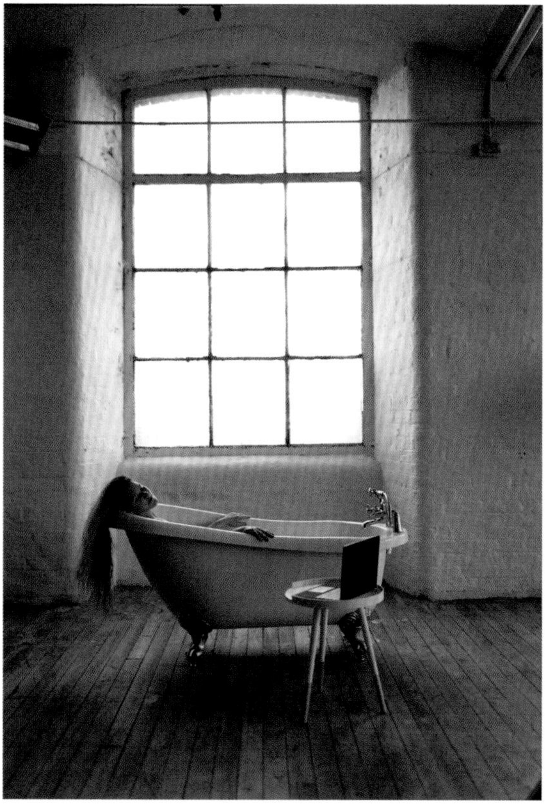

The techniques I used to create this image (and pretty much every image) are like a big bag of pick 'n' mix. I started by changing the canvas size of the image – this makes it sit better on my Instagram feed, where most people will view it. I didn't want the window to be cut off, so instead, I made it smaller. This was done using a simple copy, paste and fluffy Eraser brush to blend. It also helped me get rid of some of the clutter at the top of the picture, keeping the focus on my mermaid-self.

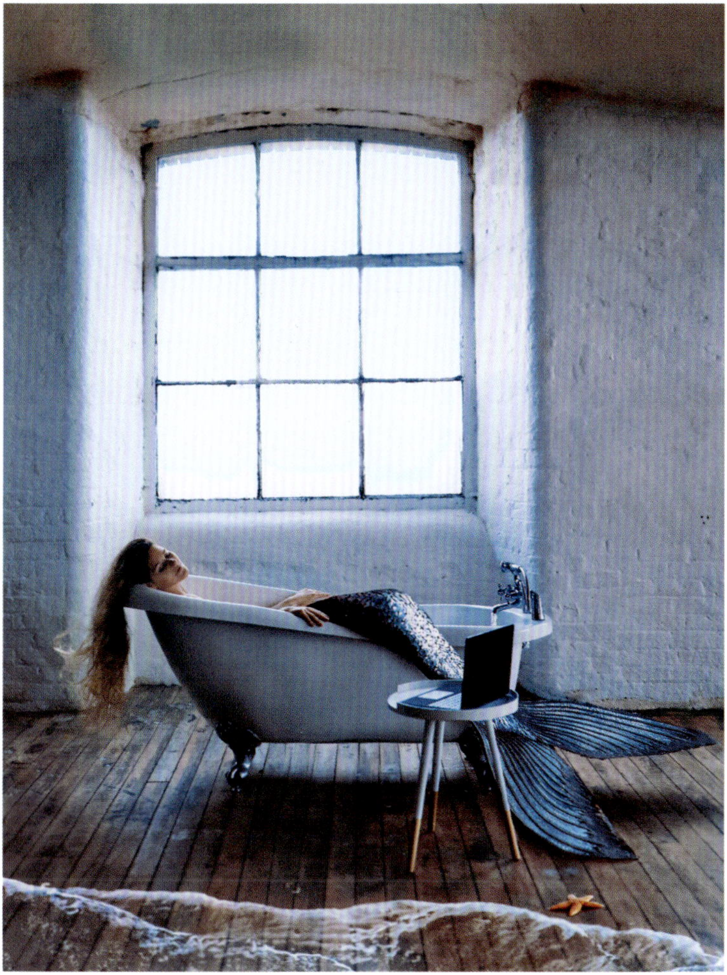

Adding the mermaid tail was by far the hardest part of this edit. Unfortunately, I didn't have a realistic mermaid tail to hand (but you can find some wonderful ones online if you have the budget), so I used a stock image instead. I use Shutterstock as my main stock website, but there are great paid alternatives like Adobe Stock and iStock or free websites like Unsplash. When searching through all the pictures of tails, I wanted one that had a bend in the knee to suit my pose in the bath. It took an hour or so to find the right tail, but the difference it makes to the final image was definitely worth the time.

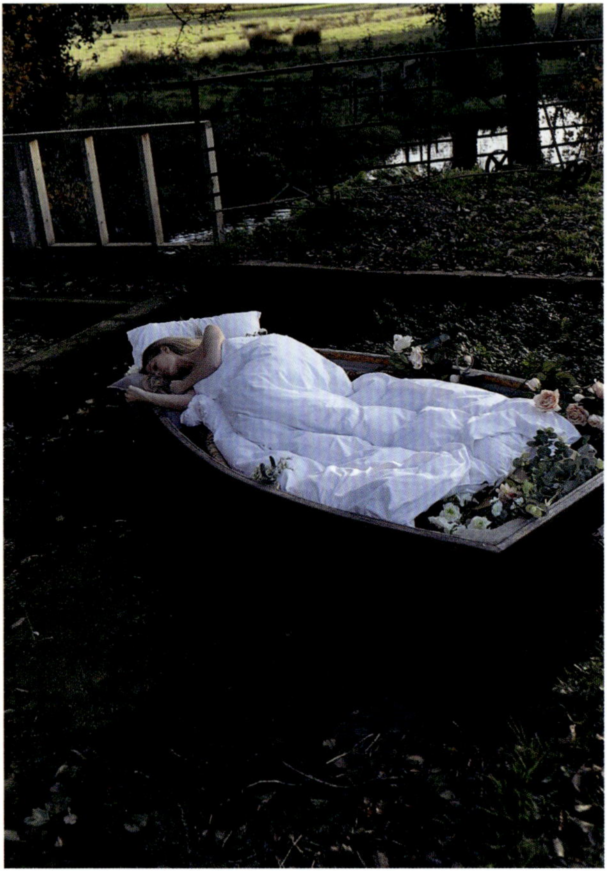

Shooting this image was great fun – who doesn't want to be cosy and warm in a big old duvet on a boat? But editing it was far more challenging. It's really useful to shoot pictures of other things you might want to edit into the shot later – in this case, that was the river. I shot loads of pictures at plenty of angles to make sure I had variety to choose from. It's always hard to judge an edit before you're in the room doing it, so having choice is crucial. I found that when I put the boat onto a 'clean' river, it looked a lot more unrealistic, and my eyes were drawn to the reflections of the boat in the water – far harder to edit. Editing in the pictures I took with algae in the water helped take the focus off that, and personally, I feel leads to a more whimsical and interesting final result.

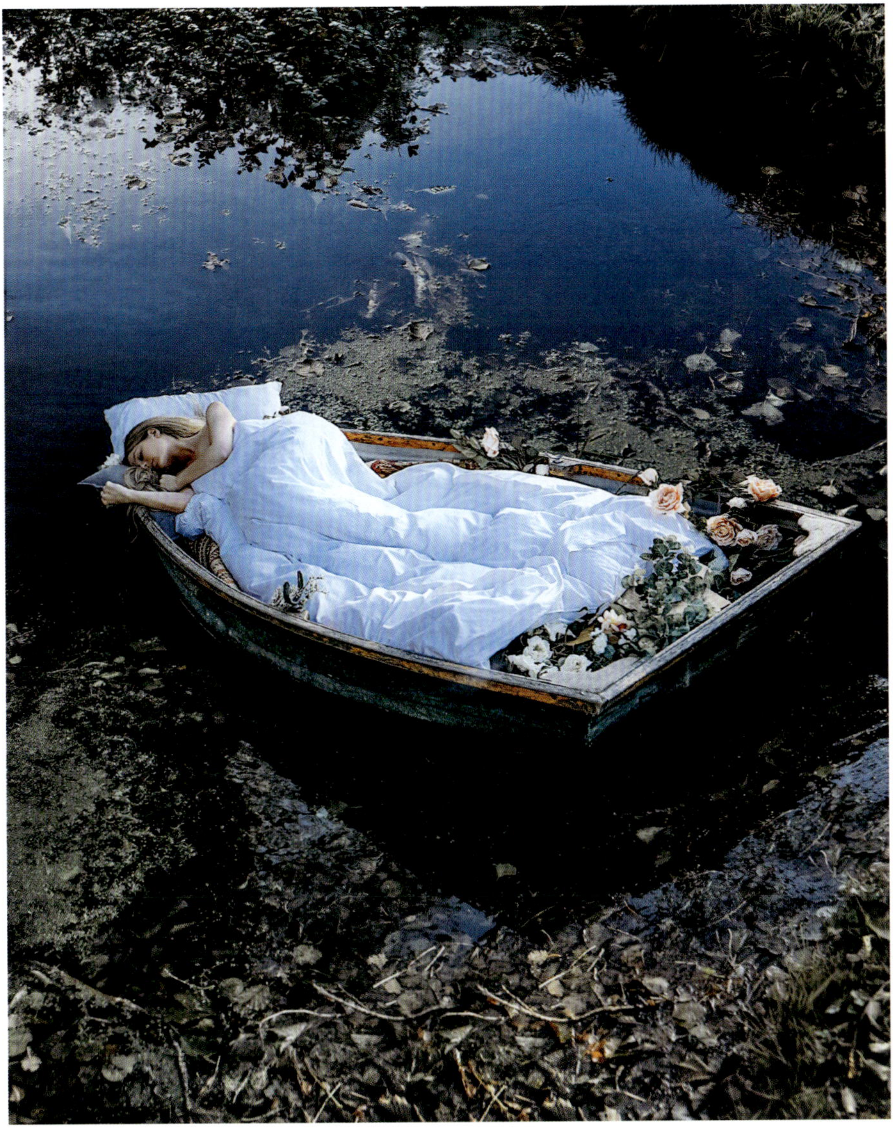

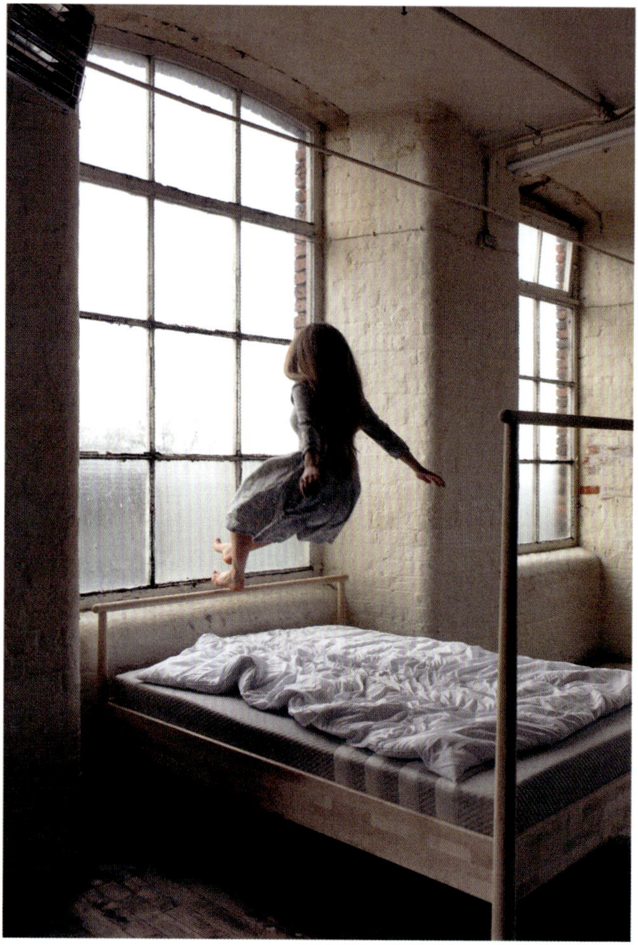

When you're doing big edits to your images, a great process to practise is that of visualizing the edit before you do the shoot. I knew I wanted to be crashing through a broken window, and therefore knew that I would need something to create the illusion of broken glass falling. I bought (and smashed) some plexi glass prior to this shoot, and was really happy with the result. Trying to find matching stock would have been really hard, given the unique lighting, reflections and colours behind the clear glass, so real-life props were my answer here. I threw them into the air separately, and selected/copied/pasted them in to my shot afterwards.

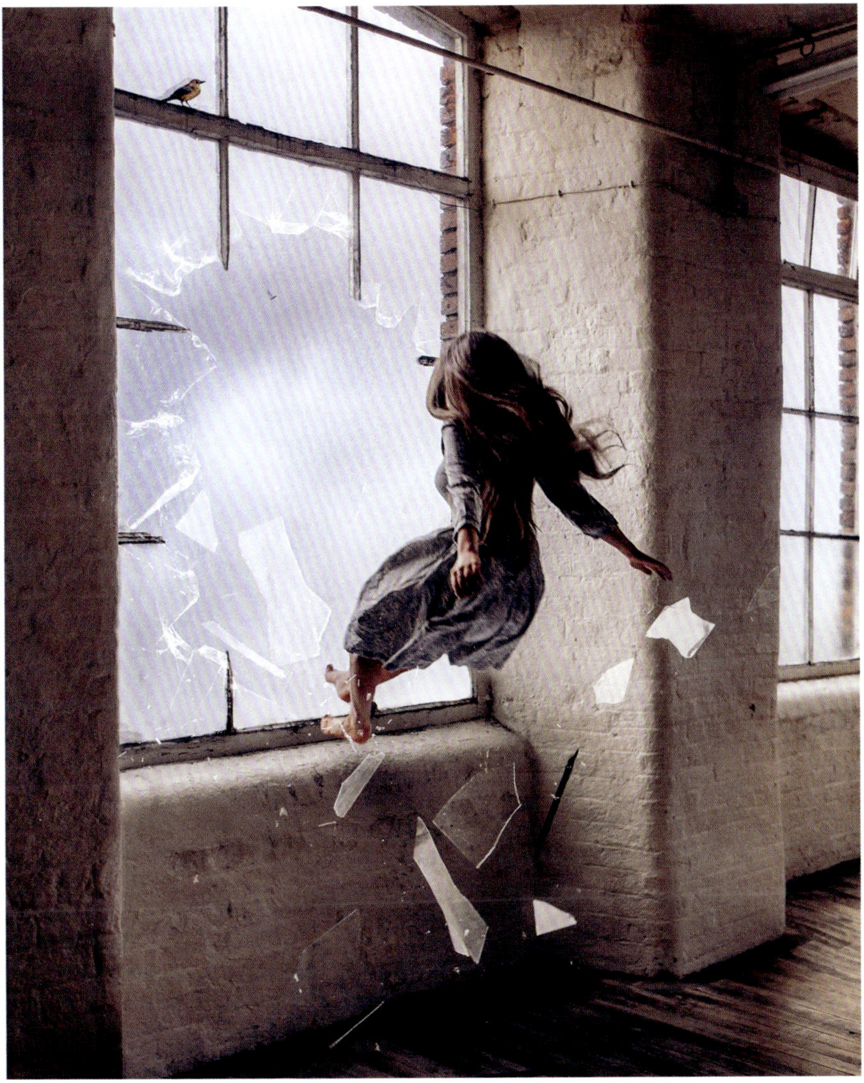

Nowadays, people are also leaning towards AI to create their stock. In this instance, using the Generative Fill tool in Photoshop, you could easily create a smashed/broken glass in the frame using prompts like 'broken window panes hole'. There are pros and cons to relying on AI for editing, which I'll talk about in more detail over the page.

USING AI

By far the biggest 'pro' of AI is lack of effort, and speedy time. You can save money on buying props or purchasing stock imagery, and all you need is to try a few prompts until the software begins to generate the idea you had in your head. However, like anything, there are some disadvantages to keep in mind.

The first I've discovered is quality – the close-up result can be very blurry and low resolution if you're generating in bigger pixel area sizes. Sticking to smaller areas (1,024 pixels or less) is the answer, but not always viable, depending on what sort of image you're looking to create.

The second issue is the potential for over-reliance on AI to the detriment of your own personal creative input. While AI undoubtedly offers a shortcut to many aspects of the creative process, there is an undeniable risk of succumbing to a formulaic approach that can compromise your own vision. How do we, as artists, retain a style while introducing AI to our work? It's a great question and each artist has to answer it individually.

Since we're on the topic of AI, another noteworthy challenge is the ethical considerations surrounding using AI-generated content. If you've been on social media in the last year, you'll likely have come across a fiery debate surrounding whether or not AI should be used at all. As technology becomes more adept at crafting realistic images, questions arise regarding intellectual property, authenticity and the potential for misuse. AI-generated photos can inadvertently perpetuate biases present in the training data used, and the ethical responsibility falls on both the creators and users to navigate these complexities. Striking a balance between innovation and ethical considerations is so important to ensuring that AI serves as a tool for positive advancement rather than a potential source of controversy.

My personal take on AI is that it is undeniably helpful – it streamlines my editing and gives me back hours of time that I could have easily spent in front of my laptop, and lets me make healthier life choices with that free time. I'm not ashamed to admit that Generative Fill creates (occasionally!) more realistic results than I could have done by myself, creating shadows, detail and, most importantly, flowing hair where I would have sometimes abandoned the image in frustration. Equally, I completely understand the wary and sceptical viewpoints. How much will it erase my competency and talent, let alone my unique style? I can't deny that in using AI, I can't take as much credit for my work as I could previously.

That said, I'm also acutely aware that times change, trains are always leaving the station and it is better to

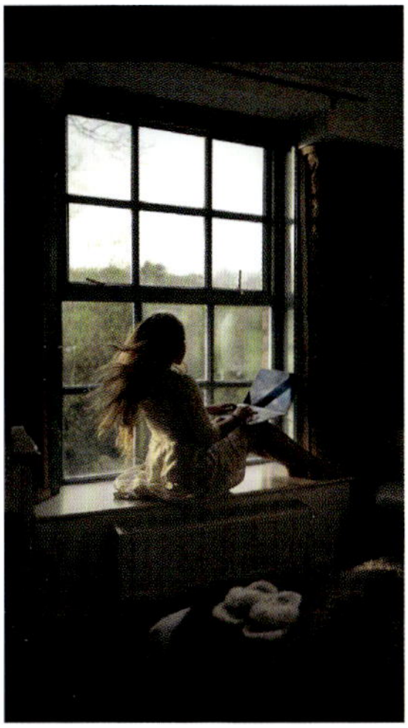 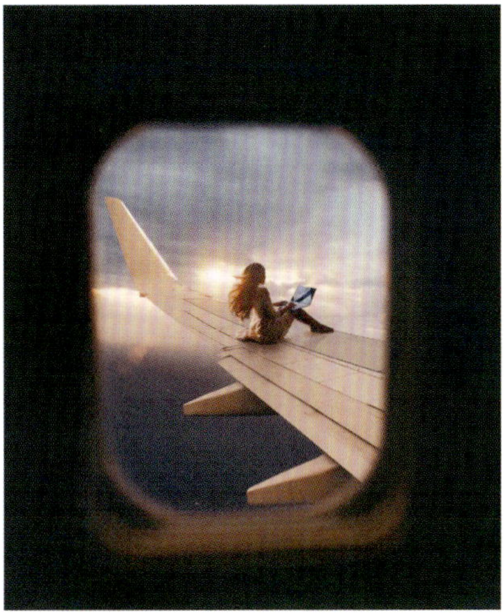

A before/after from my pre-AI era. I shot the plane window separately, and Photoshopped myself in using a similar light set-up. Spot my editing mistake...

be on that train than off it, even if just with familiarity, understanding and a balanced view of the positives and negatives. I remember vividly when I first started uploading my Photoshopped work to Flickr as a teenager, and reading many comments on how using Photoshop was cheating and impure, 'an excuse for untalented photographers'. Even correcting exposure and white balance (let alone changing the tones and colours) was a sign of my failure at mastering my camera. Nowadays, people would baulk at the thought!

Editing and photo-manipulation is considered a skill and a hard one to master at that. Courses in Photoshop are popular – editing tutorials are a huge hit on YouTube. It's an amazing program that can bring ideas (especially on lower budgets) to life – and Photoshop's existence has contributed to the way my brain and imagination interpret life in front of my eyes. I can't help but wonder if AI is just how Photoshop was perceived in the early days, and to wonder if there will be future courses on prompts and how to master it ethically and skillfully, and whether it will eventually slot into our day-to-day work/edit life as easily as Photoshop has.

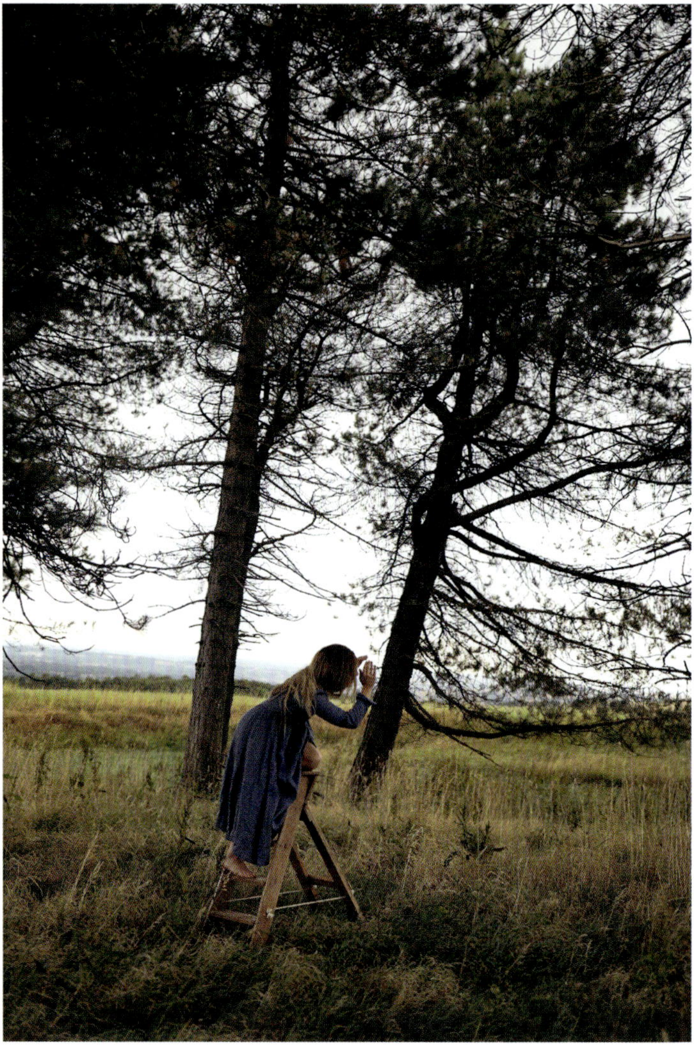

I wanted to create something that encompassed passion and creativity not being tied to expensive, shiny kit. I truly believe that you only really learn when you get out into the world and try, and fail. Break your cameras! But also be smart enough to have insurance. Chaos and order can co-exist, as can magic and reality. And sometimes, they go very well together.

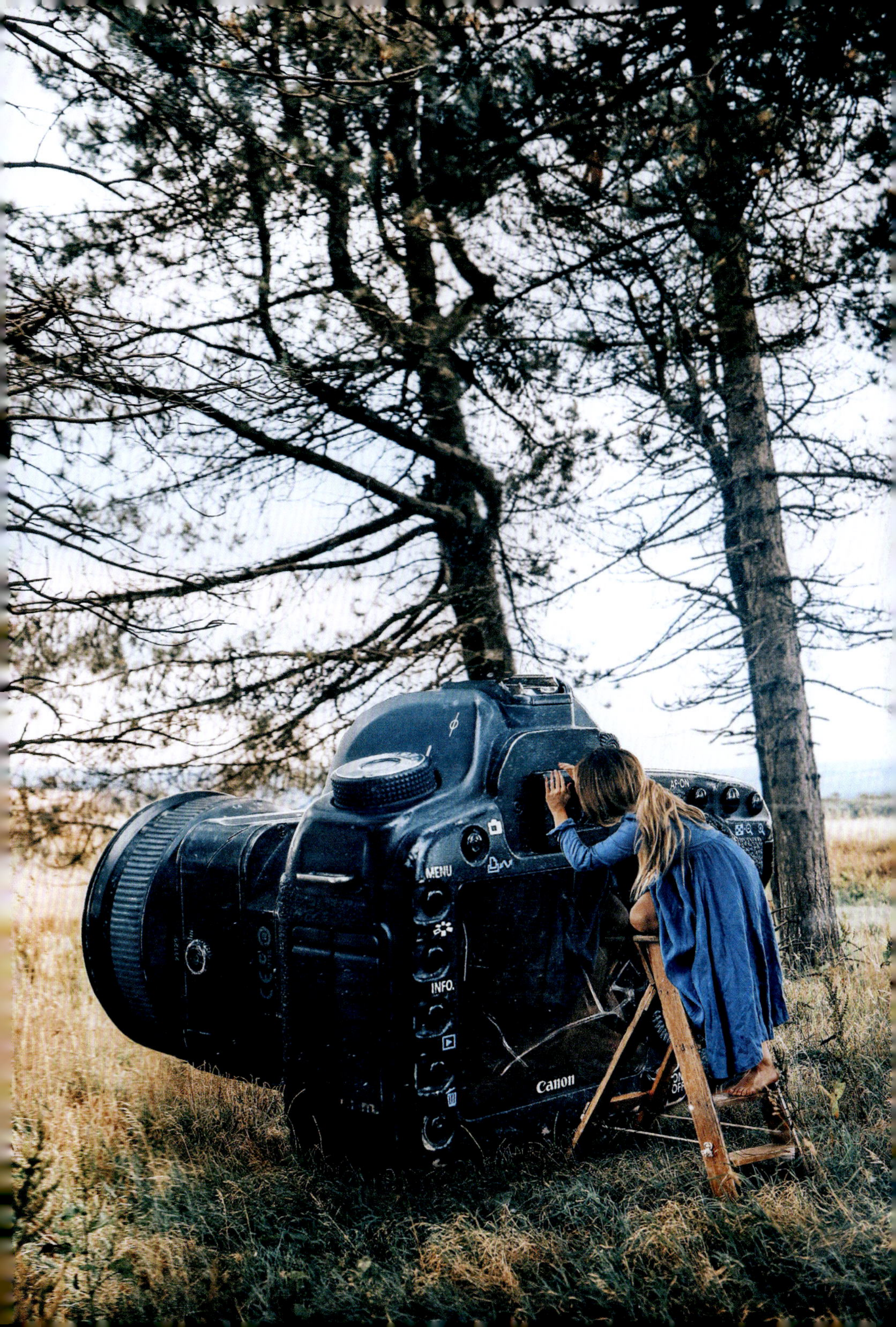
AF-ON
MENU
INFO.
Canon

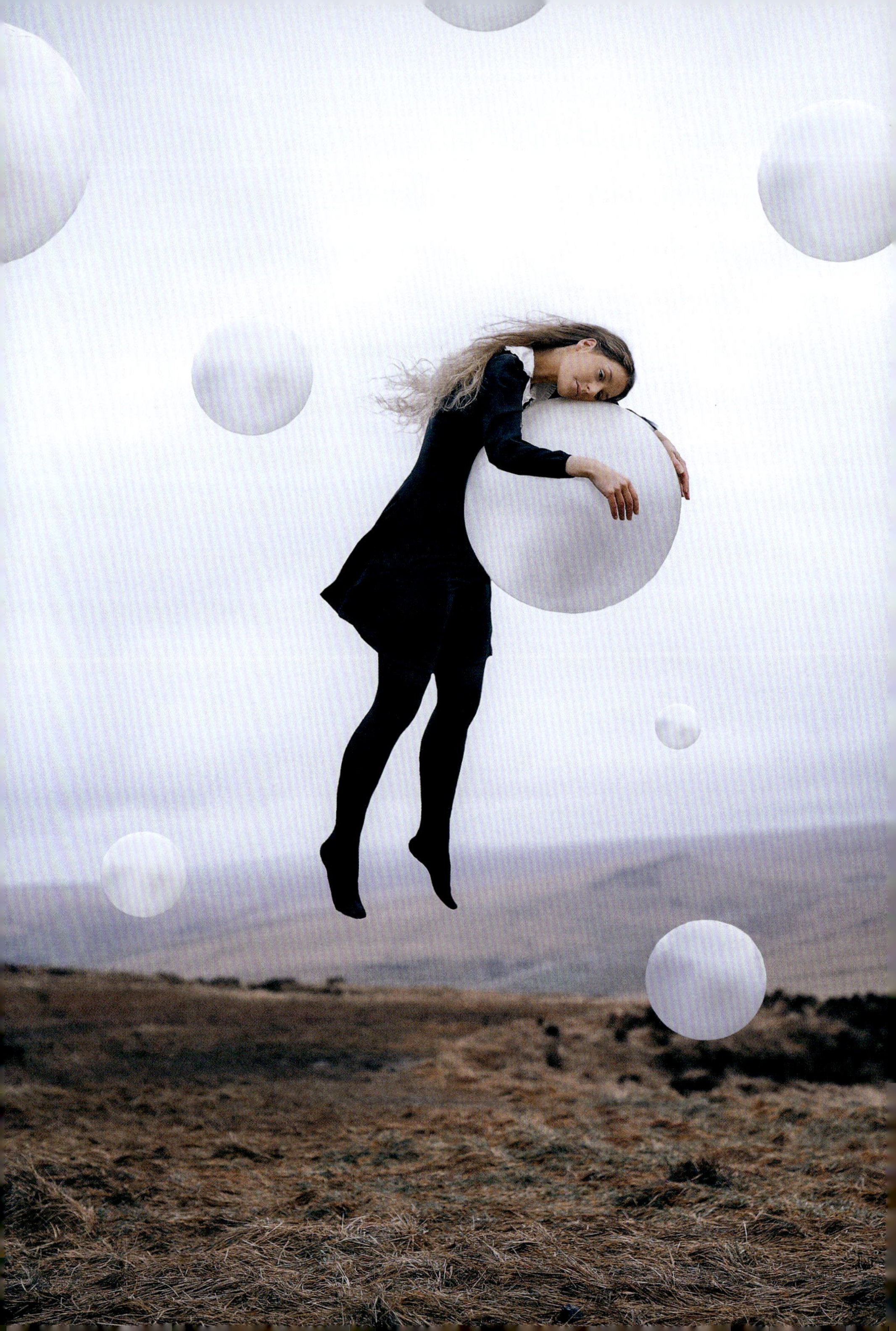

EASY, FUN IMAGE-EDITING TECHNIQUES TO TRY

LEVITATION PHOTOGRAPHY

Levitation photography creates the illusion of a person or object floating in mid-air. Here's a short but sweet overview of the process:

1. SET UP YOUR SCENE

Plan the composition and background for your levitation shot by choosing a suitable location.

2. TAKE MULTIPLE SHOTS

Use a tripod to ensure consistent framing. Take one shot with yourself in position and another with just the background. Ensure the camera settings remain the same for both shots.

3. POSITION THE SUBJECT (YOU!)

Strike a pose or position yourself as if you are floating. You can support yourself with a stool or chair underneath. Try not to let any of the chairs block the front of your body.

4. EDIT THE IMAGES

Open the two images in an editing software like Photoshop. Use layers to place the image with the subject on top of the background image. Erase any supporting props or platforms using tools like the Eraser Tool. Fine-tune the image by adjusting lighting, colour and contrast to blend yourself seamlessly into the background.

'Support Bubble' – 2021.

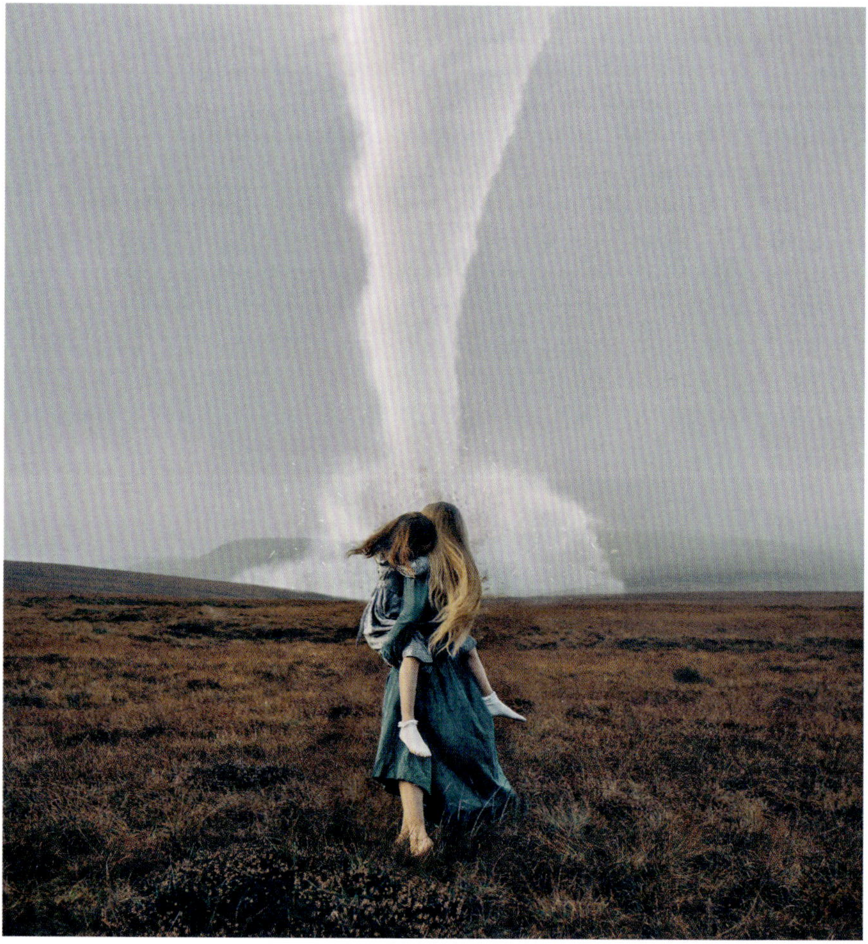

'Mother' – 2018.

ADDING EXTREME WEATHER TO YOUR IMAGE

Adding snow, rain or even a tornado can be a super-fun way to enhance the mood and atmosphere of an image. Here's the general process to achieve this effect:

1. SELECT A SUITABLE BASE IMAGE

Choose a photo that will benefit from the addition of snow or rain. Images with darker backgrounds work better for this effect, like the one in my example opposite.

2. FIND OR CREATE SNOW/RAIN OVERLAYS

Look for pre-made snow or rain overlays online, or create your own using Photoshop brushes or stock images. Ensure they have a black background.

3. ADD THE OVERLAY

Open your image and the snow/rain overlay in Photoshop. Place the overlay on top of the image using layers. Adjust the size, position and opacity of the overlay to make it appear natural. I like to do this by using the Screen blending mode in Layers. Experiment with various blending modes to achieve the desired effect.

4. REFINE THE EFFECT

Use tools like the Eraser or Layer Mask to remove or blend the effect in specific areas, such as avoiding covering the subject's face or other important details. Adjust the overall image settings like the colour temperature, contrast and saturation to harmonize the added snow or rain with the original image.

ADDING A STOCK PHOTO OF AN ANIMAL INTO YOUR IMAGE

To add a stock photo of an animal into your image, follow these six steps:

1. CHOOSE A SUITABLE STOCK PHOTO

Find a stock photo of an animal that matches the style and lighting conditions of your image. When I shoot my base image, I prefer to use backlight or shoot in shade, so I'm always looking for stock imagery that matches this. Make sure you pay attention to the perspective of both images as well as the lighting direction to ensure consistency in both, so that the stock image blends realistically and appears believable to the viewer.

2. OPEN BOTH IMAGES

Open your original image and the stock photo in an editing program such as Photoshop.

3. EXTRACT THE ANIMAL

Use selection tools like the Object Selection tool to select the animal in the stock photo. Copy and paste the selection onto a new layer in your original image.

4. RESIZE AND POSITION

Scale the animal layer to an appropriate size and position it in your image. Use transformation tools like Free Transform to adjust the orientation perspective if needed.

5. BLEND AND REFINE

Use layer masks, erasers or blending modes to blend the animal layer with the original image. Pay attention to lighting, shadows and colour adjustments to make sure the animal is naturally integrated into the scene.

6. FINAL ADJUSTMENTS

Make any necessary adjustments to the overall image, such as using an image of fur on a black background (see page 175 and the technique with snow and rain) to ensure visual coherence between the animal and the rest of the photo. Export and share!

Photo-manipulation has been such an important part of my work, and is a huge part of the reason I enjoy photography and creating so much. Mastering editing allows you to lift the limits on your creations, and set out to produce work that really hits the spot and tells a story. It really is a skillset and art form all of its own, and I implore anyone who is looking to try self-portraiture to add it to their personal Skill Utility Belt.

'Just Right...' – Part of a campaign for Unique Homestays, 2021.

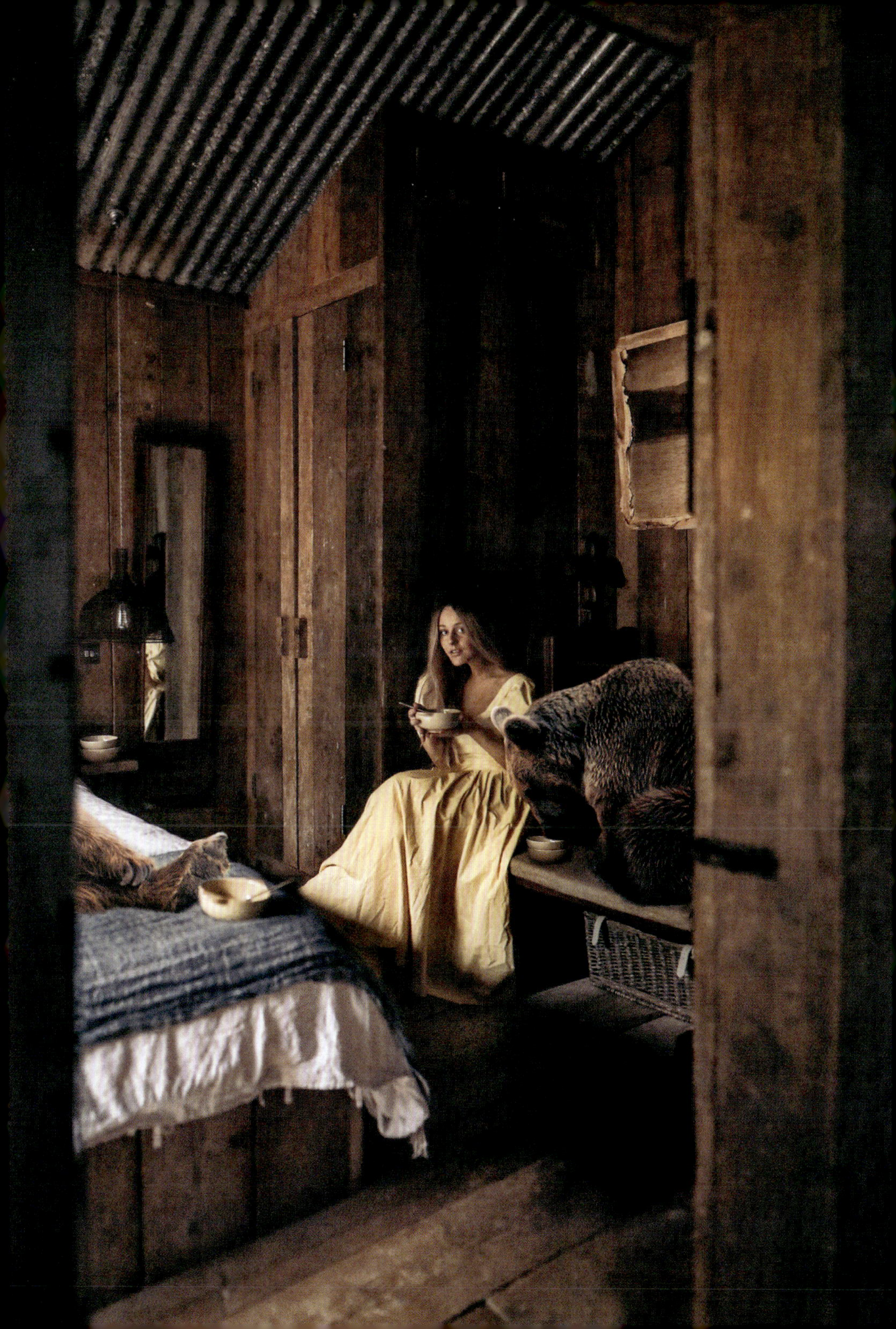

08.

GETTING SEEN

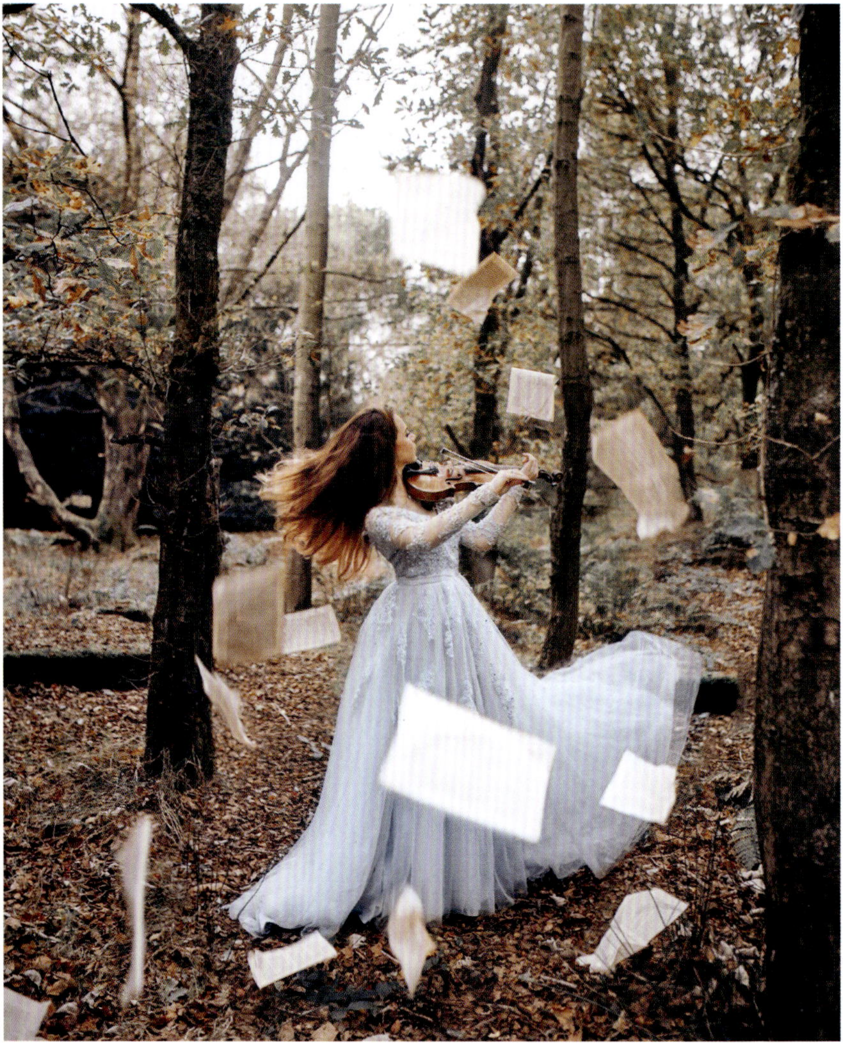

'My soul is a hidden orchestra; I know not what instruments, what fiddlestrings and harps, drums and tamboura I sound and clash inside myself. All I hear is the symphony.'

– Fernando Pessoa, *The Book of Disquiet*

SOCIAL MEDIA

The internet and social media have played a significant role in transforming the landscape of photography and self-portraiture, and were really the birthplace of my career as a photographer. There are now so many platforms that provide photographers and artists with a forum to showcase their work, connect with a global audience, gain exposure and engage with other creative individuals. Without social media, I'm not sure I'd have had the same life path, or even a remotely similar one! There are, of course, huge advantages to using social media as a photographer. Equally, there are as many pitfalls and drawbacks, and I want to talk about them in this chapter, as well as sharing my own personal tips and experiences with using the internet as your personal art gallery.

STARTING OUT – CHOOSING YOUR PLATFORMS

When I first started sharing my work online, I used websites such as Myspace, DeviantArt and Flickr. Now, we find ourselves dominated by platform options, all which have different things to offer. I'm going to talk about the four current main apps for artists: Instagram, Facebook, TikTok and YouTube.

1. INSTAGRAM

I see Instagram as a portfolio – a curation of your best work (or, in some cases, your best life). Instagram has evolved over the last few years to become more focused on reels, which are short, entertaining videos to quickly hold a viewer's attention and, hopefully, engagement. That being said, still images still have a place on Instagram. If you're looking to maximize your engagement, gain followers and create a buzz about your work, prepare yourself – it's likely you are about to take on a new full-time job! The Instagram Algorithm responds best to users who *use* Instagram. To really take off on there, Instagram would love that you post daily, or three or more main posts a week. It also would like you to comment on others' posts, engage and like on your main feed, as well as through the explore section. You'll need to use a combination of reels (which means learning to become a videographer and content creator, filming all the behind the scenes of your work) and still posts. Posting daily stories about your day-to-day life and who you are as a person helps others to connect with you, and will increase interest in your life and what you have to say. And remember to keep an eye on trends – if not be brave enough to start some of your own! Now that we are surounded by incredible, high-quality

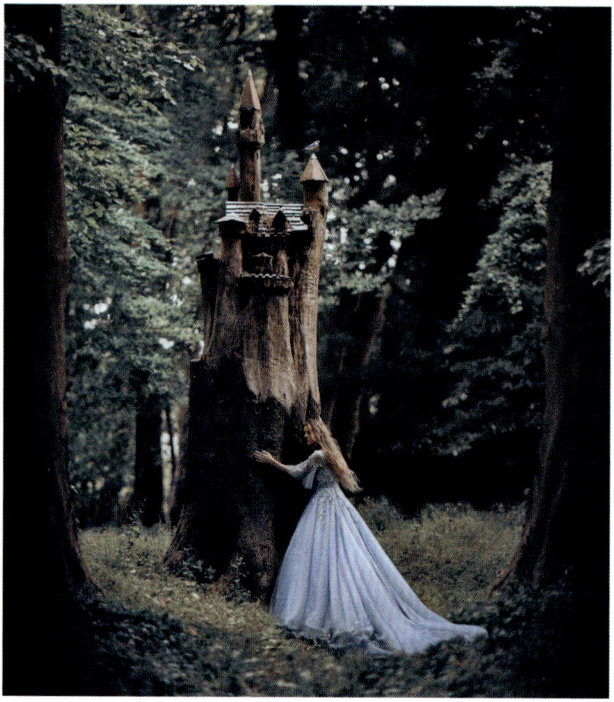

'Saying Goodbye to the Magic' – 2022.

content on a daily basis, it's important to create work that breaks the mould and is fresh fodder for our oversaturated and overstimulated brains. Sounds exhausting? It is!

I started feeling a little deflated by the energy > reward equation Instagram offers a couple of years ago. It's very difficult to pour *so* much time, energy and money (photoshoots, cameras, props and dresses aren't cheap) into a platform that makes it so difficult now to be discovered. With Instagram showing less than ten percent of your followers your work, engagement is harder to reach than ever. So, don't be disheartened if you're finding Instagram a tough cookie to crack – you are not alone. Here are my top tips for using it:

- **ENGAGE**: Social media is supposed to be that – social! While it's tempting to want to 'hack the algorithm', it's better to take it with a pinch of salt and use Instagram to genuinely interact and support artists and people that truly inspire you. By engaging authentically with other accounts, you're more likely to find your people and your personal community on there. Try and avoid starting fights in the comment section, especially if it's not your own account. Focus on finding and supporting the work that you love and be inspired! I like to use my stories to share my favourite poems, imagery and memes on a semi-regular basis. That feels sustainable to me.

- **SUSTAINABLE CREATING = SUSTAINABLE POSTING:** If it takes you a month to finish a piece of work that you feel really happy with, post once a month. If it takes a day, post once a day. The key to avoiding Posting Burnout is to create within your available energy and time. I post around once a month, and my engagement is doing well.

- **HONEST CAPTIONS:** For some creators, short, snappy, mysterious captions work great. If that aligns with your work then excellent! For me, I've found that open and honest writing alongside my work has prompted the most connection with my audience. I write about everything – from how I'm feeling, to what's exhausting me, to what's making me feel alive. Since the image-posting quality on Instagram is so high, I try and keep my captions down to earth.

- **TAG YOUR LOCATIONS AND SHARE:** It's so easy to want to gate-keep where you found your favourite location spots, dresses and props. And sadly, there are people out there who will go ahead and copy your ideas, pixel for pixel. But you should not let this sad reality keep you from what is essentially the 'Big Diamond' buried deep in the 'Instagram Mine'. People use social media platforms like Instagram to do one of three things: share their lives and their own work (check!); look at other people's lives to see what they want to add into their own (get inspired); and look at other people's lives and judge what they don't like, and don't want to add to their own (the haters). When you freely share your finds, your methods and your inspiration, you pass the spark on to others. And hopefully they take the spark responsibly and fairly into their own lives, but as artists we have to share the spark. There's no such thing as an original idea, original emotion, original thought. We stand on the shoulders of giants and we let others stand on our shoulders, too.

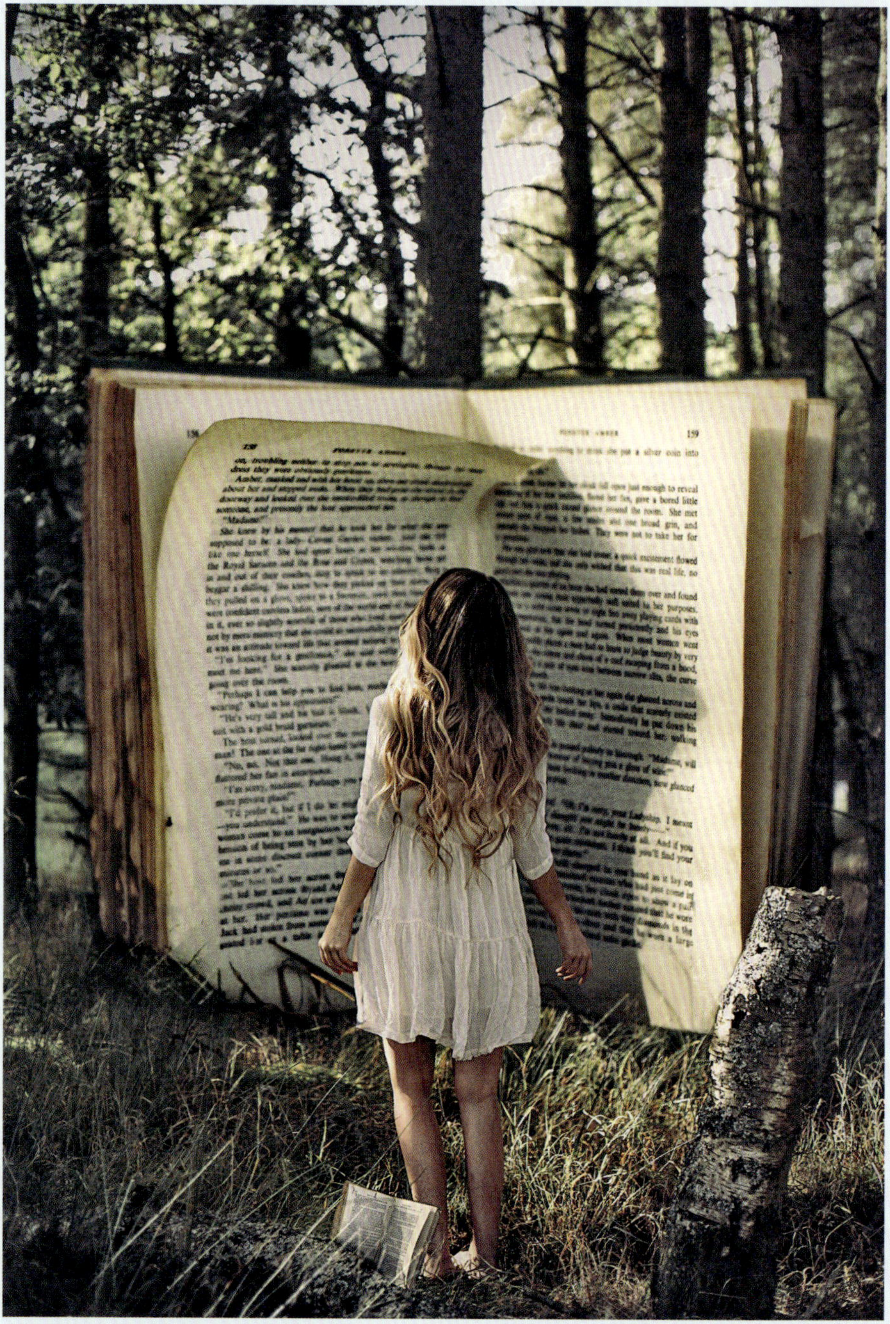

2. FACEBOOK

Facebook is still clinging on as a social media giant and rightly so. While now mostly used to silently watch our old school pals' lives evolve, it is possible to squeeze some artistic merit from Facebook. Personally, I prefer to use it to manage a micro-climate of personal life fun and what I like to call 'maybe clients'. Being friends with someone on Facebook means you have a reliable drip feed into their day and life. By posting consistently, and making it clear that you have a passion, it's possible to foster an environment of support on Facebook, which can eventually lead to jobs. By having my wedding clients upload their photo albums, and having them tag me (using the tagging feature), I've secured most of my future client work.

MY TOP TIPS FOR FACEBOOK ARE:

- **TAG, TAG, TAG:** Tagging people means your imagery will show up on their feeds. This means including as many people as you can in your work.

- **INTERACT:** Commenting on people's posts and having others comment on yours will increase your visibility across the platform.

- **BE OPEN:** You're far more likely to create great discussions, interest and buzz on your Facebook page if you write honestly about things that people can relate to. Ask for advice and opinions and always set your profile to 'Public' to boost the sharing capabilities for your posts.

One of my first self-portraits, playing with the idea of giant books.

3. TIKTOK

Photo and still-image artists continue to be frustrated by TikTok. As a video-sharing app, it's geared mainly towards short, entertaining videos, which usually do better the less professional they are and the more they feature cats. TikTok works mostly on viral videos and trends, so if you're choosing this platform, you need to be prepared to mix both those things with video and your work. Making 'behind the scenes' TikToks of you making your work and combining it with a trending soundbite is a good way of getting your work featured to new users. It's also a great place to just be real – 'storytime' videos are popular, as well as sharing your own methods and tricks when you create. This app is great for those who can embrace things going wrong – filming your camera and tripod flying off a cliff goes down brilliantly on TikTok!

TIKTOK HACKS:

- **STAY ON TREND:** Use trending sounds and filters, and take part in trending challenges. People love to see how others can interpret the same relatable sounds, music and memes into their own lives, and will often engage with your video if they feel the same.

- **THINK FUNNY:** TikToks are being watched by people looking for content to share with their friends, partners and families. When you make your content lighthearted and relatable, it is more likely to be shared.

- **SHOW YOUR PROCESS:** Sharing a series of befores and afters is a far more entertaining watch than a series of serious images. Leave that for Instagram!

Don't forget to try out new trends on social media. When Adobe released its new Generative Fill AI feature, I immediately hopped around the back of my house to this flower-less bush (next to the bins!). I created this to see just how far AI could take a very ordinary photo, and since so many other people were exploring the same function, this content performed well online.

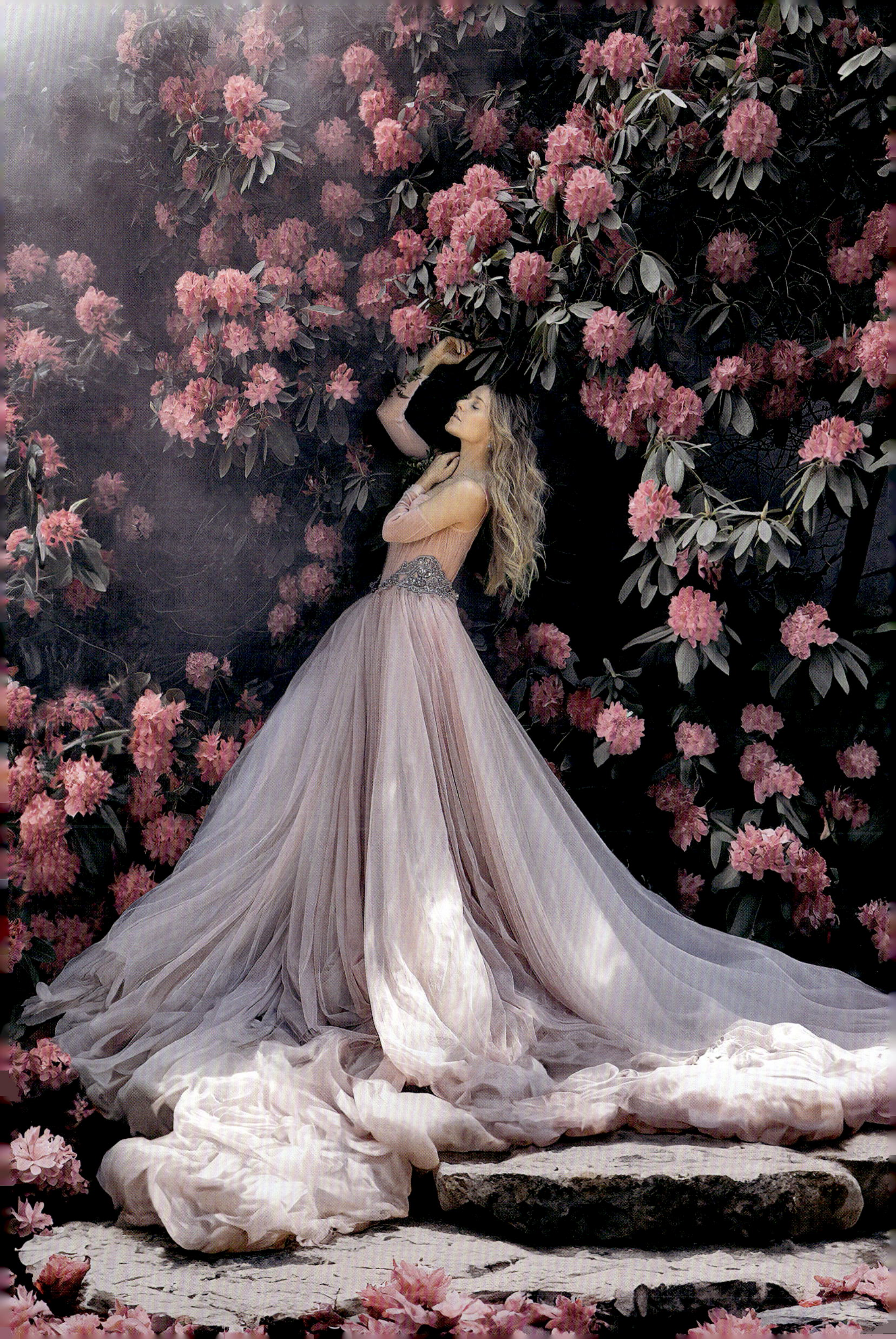

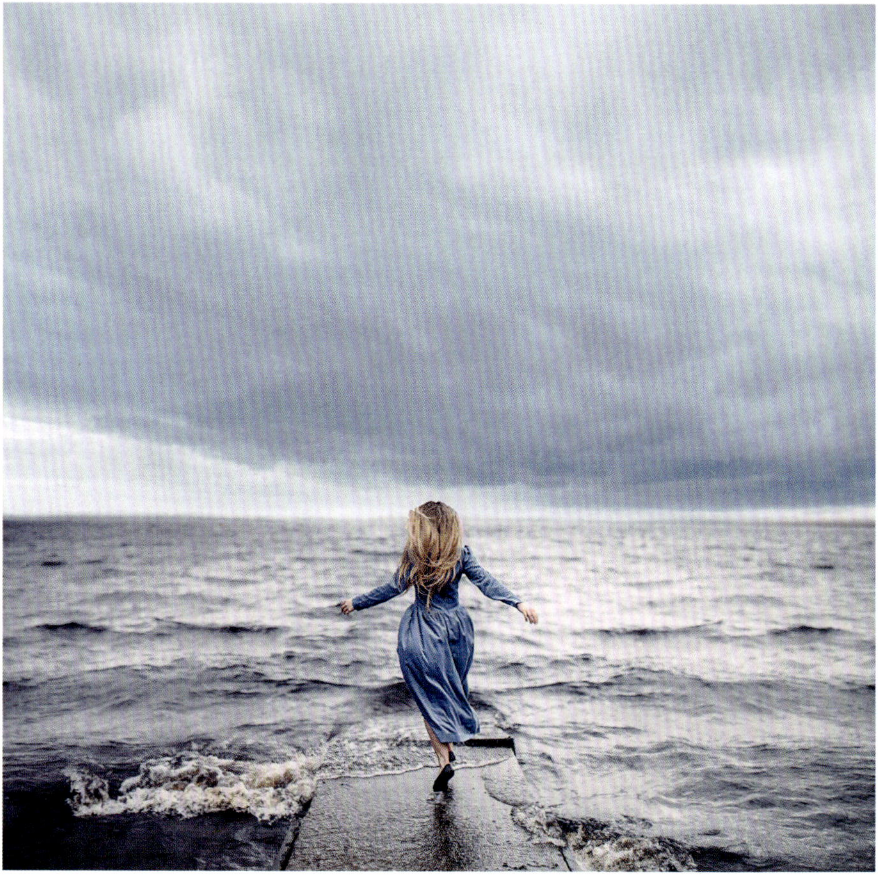

'Bird' – 2016.

4. YOUTUBE

Probably the social media equivalent of Mount Everest. YouTube is the oldest, most unchanging and strongest social media platform that continues to grow. Again, geared towards video, this platform is great for artists who want to share their honest selves, be it via in-depth behind-the-scenes videos, solo talking-to-camera videos about their photography or personal experiences, trying challenges or sharing an editing tutorial. YouTube videos are best discovered when paired with click-baity titles (DON'T FORGET TO USE CAPS LOCK AND LOTS OF EXCLAMATION MARKS!), intriguing video thumbnail pictures and a controversial topic. YouTube is great for creators who don't mind debate – the comment section is a Wild West and you have to be prepared for people to pick you (and your work) apart.

MY YOUTUBE TRICKS:

- **CHALLENGES:** As a photographer, taking part in interesting challenges is a great way to create interesting, watchable content on YouTube. Try doing a shoot using only a toy camera or teaming up with two other photographers to shoot the same model in different styles. Set a £10 budget challenge and see what you can create.

- **OPEN UP:** If you're looking to form stronger connections, then vlogging and one-on-one style chatting to the camera is a good route to try. It can feel very strange at first, but imagine you're talking with a friend instead of to a camera. Opening up in confessional-style sessions is a great way to connect with your viewers.

- **TUTORIALS:** YouTube is a great place to learn, but equally, a great place to teach. Screen-record your editing sessions to show people how you got your image from A to B.

My personal experience with social media was an unexpected one. When I first started sharing online, it was around the same time that blogging was born and I found myself accidentally building an online community. By posting my 365 self-portraits daily, and including a short write up of my day, I unknowingly became a blogger without a blog. The photography community welcomed me and grew with me, and I supported others on there as they supported me. Using social media this way means artists can connect with their fellow photographers, exchange ideas, provide feedback and collaborate on projects together. These communities really can foster creativity, nourish that little spark and provide a super-supportive environment for artistic growth.

Eventually, the more I posted, the more exposure and recognition I received online. My work in 2007 wasn't exactly high quality, but it was interesting and different enough to cause a stir online. This opportunity to reach a broader audience, gain recognition and to potentially attract clients, galleries and publications was super cool on the surface. It was nice to be regarded as a 'somebody'. But equally, you can be kicked out of favour as quickly as you can be put on the pedestal, so it's important to stay humble and not let any social media attention over-inflate your ego. A healthy self-esteem boost is a wonderful thing and it's also a good place to stop.

It's important for photographers to strike a balance between utilizing social media platforms to gain exposure and spread the word about their work, while maintaining a focus on their artistic vision and personal growth. Social media is in itself a trend – and something that you should think carefully about before selling your soul to it. How valuable is your privacy to you and the privacy of those around you? At the start of my social media journey, I shared openly to strangers, as a stranger. Now, people know the names of my parents, they can message my boyfriend, they have access to my entire life and history. The simple sharing of my inner thoughts is less possible because of this and I happily choose the balance of privacy and openness that is right for me. At the end of the day, social media is a tool of inspiration, connectivity and sharing when used right. To take you must first give – and that's a great motto to approach social media with.

'Down to Earth' – 2022.

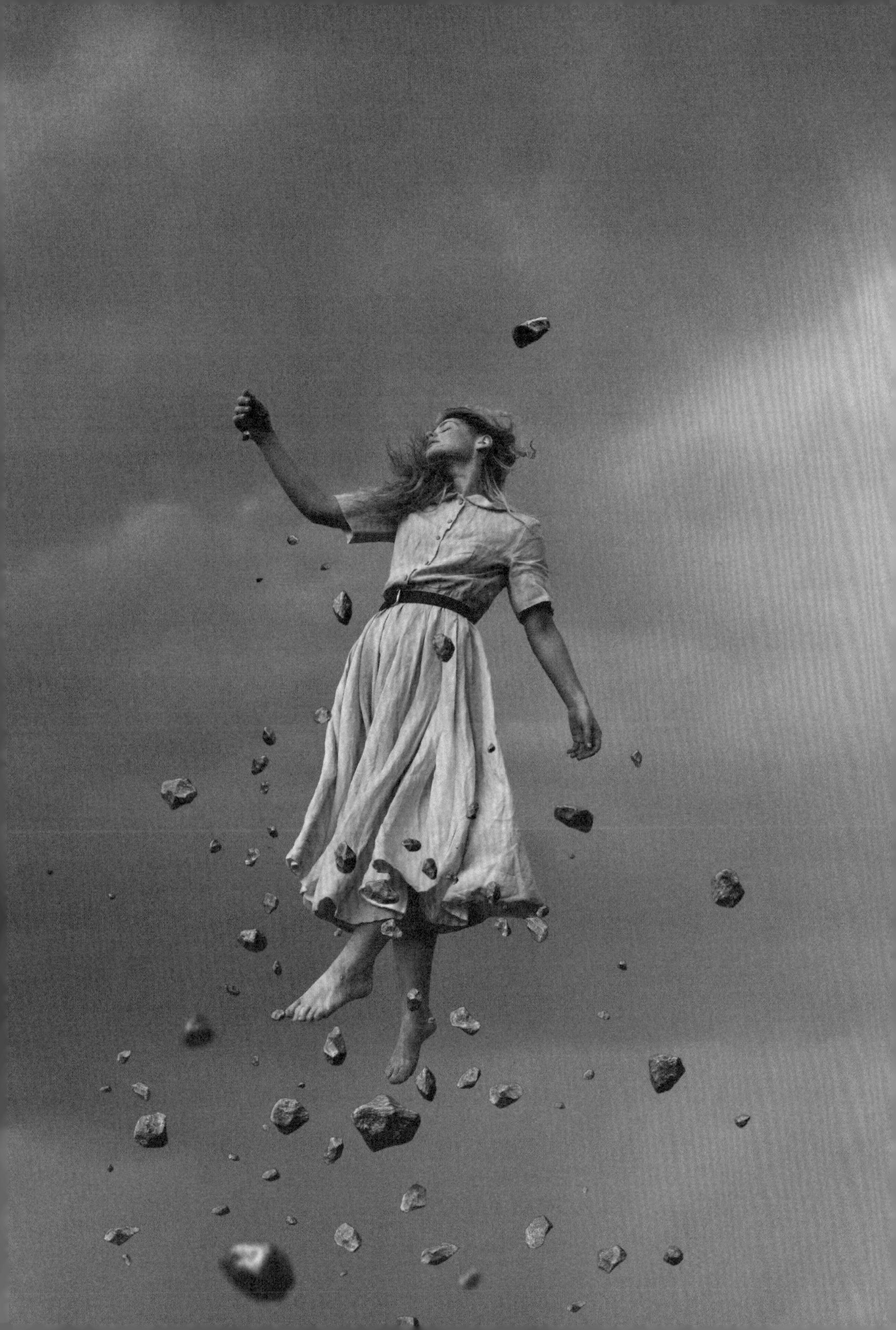

09.
WHAT NEXT?

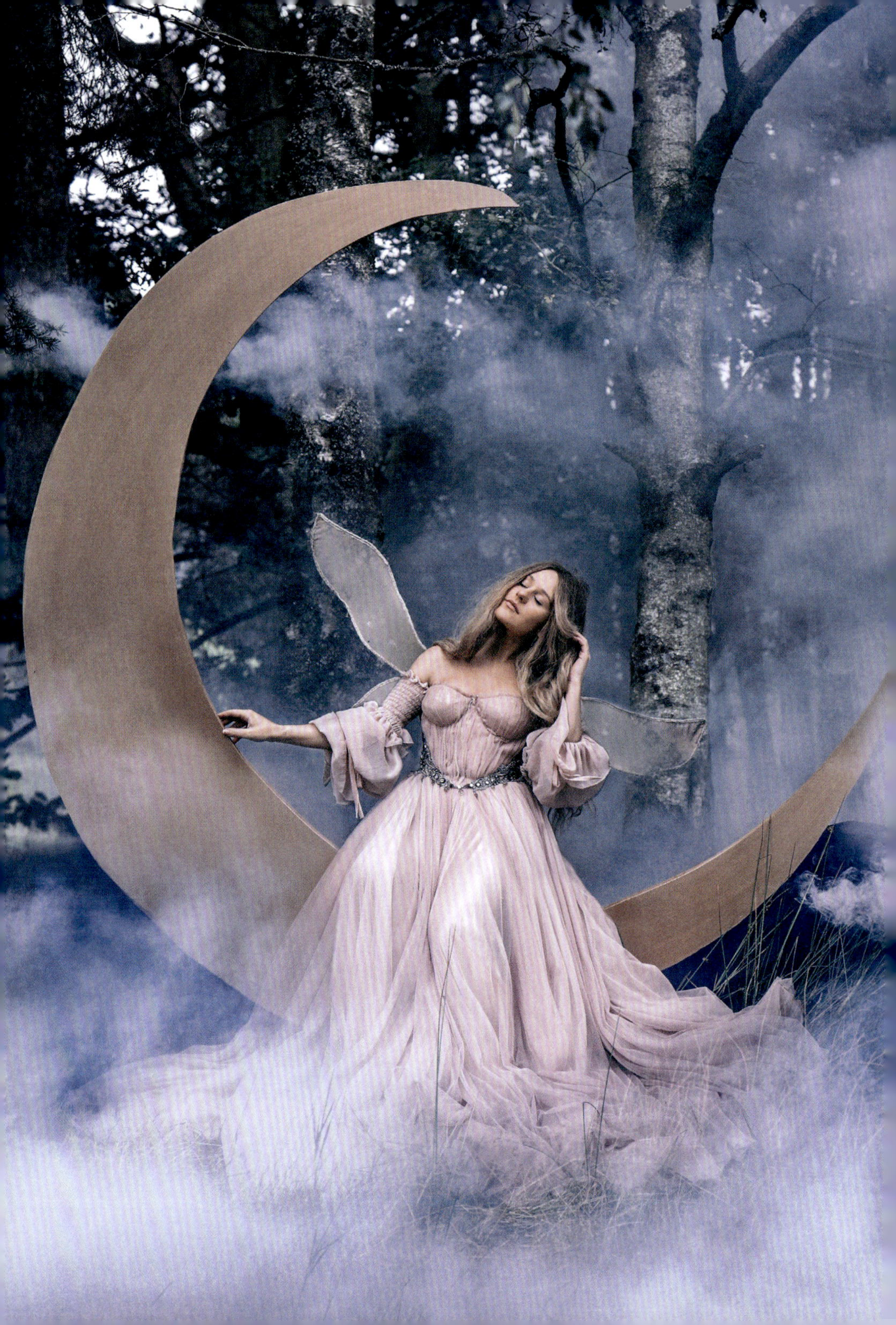

FROM HOBBY TO CAREER

Okay, so you've got the kit, you've learned how to make your ideas a reality, and now you'd like to actually know how to make some money from this whole jam you've got going on. Let me talk you through the steps I took to take my self-portraits from teenage escapism into a full-time photography career.

First of all, transitioning from being a hobbyist self-portrait photographer to a full-time professional photographer involves plenty of dedication and hard work – it's not for the work shy, or faint of heart. Make sure you're okay with the idea of loathing the same thing you've grown to love – and prepare yourself for the hard work behind the scenes. Endless hours replying to emails and thousands of pounds spent on back-up software and replacement kit can easily grind you down. It is quite alright to choose not to monetize your hobbies but it's also wonderful to do something you love every day.

Here's my step-by-step guide to becoming self-employed:

'A Midsummer Night's Dream' – Shot as campaign work for the RSC and Adobe.

1. DEFINE YOUR NICHE AND STYLE

Self-portrait photography can be a broad field, so it's a good idea to identify a specific niche or approach that sets you apart from others. When you develop a unique artistic vision that showcases your personality and creativity, it's much easier to appeal to those looking for exactly that. For me, I wanted my sector in the world of photography to be conceptual portraiture, with a side serving of storytelling fairytale vibes.

2. PORTFOLIO

Once you feel you've nailed your 'thing', the next step is to build up a strong portfolio. Over time as a hobbyist, you'll hopefully have accidentally created a decent start on one. Try and narrow this down to your best images only and if you're unhappy with your overall portfolio, arrange new shoots that complete the missing pieces. Consider seeking feedback from fellow photographers or industry professionals to identify some areas for improvement – many photographers charge small fees for portfolio reviews and advice, and this is something you can also offer in time. Display your portfolio on your website and on social media. It's also not a bad idea to carry a small version around with you, in case you ever meet potential clients in your day-to-day life.

3. EDUCATE YOURSELF

Even if you have a natural talent for photography, there are always new things to learn. Consider enrolling in photography courses or workshops to expand your knowledge and improve weaker areas, whether that be editing, lighting techniques or even things like brand building and social media. You can also consider running your own workshops if you've built up an audience and have people who like your work and style. I taught my first workshop when I was 18 years old, and had certain people online tell me I shouldn't. Part of me listened to them and believed them, but I persevered regardless and held two fully booked workshops in London. At the end of the day, if people like your work and want to learn from you, you have the right to offer up what you know.

4. TAKE ON A FEW SMALL JOBS, THEN INVEST IN EQUIPMENT

I wouldn't recommend throwing away your full-time job to go straight into being full-time in your hobby. I applaud the courage it takes, especially when you're unhappy in your current workplace, but if you can, lay the groundwork of a working business first.

To do this, take on a few small jobs, which may or may not include self-portraiture. I photographed friends' families, pets, random portraits for musicians, all for a very small fee. Almost everything I earned, I put right back into my kit, upgrading my camera, lenses, lighting equipment and any other tools I deemed necessary for improving my photography. The more I shot, the more my confidence grew and the more I knew what I was doing. After six months of shooting low-pressure work, I took on a wedding photography booking and now shoot 30 a year.

I should add: if you do take on 'non-artistic' work, don't neglect your niche. Keeping my self-portraiture alive led to most of the campaign work I get now, and while I love wedding photography, it feeds my soul in different ways to my art work and that's okay.

5. BUILD A PROFESSIONAL WEBSITE

Creating an online platform to showcase your work and present yourself as a serious professional is a great way to transition to a pro. This way, other people can find you, contact you and hire you for work. Use a website builder (I use www.format.com) or hire a web designer to create a visually appealing and user-friendly portfolio website. It really is worth the investment.

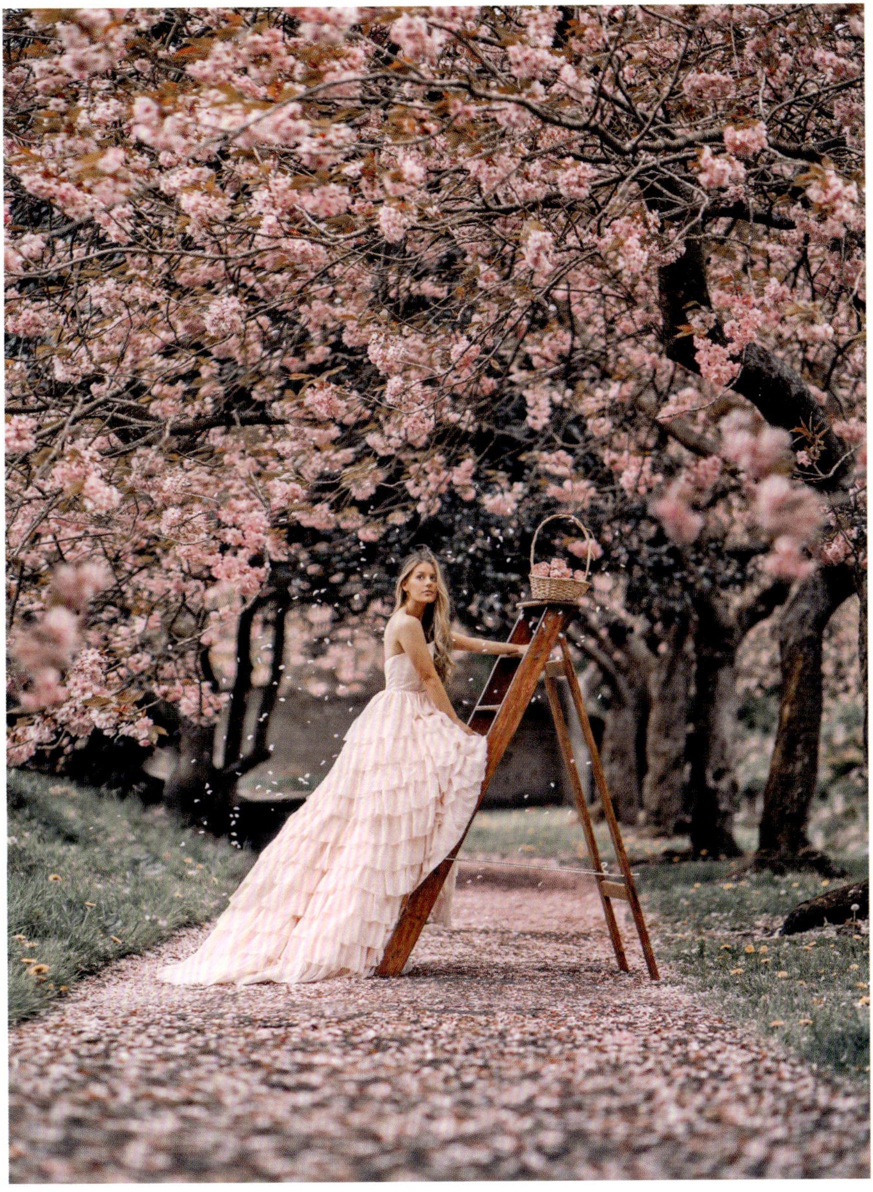

'In Full Bloom' – 2021.

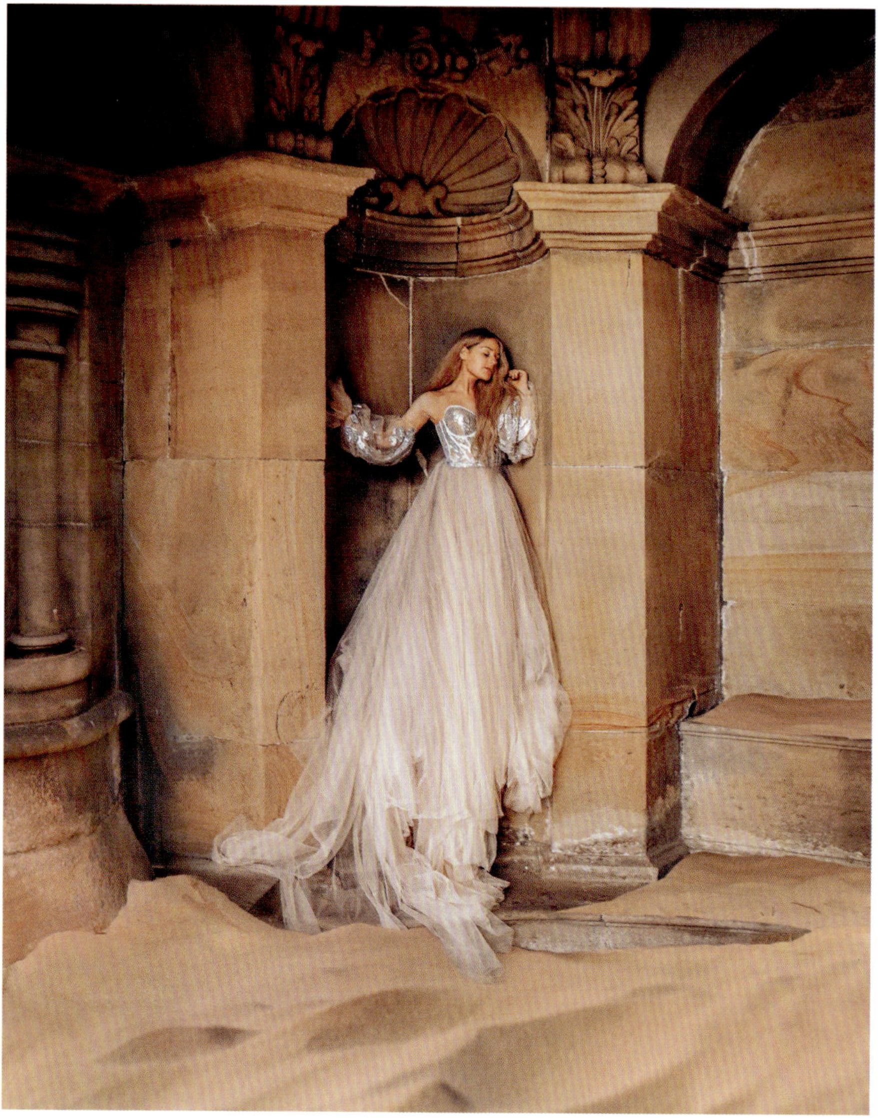

This beautiful gown was lent to me for this shoot by the very talented dress designer Chotronette.

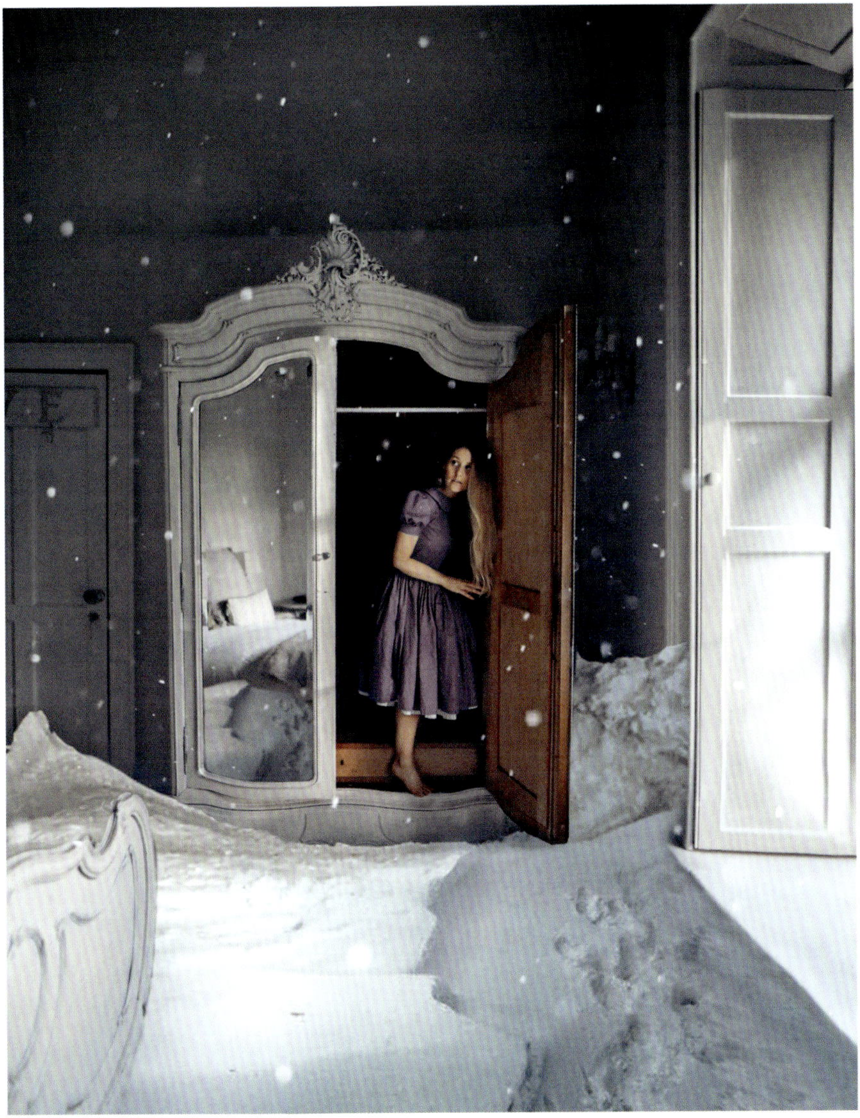

'Discovering Narnia...' – Part of a campaign for Unique Homestays, 2021.

6. SOCIAL MEDIA PRESENCE

Hopefully you already completed this in the hobbyist stage, but leveraging your social media platforms like Instagram, Facebook, TikTok and YouTube will help you reach a wider audience and connect with potential clients. Regularly post your self-portraits (as much as possible, as discussed in the previous chapter), share your behind-the-scenes content and engage with your followers to build a loyal fan base.

7. NETWORK AND COLLABORATE

Networking doesn't always mean attending business-type events. For me, I learned the importance of natural networking – chatting to people who see me shooting, telling people what I do and asking them about themselves, making people feel welcome and comfortable in your presence. When it comes to hiring others, nobody wants to pay someone to turn up and bring the vibe down, and people will often place the value of feeling comfortable with someone over their experience and price. When you network, do it honestly and authentically – and be wary of making people feel as though you're social climbing at their expense. Let people offer opportunities naturally, rather than trying to persuade people to give you them. Show genuine enthusiasm about the things they love and build other people up. If it comes back around, fantastic. And if it doesn't, you still leave on a gain, for making someone's day brighter.

To collaborate, find photography events, workshops and conferences to meet other photographers, potential clients and industry professionals. Get to know the models, makeup artists, stylists and other photographers you work with, as this will help to expand your network and leave you a well-recommended person to have around.

8. CREATE A BUSINESS PLAN

An ex-boyfriend of mine once gave me some pretty good advice. He said the best way to create a business plan is to imagine the end point first. What does being a successful photographer mean to *you*? (I should add, there is no right answer to this. Mine involves frolicking in fields, having plenty of free time for my partner and cat, and doesn't involve being featured in *Vogue* at all – sorry not sorry!)

Once you've established what it might look like to be a successful artist, then you can start to break down the steps it would take to get there. If it is having ten magazine covers on established name-brand mags, then what would it take to be hired for one? Maybe that means you'll need to shoot for a few big clothing brands before that happens. Or connect with a few celebrities for shoots. There are many ways we can break big goals into smaller, more achievable ones. I remember one day deciding that

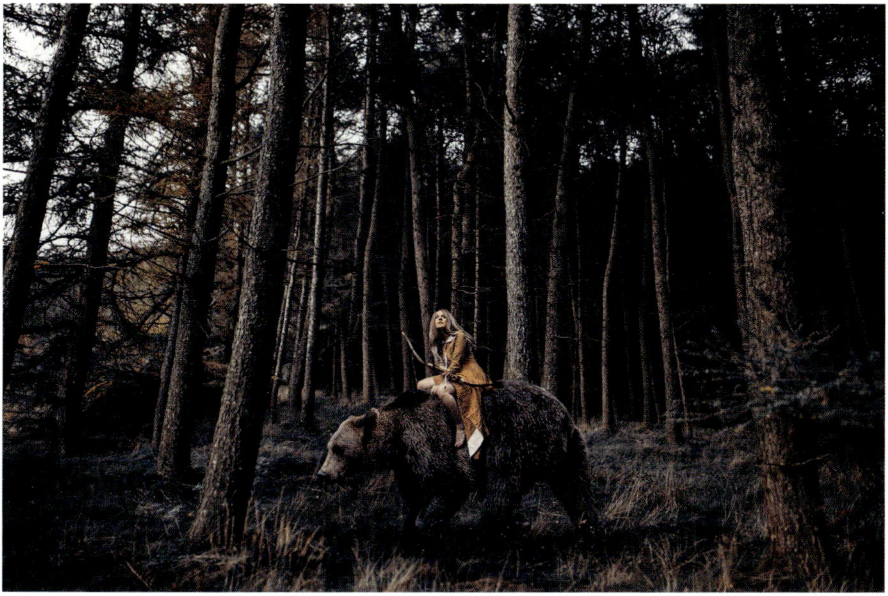

'Once More unto the Breach' – 2015.

I wanted to shoot celebrities – and contacting different agents directly using their email addresses I found on X (previously known as Twitter). I sent so many emails, offering free shoots for the different celebrities on their rotas. I told the agents that if they liked the images and wanted to book me for more, we could discuss payment after the first shoot. This was incredibly successful, and a few months later I found myself in Paris in a hotel by the Eiffel Tower, shooting with a well-known TV star. Spoiler though, I later found that I absolutely loathed the controlled and specific nature of celebrity shoots, and decided that it did not, in fact, fit my vision of feeling like a happy, successful photographer.

Developing a detailed business plan is a great way to turn your photography hobby into a full-time career. Define your target market, set realistic financial goals and outline strategies for marketing, sales and growth. You can also use the playful 'Low Price/High Sales and High Price/Low Sales' strategy. Try and come up with five ideas, five things to offer people, that are both low and high in price. 'Low Price' might be a family photoshoot, whereas 'High Price' might be wedding photography. Fit ten 'Low Price' shoots into one day, to make the same (if not more) than one day of your 'High Price' shoot. The more experienced you get, the more vast this difference in price and offer will become. I still offer family photoshoots at a low price, but now I offer them in low season, knowing those smaller shoots will come in handy in quieter seasons.

9. PRICING & CONTRACTS

Both are equally tricky. Determining a fair pricing structure is imperative to being able to sleep at night, and should be based on your skills, experience and market demand. I can't stress enough how bizarre it is to choose this number yourself, and if you've ever been a people-pleaser, or had low self-esteem, prepare to sweat!

I shot my first ever wedding for £200, and immediately raised the price to £500 (and this was back in 2010). It's a great idea to second-shoot/assist another photographer before setting your prices – this is something I wish I'd done. I had no idea about the workload, time and pressure that shooting a wedding would hold, and grossly undercharged. My current fees for weddings (as of 2023) are between £2,000–5,000, depending on the needs of the client. This is actually considered low – I know some wedding photographers who charge £20,000 as their starting rate.

Next up, contracts! The hardest lesson every photographer learns is what on earth to do when you have your first unhappy client, especially when you feel you did a good job. This is why establishing clear, well communicated contracts for your clients is imperative. Outline the scope of work, any usage rights, the payment terms and all the other important details. There are plenty of photography contract templates you can find online, and it's never a bad idea to run yours past a lawyer to check you're well protected.

10. OFFER SERVICES BEYOND PHOTOGRAPHY

By diversifying your offerings and providing services such as workshops, tutorials, prints and merchandize featuring your self-portraits, you can earn a little extra and keep your niche alive. During the Covid-19 pandemic, my editing tutorials actually became my main source of income.

11. MANAGE YOUR FINANCES – AND PREPARE TO CRY WHEN YOU DO YOUR TAX BILL

As you transition to a full-time career, it's super important to manage your finances carefully. I registered as a sole trader for my business at 18 years old, and have been keeping track of my income and expenses, budgeting for equipment upgrades, software costs and all kinds of photography related

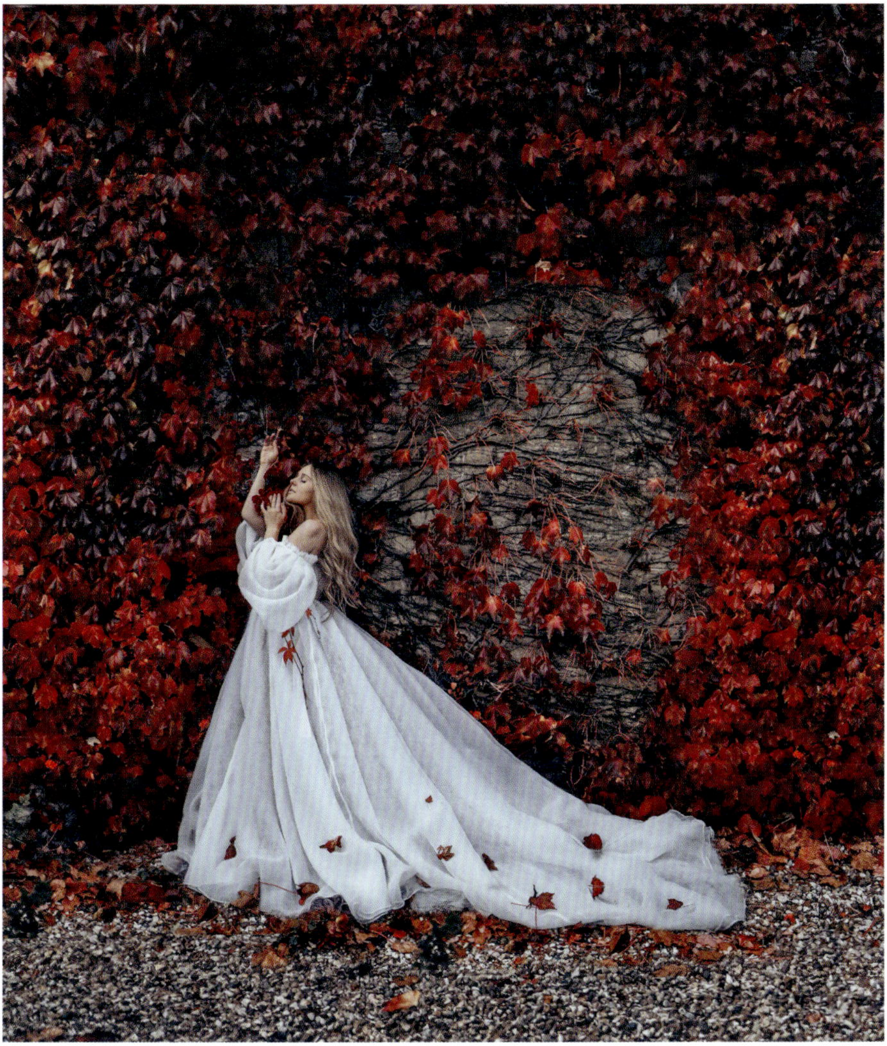

'As if I Had Wings' – 2019.

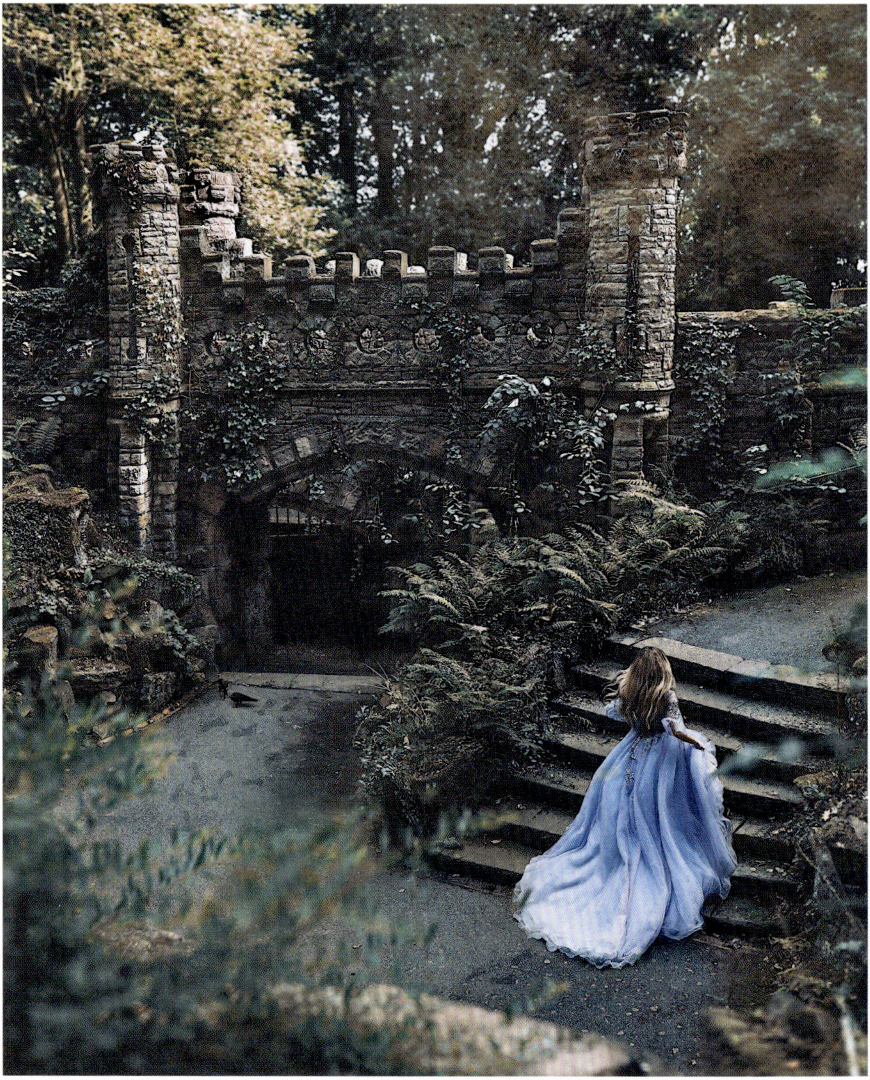

'Cinderella' – 2018.

expenses ever since. Prepare to pay a lot in tax – as a sole trader, my average tax each year is 29 percent of my income, and then 40 percent on any profit I make over £50,000 per year. I think my worst ever tax bill was £16,500 – it was my entire savings. I cried and cried and cried, told my parents I was moving off grid to live in a treehouse, and despised that I was forced to partake in such a world where I would have to give 'my' money to the government. But, having grown up a little since then, I now realize that the money I pay into my taxes comes right back out into the world I benefit from, and I now treat 29 percent of my income as not mine to spend at all.

12. FIND YOUR BALANCE

Try to understand that transitioning to a full-time career takes time and involves some financial risks. As mentioned earlier, starting part-time or working on freelance projects while gradually building your photography business is a safer way to enter the photography industry. Focus on nurturing your love of creating, and your skills and experience, before taking major risks.

Remember that turning photography into a full-time career requires persistence, patience and a commitment to continuous improvement. It's essential to stay true to your artistic vision, while also adapting to whatever the market demands and trends might be. But, with dedication and passion for your craft, you can transform your self-portrait photography hobby into a rewarding and fulfilling career – it can and does happen, I promise!

THE ARTIST EMERGES

Often, feeling like your true, authentic self as an artist has nothing to do with being successful. Many people work for years, exhausting themselves by trying to score goals into constantly moving goalposts, only to find that they neglected the very things that give their lives meaning: our art, our families and friends, our lovers, our pets, the poems and the songs. Success comes in many shapes and forms, but to me, the perfect shape of happiness is misshapen; it hurts sometimes, has room for failure, heartbreak, loss, all the things that really teach us who we are and our unbelievable capacity to overcome the pain we are dealt in this lifetime.

It can be so easy to become swallowed up in the 'keeping up' – in our Instagram followers, in booking celebrity clients, having the perfect skin, a full head of hair. We are all searching for that thing that will complete us. But it isn't a person, a job or a house. It's not the amount of money in our bank account, or the right number of children sitting in the backseat of the right brand of car.

Show me a life that leaves room for swimming in the sea, stroking the cat and picking flowers with my children. Show me a life that means I get to create meaningfully, honestly and vulnerably, that at the same time, earns me a comfortable and modest living. Show me someone with the courage to walk into situations that might break apart their peacefulness, their comfort and their ideas of what this life means – and someone who takes the time to explore this, to rebuild themselves, to become wiser, kinder. Show me this kind of life, this kind of person and I would very much like to see their self-portraits.

Here's mine.

'Self-portrait' – Rosie Hardy.

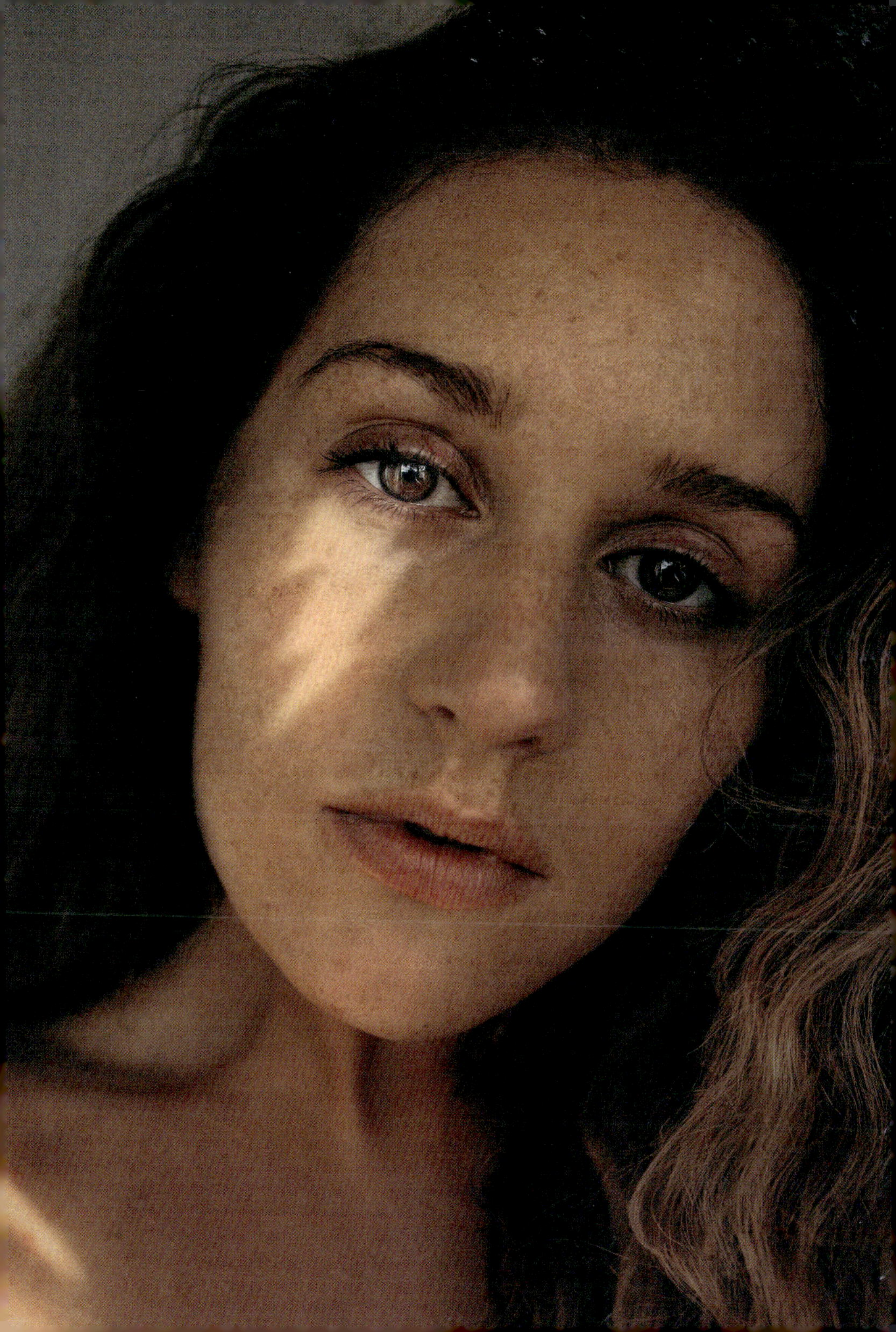

ACKNOWLEDGEMENTS

I am profoundly grateful to my family and friends. Their unwavering love, support and encouragement has been the cornerstone of my spirit. This also includes every single person on the internet who has sat with me in the darkness, our keyboards connecting our hearts. Your kindness and belief in me have been a life-cherishing force throughout this journey.

My therapist once sat with me, listening, while I explained that I didn't think I'd ever find someone who would love me, given my history. It was too much for me to carry sometimes, let alone someone else. He told me, 'Rosie, it's not too much. You deserve someone with big hands.'

Huge gratitude to the wonderful team at Ilex/Octopus for their collaborative efforts and hard work – your contributions made this book possible. Thank you.

To Ash, who has the hands of a giant, and an equally massive heart, made entirely of gold:

Thank you for loving me as I am. You are the calm to my chaos.

PICTURE CREDITS

6 Metropolitan Museum of Art, Bequest of Benjamin Altman, 1913; 7 Alamy Stock Photo/Archivart © Banco de México Diego Rivera Frida Kahlo Museums Trust, Mexico, D.F./DACS 2024; 8 Yelkrokoyade, Public domain, via Wikimedia Commons; 9 Courtesy the artist and TJ Boulting